W9-BPM-976

FREE UNION COUNTRY SCHOOL'S

THE FAMILY FIELD GUIDE
TO CHARLOTTESVILLE AND BEYOND:
GREAT OUTINGS WITH CHILDREN

BY SUSAN T. HAAS

AND THE FAMILIES AND FRIENDS
OF FREE UNION COUNTRY SCHOOL

http://avenue.org/familyfieldguide

Copyright 1999 Free Union Country School.
All Rights Reserved.

Cover Illustration by Gail McIntosh

Other Illustrations by Students of the
Free Union Country School

Design by Payne, Ross and Associates, Inc.

Published by Free Union Country School
P.O. Box 250 Free Union, Virginia 22940
1.804.978.1700

ISBN 0-9671380-0-0

Dedicated
to the families who founded Free Union Country School.

Founded in 1984, Free Union Country School is an independent preschool and elementary school devoted to challenging each student in a stimulating and supportive environment that promotes the development of imaginative critical thinkers who are compassionate members of society. At its inception, the school's mission was to incorporate a strong working relationship between parents, teachers and students. The school's multilayered programs combine innovative curriculum with the cultivation of lifelong love of learning. Classes have low student/teacher ratios that support the building of self-confidence by developing an individual's most effective learning style. Free Union Country School campus is in a rural community fifteen minutes from Charlottesville, set along the backdrop of the Blue Ridge Mountains. Simply, Free Union Country School is a community where learning is valued, individuals are respected, diversity is understood as a strength, and teamwork is rewarded.

Free Union Country School is located at 4220 Free Union Road in Free Union, Virginia. (804) 978-1700.

TABLE OF CONTENTS

FOREWORD

What could be more audacious (or bodacious!)...and more American than starting a school from scratch? No textbooks, no pre-existing philosophy and curriculum, no schoolhouse. No *Field Guide to Opening Your Own School*. Just simple idealism, common sense, love and understanding of children...and a knowledge of construction!

We dedicate this book to the families who founded Free Union Country School fifteen years ago. Those families, the neighbors who supported the endeavor, and the families who have continued to shape and build the school are entrepreneurs at their best. They believed enough in their families, their community, and their understanding of child development and learning to create a brand new school. Their common-sensical approach to education—learning through exploration and experience, consideration of the whole child, active partnership between home and school, social and personal responsibility—was deeply rooted in well-established principles of education dating to the turn of the century.

This book is another audacious undertaking by the families of Free Union Country School. Until we pooled our experiences of favorite activities, hikes, theaters, restaurants, and shops, we had no idea there was so much for families to do in the greater Charlottesville area. And we know that there are places we've missed! This book has turned out to be a much greater endeavor than we ever anticipated, and we are tired but delighted for it.

We thank all the families and friends of the school—and especially the children—who visited and reviewed attraction after attraction and then shared with us artistic renderings of their trips.

Our greatest thanks go to Susan Haas, the writer of children's novels who singlehandedly created order out of the piles of reviews, producing a text that is both a breeze to read and chock full of pertinent and necessary information. We are in awe of her enthusiasm, determination, energy, wit, and talent.

This book would not have happened if Carolyn Lawlor, the school's new Director fresh from Alexandria, had not asked, "Why don't we write a book about what to do with children in Charlottesville?"

Without the careful and patient editing, checking, proofing, reading and re-reading by Jolee Horn, Carolyn Lawlor, Jane Paxton, Aaron Sheehan-Dean, Erin Smith, and Lois and Shorey Myers this book would still be a draft. The indomitable Myers were relentless in their editing and determination to create a terrific resource for families. Patrice Kyger brought style and a meticulous eye to the book; we learned a great deal from Patrice.

Jacqui Frank provided the utmost help in taking the book (it seemed like magic to us....we know it wasn't!) from draft to edited digital copy, and in keeping us all on track.

Digging into the deepest reaches of her patience and wisdom, Jolee Horn kept us sane, safe, and on schedule, a mighty task. Jeri Goldstein generously shared her knowledge of down-to-earth, here's-how-you-do-it self-publishing.

Our thanks to Pete Myers for designing our webpage and to Andrea Larson for helping to plan the book's future. Thank you to our two photographers for their enthusiastic support, from conception to darkroom to print.

To the spouses, children and friends of our book team, our love and gratitude for your patience and support, even as the laundry piled up and up. From the cast of characters, you can see that this book is a classic Free Union venture—everybody in!

We thank the gifted Gail McIntosh, whose watercolor graces our cover and captures the spirit of our school so well. Susan Payne and Lisa Ross of Payne, Ross and Associates, Inc. gave us the beautiful cover design, the layout, much sage advice, and their enthusiastic support for this project. Their love for the Charlottesville community bubbled up in every decision we made together—from artists to consider—to printers to hire. They managed the nuts and bolts design and production of this book; without them and their support, this book would still be a dream.

We have turned ourselves inside-out trying to get every detail right. The opinions are ours and those of our school families and friends. We welcome your opinions as you visit these and other attractions—write us c/o Free Union Country School or respond through our webpage (http://avenue.org/familyfieldguide). As the attractions say, "fees and hours are subject to change at any time without notice." Take this to heart and call the attractions or check their website to ensure that your foray will be a great success.

The Family Field Guide to Charlottesville and Beyond: Great Outings With Children was conceived, written, and published entirely in Albemarle County. It celebrates Charlottesville and the surrounding communities. We wish you, the families of Charlottesville and beyond, great adventures together. Have a bodacious time!

Free Union Country School
4220 Free Union Road
P.O. Box 250
Free Union, VA 22940

http://avenue.org/freeunion

TO GET THE MOST FROM THIS BOOK...

If your family is anything like ours, life is a whirlwind of laundry and groceries and work and laundry and homework and laundry. The thought of fun, family-oriented activities is as fleeting as a newspaper clipping or a television blurb. Then it happens. We're hit between the eyes with a rainy day or a rare free weekend. We try in vain to recall even one of those fun activities. Why isn't there one place we can go to find out about everything fun for kids in Charlottesville? And what about visitors? If those of us who live here are at a loss, visitors must be especially frustrated.

We, the parents of Free Union Country School, decided to take matters into our own hands. Why not create a family-oriented guide that would not only list attractions but describe the best way to visit them with children? Our school families, although small in number, are diverse, including a seasoned tour guide at Monticello, backpack trip leaders, theater and music lovers, and more. So we hit the road, searching every nook and cranny for family-oriented activities, naively thinking our efforts would yield a slim little volume. We were delighted to find many more family-friendly attractions than we had ever dreamed.

We had to make some tough decisions along the way. To create a comprehensive guide, we included some attractions even though they do not reflect the philosophy and values of Free Union Country School. Inclusion in this books does not represent an endorsement by the school. We also included only activities that do not require registration, membership, or on-going classes. Thus, many wonderful family places such as Little Gym, Fry's Spring Beach Club, and the YMCA are not reviewed in this book.

1   *Use your judgment.*

We have provided the basics, but only you can decide what fits your family's values, taste, and budget. If you have specific concerns about safety, age-appropriateness, etc., call ahead, which brings us to....

2   *Call ahead and verify information.*

We bent over backwards to bring you an up-to-date guide and, while we are pretty sure Monticello isn't going anywhere, attractions do move, change fees without notice, and alter operating hours.

3   *Consider the "schlep factor."*

The schlep factor is a tongue-in-cheek indicator of how much "trouble" an attraction is for adults, including prep time, driving time, parking, and touring. Schlep is an old Yiddish term meaning "to drag", as in "how much stuff do we have to schlep along?" A low schlep factor means the attraction takes little overall effort. A high schlep factor means the attraction is going to take some work.

4 *Don't curse Route 29N...*

...or at least don't condemn us for giving all directions from this point. While locals know that Route 29 is not always the best starting point, out-of-town guests will be likely to find their way to this main drag.

5 *Plan ahead.*

If you would like to make a day out of an out-of-town attraction, check out the chapter of maps and the index by location. Also consult the Seasonal Calendar events chapter.

6 *Check out our webpage at http://avenue.org/familyfieldguide*

As we receive information on new or old attractions, changes in fees or hours, etc., we will post the information on the book's webpage.

7 *Be a "Timetraveler" (sites are indicated with this mark ★).*

This program, sponsored by the Virginia Historical Society, is our favorite ongoing program for families. Pick up a Timetravelers passport for kids (K–12th grade), available at the information desk of all Jefferson-Madison Regional Libraries or from their website (see below). When your family visits any participating location between April 1 and November 1, have the passport stamped and signed. You might get free or discounted admission, and your child may receive an optional report card to fill out for the attraction. When kids have collected six stamps, mail in the passport for a free Timetravelers T-shirt and a certificate from the Governor. Kids who send in their passports are automatically registered for a drawing for other neat prizes, too. For more information, including an updated list of participating sites, or to download an attraction, check out their website (http://www.state.va.us/timetravelers).

So, here it is, all in one place. Everything fun for families in Charlottesville. The new, the old, the educational and the just plain fun. Now quick—before the laundry piles up— have a great time with your kids! We'll see you on the road!

HISTORIC

Historic tours that actively involve children are one of the best ways for kids to learn about our past. The historic sites in this chapter, as well as those in our Richmond and Northern Virginia chapters, were considered exceptional by Free Union families in tailoring tours to meet the needs of families. Even families with very young children can enjoy many of the attractions. The grounds of many of these sites have hands-on activities during the tourist season and gardens that can be explored any time of the year. Our families found that touring the inside of historic homes was easiest if they had an adult for every child under age 5 or if parents took older children through the home while another adult watched younger children outside.

Attractions marked with a ★ are part of the Timetravelers program. As Timetravelers kids can collect six stamps at these attractions and send them in for a free T-shirt and a chance at other neat prizes. Many participating locations give discounts on admission to Timetravelers and their families. See the chapter Getting Started.

★ ## Ash Lawn-Highland

James Monroe Parkway (Route 795), Charlottesville
(804) 293-9539

WEBSITE: http://www.avenue.org/ashlawn

HOURS: March–October 9 AM–6 PM, November–February 10 AM–5 PM, closed Thanksgiving, Christmas and New Year's Day.

ADMISSION: Children under 6 for free, $4 for children 6–11, $7 for adults, $6.50 for seniors. For residents of Charlottesville, Albemarle and adjacent counties, $4 (ID required) or free with a guest (one free admission for one paid admission). AAA and group discounts available.

Ash Lawn-Highland, home of our fifth president, James Monroe, is an excellent historic site for kids during the March through October tourist season. During these months, costumed guides demonstrate cooking, weaving, spinning and other plantation chores at the outbuildings around the property. Kids can try their hand at hoop rolling or lawn bowling, and animals such as chickens, peacocks and sheep roam the grounds. The towering boxwood gardens have secret paths running inside the hedges, great for hide-and-seek and exploring. Since the original portion of the Monroe house was a modest five-room home, the house tour is brief (about 30 minutes). At the end, guests are brought outside to view the kitchen, where several hands-on activities await young visitors. Although tours vary depending on the guide and the group, most guides go out of their way to include children. The rooms in the house, however, are very small, making the house tour difficult with toddlers. The home is handicapped-accessible, but strollers must be parked outside.

Several special events make Ash Lawn-Highland particularly appealing for families. On Kite Day in May, the fields are opened for kite flying. All visitors with a kite are admitted free, and the fields fill with children and colorful kites of all shapes and sizes.

Plantation Days Weekend, held on the weekend closest to the Fourth of July, features 20 period crafts demonstrated by costumed guides. The guides who participate in Plantation Days are selected from craftspeople from all over the Eastern seaboard and do a wonderful job explaining their crafts to children. Folk music, food and a Revolutionary War encampment round out the festivities.

On Saturday mornings in July and August, families are treated to puppet shows and other theatrical works, including one by the Ash Lawn-Highland Opera Company (see Music and Theater chapter for details).

At Christmas, the house is decorated for the holidays. On the grounds is a Christmas tree farm where visitors can cut their own trees. Storytelling, decoration-making workshops and other Christmas programs make Ash Lawn-Highland shine during the holidays.

SCHLEP FACTOR: Fairly low, but we recommend visiting Ash Lawn-Highland during high season. Visitors during the off-season will get a much more limited view of the property, as the outbuildings will have only placards as guides. During late April and the day after major holidays Ash Lawn-Highland can get busy, but lines are never as long as those at Monticello. A nice gift shop offers lots of children's selections as well as restrooms, vending and limited snacks.

DIRECTIONS: Take I-64 to Exit 121A (Route 20S). Follow Route 20S through one set of lights to a left onto Thomas Jefferson Parkway. Take the Parkway past Monticello to a right onto Route 795 to Ash Lawn-Highland.

Guests coming from downtown Charlottesville head south on 9th Street NE, which becomes Avon Street. Turn left onto Monticello Avenue, which becomes Route 20S, then follow directions as above.

Court Square

Jefferson Street, Charlottesville

WEBSITE: http://www.avenue.org/achs

HOURS: Twilight Tours are offered Saturdays from Memorial Day–Labor Day and begin near the Omni Hotel on the Downtown Mall. Purchase tickets at time of tour. No reservations necessary, but call the Historical Society for current times.

Standard Historical Society tours offered Saturdays at 10 AM, April–October. Meet at the Historical Society building at 200 2nd Street NE.

Call the Albemarle County Historical Society, Monday–Friday 9 AM–5 PM or Saturday 10 AM–1PM at (804) 296-1492.

ADMISSION: Free, but a donation of $3 per adult is suggested.

The buildings along Court Square near the Downtown Mall date back to the early 1800s (one still stands from the late 1700s) and in their heyday were the most important, prestigious buildings in town. Families with kids under 8 should pick up a self-guided tour brochure and stroll down the treelined streets around the square. The Albemarle County Historical Society on 2nd Street NE (facing Lee Park) has one such brochure and is in the process of putting together a longer booklet describing the historic buildings in the Court Square area. The Charlottesville Downtown Foundation (804) 296-8548 also publishes an excellent walking tour brochure that offers information about the past uses of each historic building. The County Courthouse, Levy Opera House, several taverns and Magruder Sanatorium (Charlottesville's first hospital) are a few buildings along the route, and although there are no placards on the buildings themselves, the brochures do a nice job of filling in details. The buildings are not especially interesting for kids, but the walk is perfect for strollers and small, shady McGuffy Park is located at the end of the walking tour.

History-loving kids over 8 may enjoy guided tours of the Court Square area, led by the Albemarle County Historical Society. Our favorite guided tour for families is the Twilight Tour, a theatrical tour led by a costumed guide who acts the part of a local historic resident. Different eras in Charlottesville's history are portrayed each week including the Jefferson, Civil War, Antebellum, Gilded Age, and Roaring Twenties eras. Another tour, geared toward adults but fine for older children, is the standard Historical Society tour that explores the history of the courthouse area. In late October, the Historical Society hosts evening Spirit Walks where guests encounter authentically-costumed spirits from Charlottesville's history. This exceptional tour always sells out well in advance. Members of the Albemarle County Historical Society get first crack at the tickets (hint, hint). Call for reservations and membership information.

Around Thanksgiving each year, Grace Covenant Church and the City of Charlottesville sponsor "Governor Jefferson's Thanksgiving Festival", a huge living history event held in the Court Square and Downtown Mall area. Families can choose from over 50 activities including children's games and crafts, carriage rides, reenactments and much more. In addition, guests can converse with a variety of living history interpreters playing the roles of famous Charlottesville residents of the Revolutionary War era. This free, three-day event is great for the whole family. For details call (804) 978-4466.

SCHLEP FACTOR: Pretty high. Realistically, with the exception of Governor Jefferson's Thanksgiving Festival (which makes the area accessible to all ages) and the Twilight Tours, Court Square is mostly interesting to adults or older children. Families with younger children should combine a walking tour with a trip to McGuffy Park, the Ice Park or the Discovery Museum, or buy a round of ice cream cones at Chaps and stroll towards Court Square. Charlottesville Downtown Foundation self-guided walking tour brochures are available at kiosks along the Downtown Mall (in the summer), at the Downtown Foundation offices, the Nook Restaurant, the Ice Park, and Omni Hotel (all on the Downtown Mall) or at the McGuffy Art Center on 2nd Street NW.

DIRECTIONS: From Route 29, take the 250E Bypass to a right onto McIntire Road. At the Preston Avenue light, turn left onto Preston/Market Street. Turn left at the first traffic light onto 1st Street N. Go 1 block and turn right onto Jefferson Street. The Albemarle County Historical Society is located at the corner of Jefferson Street and 2nd Street NE and Court Square begins near the courthouse on Jefferson Street.

Free 2-hour parking is available on the street, or you can pay to park in the Market Street garage located at E. Market Street and 6th Street.

★ Michie Tavern

Thomas Jefferson Parkway (Route 53), Charlottesville
(804) 977-1234

Website: http://www.michietavern.com

Hours: Daily 9 AM–5 PM year around, last tour at 4:20 PM.
The Ordinary buffet lunch available from 11:15 AM–3:30 PM, April
through October and 11:30 AM–3 PM, November through March.

Admission: Free for children under 6, $4.95 for children 6–11, $10.50 for adults.
Beverage, dessert and taxes additional.

Tour is free for children under 6, $2 for children 6–11, $6 for adults.
Albemarle County and Charlottesville residents admitted free.

Michie Tavern, built near Free Union in 1784 on land owned by Patrick
Henry's father, provided weary travelers with food, drink and lodging. In
1927, the tavern was moved close to Monticello. Today, Michie Tavern
boasts one of the most family-friendly tours in the area. During the
summer, children are given cards listing items found on the tour and are
challenged to find each item. Kids will learn about the hauntings in the
tavern and about how travelers were lined up horizontally on the beds to
make room for everyone (makes sharing a room sound like a piece of
cake!). The tour continues outside where the numerous outbuildings of
the tavern can be viewed.

The tour is given by guides in period costume from April through
October but is self-guided with taped messages in each room during the
rest of the year. During self-guided tours a costumed hostess is available
to answer additional questions.

If you visit midday, have lunch in The Ordinary, the tavern's dining
room. The buffet-style meal of fried chicken, black-eyed peas, stewed
tomatoes, biscuits and more, cooked from recipes dating back to the
1700s, is a tasty way to broaden kids' understanding of history and is
plain enough to appeal to most children. There is a tavern gift shop, but
kids will prefer to walk next door to The General Store, a converted grist
mill built in 1797, which offers a variety of Virginia-made products and
kid-pleasing souvenirs.

Schlep Factor: Moderate. Michie Tavern is conveniently located near Monticello and
Ash Lawn-Highland, although that proximity means it can be busy
during high season. We recommend families try to avoid visiting the day
after major holidays and plan to arrive early in the day in April and
October. Plenty of parking is available, but you will need to climb quite
a few steps to get to the Tavern and The Ordinary. A ramp serves
wheelchairs and strollers.

Directions: Take I-64 to exit 121A (Route 20S). Go through one set of lights to a left
onto Thomas Jefferson Parkway (Route 53). Michie Tavern is on the
right. Guests coming from downtown Charlottesville head south on 9th
Street NE, which becomes Avon Street. Turn left onto Monticello
Avenue which becomes Route 20S then follow directions as above.

★ Monticello

Thomas Jefferson Parkway (Route 53), Charlottesville
(804) 984-9808

WEBSITE: http://www.monticello.org

HOURS: Daily 8 AM–5 PM March–October, 9 AM–4:30 PM
November–February

ADMISSION: Children under 6 for free, $5 for children under 12, $9 for adults.
Admission for residents of Charlottesville and Albemarle County is $5
(ID required) or free with a guest (one free admission for one paid
admission).

Tours: Family tours are offered on the hour from 9 AM–3 PM June
15–August 23. Family tours are included in the general admission fee;
register at the ticket office. The Learning Center is located inside the
Monticello Visitor Center on Route 20 and is open daily (10 AM–
4 PM June 15–mid-August) although special events may cause the
Learning Center to close.

Over the last few years, Monticello, the mountaintop home of Thomas
Jefferson, has become much more accessible to children. During the
summer, special tours for families with children ages 4–11 bring
Jefferson's life and accomplishments to a level children can appreciate
and understand. These tours allow children to touch and hold select
replicas of artifacts, and focus primarily on the children in the group.
Families must register at the ticket office for the family tour, then walk
or take the free shuttle to the house. Since the walk is steep, we
recommend families take the shuttle up. If kids are still energetic at the
end of the day, walk back down.

Regular house tours are available year-round and require no ticket
office registration. Guests take the shuttle up the mountain then queue
up at the house. When the wait for a tour exceeds 45 minutes, a Visitor
Services representative will be on hand to pass out time cards that allow
guests to walk around the gardens and grounds instead of waiting in line.
Inside, most kids over 8 are fascinated by the innovations Jefferson used
in the house and are attentive guests. As a courtesy to others, however,
parents of antsy children will be asked to leave. Parents of toddlers will
most likely want to try a tag-team touring approach.

The grounds are amazing, and families should visit even if they
decide not to tour the house. Dependencies include the smokehouse,
cook's room, cellars, stables, ice house, and kitchen with an all-weather
passageway underneath the main house. These areas are self-guided with
placards describing former uses. Families can stroll down Mulberry
Row, the center of the Monticello slave community, and through the
extensive vegetable and flower gardens. Mid-April through October, a
garden tour and a Plantation Community tour are offered. Families can
drop in and out of these 45-minute tours depending on their children's
attention spans. Below the house, guests can view the cemetery where
Jefferson is buried, then continue downhill to the entrance or walk back
uphill to the house for the shuttle.

Families visiting from mid-June to mid-August should also stop by the Learning Center located inside the Visitor Center for more hands-on children's activities. Kids can write with a quill pen, try out a polygraph modeled after one Jefferson owned, and guess the uses of different artifacts at the "What Is It?" table. The Visitor Center also has year-round exhibits about Monticello, and is located right down the street near the intersection of Route 53 and Route 20. Hours are 10 AM through 4 PM.

In the winter, Monticello offers a series of Family Workshops that explore topics ranging from tin lantern making to African American stories, games and songs. All focus on life at Monticello and are offered for two separate age groups (1st through 3rd grade and 4th through 6th grade). Monticello also offers a summer day camp for kids 4th through 6th grade to explore archaeology, Monticello history, and all aspects of Monticello as it relates to children. For information on both programs, call the Monticello Education Department at (804) 984-9853.

SCHLEP FACTOR: Moderate. The line-release system keeps kids from standing in line excessively, but families may still want to avoid visiting the day after major holidays when the wait for a tour can be over two hours. During tourist season in early spring, summer and October, plan on arriving when the gates open to avoid lines. Whenever you choose to visit, be sure to dress for the weather, since much of Monticello is outdoors.

Near the entrance, guests will find restrooms, a garden shop, and a snack bar, the Little Mountain Luncheonette, that serves drinks, ice cream, and sandwiches. Both the garden shop and snack bar are open April through October. The gift shop near the house offers lots of quality children's souvenirs, soda/juice machines, a few snacks and restrooms. The grounds are stroller- and handicapped-accessible, but strollers must be parked outside for the house tours.

DIRECTIONS: From Charlottesville, take I-64 to Exit 121A (Route 20S). Go through one traffic light (passing the Visitor Center on the right) and turn left onto Thomas Jefferson Parkway. Follow this road past Carter Mountain and Old Michie Tavern, then turn left into the Monticello entrance. Continue past the gatehouse to the parking lot on the right. Guests coming from downtown Charlottesville head south on 9th Street NE, which becomes Avon Street. Turn left onto Monticello Avenue which becomes Route 20S then follow directions as above.

University of Virginia (U.Va.)

University Avenue and Emmet Street, Charlottesville
(804) 924-0311

WEBSITE: http://www.virginia.edu

HOURS: The Rotunda is open daily from 9 AM–4:45 PM.

ADMISSION: Free.

Thomas Jefferson's Academical Village, with secret gardens, tunnels, and wide grassy areas, is an inviting place for kids. On the Lawn, the Rotunda is a great place to introduce children to the classical style of architecture Jefferson brought to this region. Symmetry (dual staircases, columns, etc.) and innovation (kids find the oval rooms intriguing) are hallmarks of Jeffersonian style that are easy to identify in the Rotunda without a formal tour. Before you leave, pick up brochures for self-guided tours of the Grounds and of the Pavilion Gardens that encircle the Lawn. Take a romp down the Lawn for antsy little ones, then follow the paths from the Lawn to the Pavilion Gardens. Feel free to enter any garden with an open gate (if the gate is closed, please respect the privacy of the people living in the adjoining Pavilions). Each garden is different, but all are enclosed by serpentine brick walls and feel like secret gardens. Facing McCormick Street (between the Lawn and Alderman Library), you'll find Edgar Allen Poe's room glassed for public display and furnished to appear as it did when Poe was a student at U.Va..

SCHLEP FACTOR: Low. Your kids don't need a formal tour to learn about and enjoy the U.Va. grounds. Parking is now easier thanks to the new parking garage. Pack a picnic to enjoy on the Lawn or check out the Newcomb Hall Dining Room, which is set up like a food court. The restaurants across the street on The Corner welcome families as well.

DIRECTIONS: Take Route 29S from Barracks Road to the intersection of Route 29 and University Drive. Continue on Route 29 for one block to the parking garage on the left. Newcomb Dining Hall is located near the top of the parking garage and the Lawn is a 5-minute walk away.

AND BEYOND CHARLOTTESVILLE...

★ **Exchange Hotel and Civil War Museum**
400 S. Main Street, Gordonsville   (540) 832-2944
WEBSITE: http://www.gemlink.com/~exchange-hotel/home.htm
HOURS: Tuesday–Saturday 10 AM–3:30 PM, mid-March–mid-December, closed rest of the year.
ADMISSION: Children under 6 for free, $1 for children 6–17, $4 for adults, $3 for seniors.

Visitors to the Exchange Hotel and Civil War Museum in Gordonsville tour the hospital where sick and wounded soldiers were brought during the Civil War. The guided tour begins on the first floor with a brief history of the Gordonsville area. On the second floor, guests learn about the Civil War period in Gordonsville. The top floor has been reconstructed into a receiving hospital which includes a surgical ward, where everything from tooth extractions to amputations were performed, and the hospital ward where soldiers recuperated. Actual surgical instruments used during the war are on display and the guide gives detailed descriptions of surgeries performed.

Since tours are conducted as guests arrive, families will have a docent to lead them through the museum. Tours are tailored to the needs of each family. Families with children may request a shorter and less graphic tour.

Two reenactments are performed at the hospital each year, typically in April and October. Real doctors portray Civil War doctors performing various surgeries in the receiving hospital. Outside, a field hospital is set up in tents with each tent demonstrating some facet of Civil War medicine. The pharmacy tent, for example, has a pharmacist demonstrating and describing pharmaceutical practices during the war. The reenactments are quite realistic and may be too much for squeamish guests. The outside tents, however, are fine for children of all ages.

SCHLEP FACTOR: Moderate. This is a great trip for families with middle grade children studying the Civil War, but it may be too intense for younger children. A small museum store on the ground floor offers some children's books and souvenirs, all related to the Civil War. The museum is not handicapped- or stroller-accessible beyond the first floor.

DIRECTIONS: Take Route 29N to a right on Route 33E at the main intersection in Ruckersville. Follow Route 33 through Barboursville and continue for another 5 miles to Gordonsville. At the traffic circle in Gordonsville, go halfway around the circle to Main Street. Go under an underpass, and the Exchange Hotel will be on the left just before the fork in the road.

Hatton Ferry

Scottsville

WEBSITE: http://www.hattonferry.org

HOURS: Friday, Saturday and Sunday, 9 AM–5 PM, mid-April–mid-October, but entirely dependent on the water level in the James River.

There is no direct phone number for the ferry, but their brochure advises visitors to call the Visitor Center at (804) 293-6789 or the Albemarle County Historical Society at (804) 296-1492 to make sure the ferry is running.

ADMISSION: Free.

One of only two poled ferries left in the United States, the Hatton Ferry was used to carry goods and passengers across the James River in the 1800s. The ferry still runs on weekends in spring through early fall, giving passengers a fun and free 15-minute ride across the river. This is no tiny raft; the ferry can even take your car across. One hitch: the ferry doesn't run if the water is too high or too low, but there is no direct number to find out if they are running on any particular day. Their brochure advises visitors to first call the Visitor Center or the Historical Society.

SCHLEP FACTOR: High. Hatton Ferry is 25 miles south of Charlottesville, so combine this with a trip on the river with the James River Runners (just across the parking lot).

DIRECTIONS: Take I-64 to Exit 121A (Route 20S). Follow Route 20S for 17-1/2 miles (the road narrows). Fifty feet beyond the "Welcome to Scottsville" sign, turn right onto Route 726. Go 1 block to the stop sign, then continue straight for 1/4 mile to a 2nd stop. Turn right (you will still be on Route 726) and go 3 miles to a left on Route 625. Go 2 miles to the Hatton Ferry.

★ Montpelier

Route 20N, Orange   (540) 672-2728

WEBSITE: http://www.montpelier.org

HOURS: Daily 9:30 AM–5:30 PM April–November, 9:30 AM–4:30 PM December–March. Closed first Saturday in November, Thanksgiving, Christmas and New Year's.

ADMISSION: Children under 6 for free, $3.50 for children ages 6–11, $7.50 for adults, $6.50 for seniors. AAA and senior discounts available. Family programs require advance registration. Call the education department at (540) 672-0025 to get on the Family Programs mailing list or to register for programs.

James Madison, fourth President of the United States and the Father of the Constitution, lived at Montpelier with his wife, Dolley, for many years. After Madison's death, Dolley sold the house, which then passed through a series of owners and underwent three major additions. Montpelier today, therefore, bears little resemblance to its appearance during the Madison years. Instead of offering a typical historic home tour, Montpelier is the site of exciting ongoing architectural research and archaeological excavations and is a very child-friendly, eclectic historic site.

Guests begin their tour at the gift shop with a 15-minute orientation video about Madison's political career and the history of Montpelier. The film is well-done and can be enjoyed by children as young as 7 or 8. Afterwards, a shuttle brings guests to the main house for an introduction to Montpelier's changes over the years. Most visitors will then opt to use the free Acoustaguide audio equipment to tour the house and grounds. Since the Acoustaguide tour takes nearly three hours, we recommend that families with children instead ask one of the interpreters in the house for an abbreviated tour. The interpreters are very friendly and knowledgeable and more than willing to show children exhibits. Several pieces of original furniture, Dolley Madison's engagement ring, a reproduction of one of Dolley's gowns, and various artifacts found at the site are but a few items guests will see in this gallery-style tour. Cutaways in the walls of the house expose the original brickwork. In the winter, archaeologists are often working in the house and gladly answer questions about their research.

Outside, visitors can see the foundation of the original kitchen, the chimney foundation of the slave quarters, a temple built by Madison's slaves that doubled as the ice house, the slave cemetery and the Madison cemetery where James and Dolley Madison were laid to rest. Next to the Madison cemetery is the site of the first Montpelier house, built by James Madison's grandparents in 1732. During weekdays in the summer, kids can watch the archaeological excavations going on at the site. Behind the main house, a restored pony barn houses the Education Center with changing exhibits, some of which are good for children.

Several special events at Montpelier are geared toward families. Our favorite is Constitution Day, held on the Saturday closest to September 17th (the day the Constitution was signed). The Colonial Williamsburg Fife and Drum Corps plays throughout the day; living history interpreters, playing Madison, the town crier and Revolutionary War soldiers are on hand; and kids can try their hand at a variety of colonial games such as hoop rolling and Games of Graces. In the temple, a replica of the Constitution, on real parchment paper, is laid out for kids to sign. Kids get an "I Signed the Constitution" button, and afterwards, the parchment papers are preserved in the Archives of the Constitutional Center in Philadelphia. Admission is free, balloons are handed out, and cake and punch are served.

Celebrations are also held on James' and Dolley's birthdays, March 16th and May 20th, respectively. Admission is free, cake is served and several special events typically happen those days. Watch for other family-oriented events such as Big Woods Walks when a naturalist gives guided hikes around the 2,700 acre property.

Montpelier also hosts family programs throughout the year ranging from a really scary haunted barn and Halloween party at Halloween to Christmas family events with different hands-on workshops each year. Summer brings Summer Fun Programs for kids 3 through 12 and the Montpelier Natural History Day Camp for 4th through 8th graders. Registration is necessary for all family programs and camps and can be made by calling the Montpelier Education Department at (540) 672-0025.

SCHLEP FACTOR: Moderate. Montpelier is a 40-minute drive from Charlottesville. If possible try to avoid touring around major holidays. May, July, and October are the busiest months and Monday and Tuesday the quietest days. Families visiting at quieter times will get more hands-on help from the staff. A gift shop offers lots of children's selections, and there are drinking fountains, restrooms and drink machines on site. The property and house are stroller- and handicapped-accessible.

DIRECTIONS: Take Route 29N to a right on Route 33 in Ruckersville. Follow Route 33 for 7 miles to a left onto Route 20N. Take Route 20N about 8 miles to Montpelier on the left. Signs on Routes 33 and 20 will guide you.

Revisiting the Virginia Gold Rush

Lake Anna State Park, Spotsylvania County   (540) 854-5503

WEBSITE: http://www.state.va.us/~dcr/parks

HOURS: Gold panning available weekends only, one tour per day, Memorial Day–Labor Day. Call ahead for times.

ADMISSION: $1 for kids, $2 for adults (subject to change)
Tours: Free, no reservation necessary, meet at the Visitor Center.

We love the Gold Rush tour at Lake Anna for a couple of reasons. One, you will find many adults who don't know Virginia was the site of a major gold rush, yielding some of the largest chunks of the precious metal ever found in the United States. Second, Lake Anna park officials not only tell kids about the gold rush, they let them try panning for gold in the very stream miners flocked to in the 1840s. That kind of hands-on learning really helps kids digest information and makes for a memorable visit. The information portion of the tour is pretty short, and afterwards, kids can pan for gold until the sun goes down. The original mine shaft is still on the park premises, although presently obscured by overgrowth. Future plans are for the area to be cleared and for guided excursions to the mine site to be added to this fun and educational outing. Afterwards, take a dip in Lake Anna, go for a pontoon boat tour or let kids try their hand at fishing in the children's fishing pond.

SCHLEP FACTOR: Fairly high from Charlottesville, as the park is over an hour away. Plan to spend the day, as there is plenty to keep the whole family happy. The lake and beachfront are really well-maintained. A large snack bar (more like a restaurant) provides plenty of food options.

DIRECTIONS: Take I-64E to the exit for Route 208N. Go north on 208 to the town of Louisa. Turn right on Route 22/Route 208 to the town of Mineral. In Mineral take a left on Route 522 (take care to stay on Route 522 in this area as the road makes a left turn beyond the railroad tracks). Stay on Route 522 for about 5 miles. Turn right onto Route 208. Go 7.5 miles to a left on 601. Go 3 miles to the park on the left. (From Route 208 in Mineral there will be signs to guide you.)

★ The Stonewall Jackson House ·

8 E. Washington Street, Lexington   (540) 463-2552

WEBSITE: http://www.stonewalljackson.org

HOURS: Monday–Saturday, 9 AM–5 PM, Sunday, 1 PM–5 PM, open until 6 PM June 1–August 31, closed major holidays

ADMISSION: Children under 6 for free, $2.50 for children 6–18, $5 for adults. AAA and group discounts available.

Tours: On the hour and half-hour, the last tour begins half-hour before closing.

Tour organizers at The Stonewall Jackson House, who obviously understand how hard it can be for kids to tour historic homes, have devised a ploy to keep kids awake and listening as General Jackson's life in Lexington is recounted. Upon entering the house, children are given slates listing items found in the house and are challenged to find and check off each item during the tour. In addition, guides try to engage and interest children throughout the half-hour tour, making this an excellent stop for families with school age kids. Guests who visit the house on Jackson's birthday, January 21, are treated to birthday cake and free tours. Other special events include cider pressing one weekend in October and a Christmas event on the first Saturday in December. An adjacent garden and gift shop are free to the public.

SCHLEP FACTOR: Pretty high, since Lexington is a 1-hour drive from Charlottesville. The house has restrooms and a gift shop and is handicapped-accessible. After your tour, take a 2-block walk down Washington Street to Sweet Things Ice Cream Shoppe for homemade ice cream. If your kids have been studying the Civil War, we highly recommend combining a trip to Jackson House with a trip to the Lime Kiln to see their cornerstone production, "Stonewall Country". Although babies are welcome in the tours, stairs in the house mean strollers should be left outside.

DIRECTIONS: Take I-64W to Staunton, then I-81S to Exit 188B (Route 60W) towards Lexington. In Lexington follow the blue and white trailblazers signs (clearly marked every mile or so, but watch for one turn in town) to the Visitor Center on the right. Park at the Visitor Center and walk 1-1/2 blocks west to Jackson House.

Note: The Visitor Center has a slide show and a wealth of information about Lexington, and is a good starting point for families who have not visited the town before.

★ ## Woodrow Wilson Birthplace

18-24 N. Coalter Street, Staunton   (540) 885-0897

WEBSITE: http://www.woodrowwilson.org

HOURS: Daily 9 AM–5 PM March–October, Monday–Saturday 10 AM–4 PM, Sundays noon–4 PM November–February, closed major holidays.

ADMISSION: Children under 6 for free, $2 for children 6-12, $4 for students, $6.50 for adults, $6 for seniors. Group, school, and AAA discounts available.

The Woodrow Wilson Birthplace, restored to look as it did when our 28th president was born here in 1856, got a thumbs-up from our families who visited with children 7 and older. Original furnishings, including Wilson's crib, are on display. The guided house tour lasts about 45 minutes and is the only way guests can view the home; however, the museum is self-guided. In the museum, kids especially enjoy Wilson's restored 1919 Pierce Arrow automobile and other personal possessions. While many kids may not understand Wilson's place in history, they are still intrigued by these blasts from the past and how life has changed since the early part of the century. One mom noted that the memorabilia engaged her daughter long enough for her to read some of the more grown-up displays. Even the controversial issues regarding Wilson's life (e.g., as president he didn't support women's suffrage) are covered in this comprehensive museum. Afterwards, browse the large gift shop or allow kids to run off a little steam in the boxwood gardens.

SCHLEP FACTOR: Fairly high, mostly because of the drive. The house is stroller- and handicapped-accessible, so babies would be fine here, as would kids 7 and older, but toddlers and preschoolers will get antsy. The house is in downtown Staunton and is an easy stroll to a restaurant or cafe. On site, you will find vending machines and restrooms with a changing table.

DIRECTIONS: Take I-64W to I-81N. Take Exit 222 and follow Route 250W into town. Route 250 veers to the right then splits into 3 parts; go straight up N. Coalter and turn left onto Frederick Street. Follow signs to parking.

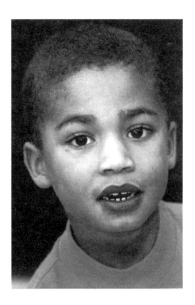

MUSEUM

While Central Virginia may not be a museum Mecca like D.C., the Charlottesville area does boast a wide variety of museums without the two-hour drive or the parking hassles. Families can choose from a rambunctious afternoon at the Virginia Discovery Museum, hands-on learning at the Frontier Culture Museum of Virginia, or a thought-provoking visit to the Bayly Art Museum just to name a few. And don't overlook Richmond and Northern Virginia in your museum-hopping. Check out those chapters for more great museums the whole family can enjoy.

Attractions marked with a ★ are part of the Timetravelers program. As Timetravelers kids can collect six stamps at these attractions and send them in for a free T-shirt and a chance at other neat prizes. Many participating locations give discounts on admission to Timetravelers and their families. See the chapter Getting Started.

Bayly Art Museum

Rugby Road, Charlottesville   (804) 924-3592

WEBSITE: http://www.virginia.edu/~bayly/bayly.html
HOURS: Tuesday–Sunday 1 PM–5 PM, closed Mondays.
ADMISSION: Free.

Tours: Age-appropriate tours can be arranged with docents.

The only art museum in Charlottesville, the Bayly is actually much more accessible to kids than many people realize. In addition to the permanent collection of ancient and modern works from around the world, the museum hosts nearly a dozen temporary exhibits each year, many of which are fascinating to kids. One recent temporary exhibit showed how art historians use science to distinguish real from counterfeit artifacts, with lots of opportunities for young sleuths to do their own investigations on museum samples. Two or three temporary exhibits are brought in every semester, assuring visitors that the Bayly will have a new look each time they visit. Although special programs for kids are not regularly scheduled, when a new exhibit arrives that lends itself particularly well to children, the museum will arrange hands-on adjunct activities to complement the exhibit.

Group tours are available at any time (even when the museum is closed) and can be tailored to any group's age or interest. During a preschool tour, for example, kids are outfitted in vests and become detectives in the museum. All tours are inquiry-based rather than lectures, giving kids an opportunity to interpret art through their own eyes.

Each fall, the Bayly hosts the Writer's Eye competition where authors 3rd grade and older compete for prizes in both poetry and prose categories.

Note: In the not-so-distant future, this hidden gem may gain a more prominent place in the community; the long-range plan for the museum calls for a six-fold expansion, with a cafe, gift shop and parking garage.

SCHLEP FACTOR: Low, except for parking, which can be a problem. If the patron lot is full, park in the Elliewood Street garage, which is a 10-minute stroll from the museum. The museum is small enough that even a 5-year-old can visit without totally melting down halfway through. And remember, kids can always work off a little steam by running around the U.Va. grounds before or after a visit. The museum has public restrooms and is handicapped-accessible.

DIRECTIONS: From Barracks Road take Route 29S to a left at the light at University Avenue. Take another left at the next light, Rugby Road. The Bayly is about 1/4-mile on the left. You will find a tiny parking lot for patrons around the back.

Jefferson at Monticello

Monticello Visitor Center, Route 20, Charlottesville
(804) 984-9855

HOURS: Daily 9 AM–5:30 PM March–October, 9 AM–5 PM November–February.

ADMISSION: Free.

This small museum details Jefferson's life at Monticello, including artifacts found at the plantation and many of Jefferson's personal possessions. Each exhibit has a placard in large print with a general description, and additional placards in smaller print with more detail. This is an ingenious arrangement for families: younger kids can just read the general placard, while older children can read the more detailed information. Families with grade schoolers will also want to see the short award-winning film about Jefferson's political career, presented on the hour from 10 AM through 4 PM in the summer and at 11 AM and 2 PM the rest of the year. During the summer, a separate Learning Center offers hands-on activities where kids can write with a quill pen, guess the original use of artifacts at the "What Is It?" table, experiment with a polygraph similar to the one Jefferson owned and more. Don't miss the adjacent gift shop which has many quality souvenirs, including heirloom plant seeds. Purchase an assortment of these seeds and plant a garden with the same species Jefferson used in the gardens at Monticello.

SCHLEP FACTOR: Low. For families with grade schoolers and older, this should be on your "visit often" list. Restrooms and drinking fountains are available and the museum is handicapped-accessible.

DIRECTIONS: Take I-64 to Exit 121A (Route 20S). Follow Route 20S to the first traffic light and turn right at the Visitor Center.

JMU Life Sciences Museum

Harrisonburg   (540) 568-6378

Hours: Monday–Saturday mornings during school time, although hours vary each semester so call ahead.

Admission: Free.

At the Life Sciences Museum in Harrisonburg, kids can observe and/or pet a variety of living animals such as an iguana, snakes and box turtles. Stuffed mammals, bones, seashells and butterflies, Native American artifacts and other gems from the natural world are also on display, but the biggest hit for kids is the dinosaur cave JMU students created. The staff is very friendly and helpful.

Schlep Factor: High, due to the irregular operating hours and the drive, but well worth a visit. We recommend combining a trip here with one of the other Harrisonburg attractions.

Directions: Take Route 29N to a left onto Route 33 at the main intersection in Ruckersville. Follow Route 33 over the mountain and into Harrisonburg. Continue on Route 33 when it crosses under I-81, then go about a mile to a fork in the road. Bear left at the fork onto Market Street E. Go less than a mile to a left on Main Street S. Go about 1 mile to a left onto Grace Street and follow signs to the Life Sciences Museum. Parking in front of the building

★ Frontier Culture Museum of Virginia

Staunton (540) 332-7850

WEBSITE: http://www.frontiermuseum.org

HOURS   Daily 9 AM–5 PM March 16–November 30, 10 AM–4 PM
December 1–March 15.

ADMISSION: Children under 6 for free, $4 for kids 6–12, $8 for adults, $7.50 for
seniors. AAA, group discounts and family memberships available.
Special events and evening performances: call for listing.

For parents who cringe at the thought of lugging kids to any place that
includes both Museum and Culture in the title, take heart. One parent
pointed out that since this is an outdoor museum, her children could run
between exhibits, and virtually everything they see is available to touch.

For the uninitiated, the Frontier Culture Museum of Virginia is a series
of four working farms representing England, Germany, Northern Ireland
and America. Visitors first tour the three European farms where they can
take part in the daily activities of life on an 18th and 19th century
farmstead. The American farm is presented last so visitors can see the
influence of the European cultures on early American farming. Each
farm has staff dressed in period costumes performing tasks such as
cooking, carving and spinning that were characteristic of each region.
Kids are encouraged to participate, but be careful, learning tends to
follow!

Look for evening programs such as barn dances and concerts, and
special children's workshops in the summer and around holidays.
Around Halloween, the museum hosts Fireside Tales where guests are
treated to spooky tales at each farm, told by the light of a lantern.
Because of the scare factor, Fireside Tales is appropriate only for
children ages eight and up. At the Holiday Lantern Tours, offered
Thursday through Sunday evenings in December, guests are led by
lanterns to each decorated farm for Christmas vignettes. Refreshments
are served following both events, and strollers should be left at home.
Reservations should be made in advance, up to two months for the
Holiday Tour, and the cost is a bit more than the usual admission fee.

SCHLEP   Very low. Although you have to bear the hour-long drive to Staunton, the
FACTOR   museum is right off the interstate. This museum is one of those rare
jewels that appeals to everyone from toddlers to adults. And since
activities are changed as frequently as a preschooler's playclothes, it is
worth visiting again and again.

A large welcome center provides restrooms, vending machines, maps
and an orientation film. Bring a stroller or backpack for small children
who may run out of steam before they run out of exhibit. The museum
also offers wagon rentals and electric mobility carts (each $2.50 per
visit) and the entire museum is handicapped-accessible.

DIRECTIONS: Take I-64W to I-81N (exit 87). Stay in the right lane and within a
1/4 mile, take Exit 222. At the end of the ramp, turn right onto Route
250W toward Staunton. Go through 2 lights (including the one under the
exit ramp) then continue for about 1/2 mile to a left at the Frontier
Culture Museum of Virginia sign.

Children's Museum
at the U.Va. Primary Care Center

U.Va. Medical Center, Charlottesville   (804) 924-5269

HOURS: Monday–Friday, 9 AM–4 PM.

ADMISSION: Free.

The Children's Museum, nestled on the first floor of the Medical Center, focuses on the healthy growth and development of little bodies. Helpful assistants weigh visitors using sandbags as counterweights, which helps preschoolers understand what the measurement actually means. Head, hands and feet are measured and the vital statistics recorded on a headband kids can keep. There is also an assortment of toys, which kids enjoy but which unfortunately don't continue the healthy bodies/medical theme.

SCHLEP FACTOR High. The staff here is friendly and attentive, but to really make this a destination for families, the museum should consider expanding its healthy bodies theme to include toys and other health-related activities. Still, what they have is well-done and worth a quick trip if you are visiting someone at the Medical Center.

DIRECTIONS: Head south on Route 29 (Emmet Street), left at the light onto University Avenue. Follow University Avenue through past the University and underneath the railroad trestle. Turn right onto Jefferson Park Avenue. Turn left at the Medical Center and park in the parking garage. The museum is on the 1st floor of the Primary Care Center.

Virginia Discovery Museum

East end of the Downtown Mall, Charlottesville   (804) 977-1025

WEBSITE: http://www.vadm.org

HOURS: Tuesday–Saturday 10 AM–5 PM, Sunday 1 PM–5 PM, closed Mondays.

ADMISSION: $3 for children 1-13, $4 for adults, $3 for seniors
$50 for families, $45 for grandparents, and $35 for individuals.
Memberships: Members receive free admission to this and all ASTC affiliated museums, a bi-monthly newsletter detailing upcoming events, and discounted admission to special programs.

There are two wonderful things about the Virginia Discovery Museum. One, the environment, activities and staff all encourage mess as the by-product of an active mind. Two, that mess is not in your living room. The front half of the museum includes a restored log cabin for imaginative play, a toddler room with a wooden ship play structure, a dress-up area, a discovery exhibit, and an activity room with a themed art project. Older kids really like the take-apart table where they can don gloves and goggles and take apart (or reassemble) telephones and other gadgets with screwdrivers and hammers. A new permanent exhibit, Jefferson's Corner, examines Thomas Jefferson, his life at Monticello, and the inventions he collected.

In the rear of the museum, visitors will find a computer lab and working beehive as well as hands-on exhibits that change every few months. Bats, mazes, and camping are just a few of the recent themes. In front, a museum gift shop sells great imagination-driven gifts, many under a dollar or two.

The museum hosts numerous classes, ongoing programs and mini-camps as well as several special events which require advance registration. Each Halloween, kids five and under have a blast at a Halloween Party that features activities, performances, games, food, and of course, a heaping helping of candy. In May at the U.Va. track, the Museum sponsors the Discovery Dash, a running race for 3- to 12-year-olds with prizes for all competitors.

The first Sunday of each month is free at the museum, although it can get very busy on those days. Rainy and snowy weekends can also pack in visitors, sometimes requiring visitors to log onto a waiting list for entry. Be sure to bring a jacket in case you are caught waiting outside.

SCHLEP FACTOR Very low. Getting to the museum couldn't be easier or more convenient and the museum volunteers go out of their way to make your child's visit special. Although most of the museum's visitors are 5 or under, many children twice that age still love to visit. If you are not a member, check out the listings of upcoming programs at the front desk. Validated parking (in the Market Street and Water Street Garages), restrooms, a changing area and coat closet are all provided. Handicapped- and stroller-accessible.

DIRECTIONS: From Route 29, take the 250E Bypass to the light at McIntire Road. Turn right and follow McIntire Road to the light. Turn left onto E. Market Street and go to the parking garage on the right. In the parking garage you will find Main Street and Market Street elevators. Take a Main Street elevator to the ground level and the Discovery Museum will be directly across the Downtown Mall.

★ Natural Bridge Wax Museum

Natural Bridge   (800) 533-1410) or (540) 291-2121 (Hotel number, but they will transfer your call)

WEBSITE: http://www.naturalbridgeva.com

HOURS: Vary seasonally, but open daily year-round, call for schedule.

ADMISSION: Children under 6 for free, $3.50 for children, $7 for adults. Multi-site tickets for any combination of Wax Museum, Natural Bridge and Natural Bridge Caverns available at substantial savings.

Educators will tell you that kids learn best through multi-sensory activities. Rather than simply reading to your kids about the history of Virginia and the Shenandoah Valley, bring them to the Wax Museum at Natural Bridge where light, sound and animation bring history to life. More than 150 wax figures guide visitors through themes such as moonshining and the Civil War, with a few biblical scenes sprinkled in. Kids ten and under especially seem to enjoy the Wax Museum. Afterwards, be sure to go downstairs and tour the factory to see how their figures are made and stored.

SCHLEP FACTOR High if you are making the hour-plus drive just for this, but low if you combine a visit here with a trip to Natural Bridge, which is right across the parking lot. For rainy day fun with kids ages 5 and up, visit the caverns and the museum, then pop over to the Visitor Center for a round of indoor miniature golf.

DIRECTIONS: Take I-64W to I-81S (near Staunton) to exit 180A (Route 11S). From the exit, follow Route 11S for about 3 miles to the Visitor Center and Wax Museum.

Virginia Museum of Natural History

104 Emmet Street (Route 29N), Charlottesville   (804) 982-4605

WEBSITE: http://www.vmnh.org

HOURS: Monday–Thursday 10 AM–4 PM but best to call before visiting

ADMISSION: Free, but donations appreciated.

Membership: $35 per year, includes a newsletter detailing upcoming events and other perks.

Visitors to the Charlottesville branch of the Virginia Museum of Natural History will get a glimpse into their own backyard, past and present. The museum features a main rotating exhibit, a permanent exhibit of Virginia animals and a toddler room with a rotating exhibit. The small museum is worth a self-guided tour, but if you really want to see the museum at its best, sign up for one of their parent/child classes. Offering an in-depth (and age-appropriate) look at nature topics such as "trees in winter," these classes are well-done and are in hot demand during the winter. The museum also offers take-home activity packets called Kids Investigating Science and Nature (KITS) which can be checked out for $15 for a two-week period. Various subjects such as snakes, bats, dinosaurs, archaeology, and solar energy are available.

Join the VMNH and receive (among other perks) the museum newsletter with a calendar of upcoming events, and priority registration and reduced fees for many classes.

SCHLEP FACTOR Moderate. You'll need to call ahead before visiting, but access and parking are pretty easy. The museum is small in scope, but not in quality. Restrooms and a drinking fountain are available, and the museum is handicapped- and stroller- accessible.

DIRECTIONS: From Barracks Road, take Route 29S to a left into the VMNH parking lot just before the Ivy Road/University Avenue light.

PARKS

We wish we had room to review all of our local parks, since each is a potential favorite. Some families love the cozy, tucked-away feel of McGuffy, while others love the neighborhood ambience of Greenleaf. The huge play structure at Tonsler ranks high with young kids, while older children give high marks to the nature trail at Pen Park. Go ahead and find your family's favorite, or better yet, try a new one each week! And our Richmond chapter offer three more parks—Belle Isle, Byrd and Maymont—that are well worth the hour-long drive.

CITY OF CHARLOTTESVILLE PARKS

WEBSITE: http://parks.ci.charlottesville.va.us

Since 1918, when local philanthropist Paul Goodloe McIntire donated the first land for a public park in Charlottesville, our park system has undergone many changes. Early visions for our Department of Recreation and Leisure Services facilities called for segregated clusters. Today, undergoing a true renaissance, the new vision is for "The City as a Park." This vision calls for trails connecting parks to neighborhoods as well as to each other, and for upgrading facilities and plantings. The new plan will consider all of our public parks not as segregated clusters but as an integrated system, while retaining the character and unique nature of each park.

The master plan will take many years to complete, but progress is well underway. The City of Charlottesville Public Works Department runs programs to allow citizens to get involved in the park system and to be a part of this transformation. Among other programs, families can choose to maintain park gardens or to adopt a city park and help with some maintenance tasks.

Below, we have reviewed some of the most popular local parks, but as the park transformation continues, you may find that some of our descriptions become dated. If you want the most up-to-date information on the city parks, visit their website.

Tip: If you visit any Charlottesville parks from November until mid-March, be advised that there will be no facilities available. Bring drinking water and consider throwing the old training potty in the back of the car for emergencies!

Tip: Many of the city playgrounds now use shredded recycled tires to provide a soft, safe surface beneath structures. The stuff washes out easily, but tends to leave your kids looking like they have been living in your carburetor for some months. A change of clothes and a box of wipes are a good idea if the kids need to look decent after play.

THE PERENNIAL FAVORITES

Greenleaf Park
Rose Hill Drive at Greenleaf Lane, Charlottesville

Technically a neighborhood park, Greenleaf has become so popular that on a nice day the tiny parking lot can overflow. The park has shade on those scorching days of August and is a favorite picnic spot. A new picnic shelter and restroom have just been built, replacing the aging structure that had served the park for years. Although the playground is fairly small, it has lots of interesting features that kids adore. Best of all, pick up the key to the sprinklers and watch every kid in the park come alive in the downpour. Bring a swimsuit and towel!

SCHLEP FACTOR: Low. Greenleaf is right off the Bypass, although you will swear you are out in the country. Water and restrooms are available at the shelter. If the lot is full, park on the street. For the sprinklers, stop by the Crow Recreation Center (804) 977-3977 during operating hours and sign out the key. The recreation center is right down the street on Rose Hill Drive and is open Monday–Friday 2 PM–9 PM and Saturday 1 PM–6 PM.

DIRECTIONS: Take the 250E Bypass to the Rugby Avenue/McIntire Park exit. Turn right at the stop sign and go to the next light. Turn right on Rose Hill Drive. When the road jogs slightly to the right, continue on Rose Hill Drive to the park on the right (it's easy to miss the brown park sign, so watch carefully after the jog in the road).

McGuffy Park
Corner of High Street and 2nd Street NW

An easy walk from the downtown mall or Court Square, McGuffy Park offers a small, shady playground with picnic tables and a basketball court. The park is nestled into a corner across from the McGuffy Art Center and feels like a secret, hidden garden. Drop by if you're on the downtown mall or before visiting the artists' studios at the McGuffy. If you are taking a self-guided walking tour of Court Square with kids in tow, reward them with a trip to McGuffy at the end of your tour.

SCHLEP FACTOR: Fairly low. You won't find any restrooms or drinking fountains in this tiny park, and the adjacent lot can fill during the week. Still, partly because of its location and size, McGuffy is one of our favorite city parks.

DIRECTIONS: Take the 250E Bypass to a right at the light onto McIntire Road. Follow McIntire to the light at Preston Avenue and turn left. Turn left immediately on High Street, then right at the first opportunity to 2nd Street NW to find the park. (The park is not visible from High Street.)

McIntire Park
McIntire Road and 250 Bypass, Charlottesville

Telling a playdate to "meet us at McIntire Park" is a bit like asking someone to meet you at the Smithsonian. There is a lot of park to McIntire, so be specific! Right off the Bypass is a playground and a wading pool. Both are great for the under-five set. Behind the playground is the nine-hole McIntire golf course. Most kids won't be able to play the course, but it makes a good practice area for budding golfers. A second smaller playground can be found back by the baseball fields. At the second playground you will find restrooms, a water fountain, and picnic shelters. This playground has a smooth rubbery fountain, and picnic shelters. This playground has a smooth rubbery surface that doesn't rub off on clothes or sweaty faces.

In the spring, the Dogwood Festival holds a carnival at McIntire. The main lot fills quickly, but if you park at the Charlottesville High School tennis courts, there is a wide trail through the woods that leads right to the festivities. On snowy days, McIntire is a popular sledding spot.

SCHLEP FACTOR: Low. The small park at the main entrance has excellent handicapped accessibility.

DIRECTIONS: Take the 250E Bypass to the Rugby Avenue/McIntire Park Exit. Turn left at the stop into the park. For the lower playground (visible from the Bypass), you can turn directly into the parking lot from the Bypass, but note that during much of the day, no left turn is permitted into the park. During restrictive hours, you will have to continue to the light and make a U-turn.

Meade Park
Corner of Meade Avenue and Chesapeake Street

This five-acre neighborhood park is one of the most popular parks in the city during the summer months, thanks to the Onesty Pool swimming facilities. Visitors here will find a modified L-shaped pool with a diving board and a separate fenced toddler pool. A bathhouse with changing facilities and snackbar are adjacent. Next to the pool is a playground and picnic shelter. Although the equipment is a bit outdated, it is brightly painted and a lot of fun for kids under eight. The park also has a basketball court and multi-purpose playing field. Long-range plans for the park call for new plantings throughout, construction of a new playground and children's garden, and a trail connecting the park to the Rivanna Greenbelt Trail.

SCHLEP FACTOR: Low, especially for those on the east side of town. The park has a large parking lot adjacent to the basketball court and just a short walk from the playground and pool.

DIRECTIONS: Take the 250E Bypass to a right on High Street just before Free Bridge. Bear left onto Meade Avenue at the fork and go a short distance to the parking lot on the left.

Pen Park
Park Street, Charlottesville

One of the larger area parks, Pen is home to Meadowcreek Golf Course, a big playground (sans shade), picnic shelters and several tennis courts. What a lot of people don't know is that Pen Park has a great fitness trail where kids and adults can test their strength and skill. This same trail also boasts an Interpretive Nature Trail Walk. At the beginning of the course, a box offers a brochure describing the sights and sounds of nature at each exercise station. The nature walk is about 3/4 mile long on a paved trail with some hills. The trail is not circular, so leave time to double back.

SCHLEP FACTOR: Low. Convenient location, easy parking and good facilities (during the warmer months). Water and restrooms are available at the shelter by the playground.

DIRECTIONS: Take Route 29N to a right onto Rio Road. Pen Park is 2 miles on the left. For the fitness course, enter the park, turn left at the tennis courts and park in the lot by the picnic shelters. The fitness course/nature trail begins between shelters 2 and 3.

Tonsler Park
Cherry Avenue and Ridge Street, Charlottesville

Recently rebuilt by the Charlottesville community, Tonsler Park boasts the best play structure in Charlottesville. Castles with moats, tunnels, swings and towers dominate the landscape. You'll also find four tennis courts and a new recreation building (open limited hours). Although the wooden structure is extensive, weary parents can still keep a vigilant eye from nearby benches.

SCHLEP FACTOR: Low. Definitely worth the drive from anywhere in the city. Nice clean restrooms and drinking fountains during the warmer months, and plenty of parking close to the play structure.

DIRECTIONS: Take the Route 250E Bypass to a right at the light onto McIntire Road. Follow McIntire through the Preston Avenue intersection and through the next light (at the Lewis and Clark statue) onto 5th Street. Turn right at the second light onto Cherry Avenue. Tonsler Park is on the left.

Washington Park
Corner of 9th and Preston Avenue, Charlottesville

Extensively renovated over the past year, Washington Park promises to become a showpiece in the Charlottesville park system, complete with a new playground, a wide, grassy area and a brand-new swimming pool. In the summer, Washington Park is a popular cooling-off spot for area kids. The pool, especially great for toddlers, has a sloped-in beach entry with a mushroom waterfall. Look for phase two of the renovations, including a second playground, to be completed soon.

SCHLEP FACTOR: Low. If you haven't been by since the renovations began, stop in and check it out. The new plans also improved the park's accessibility for the disabled.

DIRECTIONS: Take Route 29S to a left onto Barracks Road at the shopping center. Go 1 mile through 2 stoplights to the blinking yellow light. Turn left onto 10th Street. Pass the pool and play area, and the parking lot is on the left.

OTHER CITY PARKS

In addition to the parks listed above, the City of Charlottesville operates 12 neighborhood and mini-parks, each one a little different from the next. They are scattered throughout the city, meaning you are never far from a quick leg-stretcher. Most of these parks are fairly small, have no bathrooms or drinking fountains, and offer only curbside parking. A trip to these parks, however, is a more intimate outing and often less overwhelming for young children (or tired parents).

Azalea Park
Old Lynchburg Road
Belmont Park
Rialto and Druid Avenue
Forest Hills Park
Forest Hills Road
Jordan Park
south end of 6th Street NE
Northeast Park
Sheridan Avenue and Calhoun Street
Fifeville Park
between Grove, Spring, and Roy Streets
Starr Hill Park
corner of 7th Street NW and Elsom Street

Bailey Park
corner of Hillcrest Avenue and 250 Bypass
Quarry Park
Quarry Road and Palatine Avenue
Riverview Park
corner of Chesapeake Street and Riverside Street

The "Schoolyard" Parks

Charlottesville City Schools

Some of the best playground equipment can be found at our public elementary schools. The City of Charlottesville has an open-door policy when it comes to schools in the city limits. They encourage families to use school playgrounds after school hours as if they were public parks. Children should be supervised on the playgrounds at all times. If you are running errands in the city and the kids need to burn off some energy, check out one of the following elementary schools:

Burnley-Moran Elementary
1300 Long Street
Clark Elementary
1000 Belmont Avenue
Greenbrier Elementary
2228 Greenbrier Drive
Jackson-Via Elementary
508 Harris Road
Johnson Elementary
1646 Cherry Avenue
Venable Elementary
406 14th Street NW

ALBEMARLE COUNTY PARKS

The Albemarle County Park system is not nearly as extensive as that of the city. The county-run parks include Darden Towe Park, which is run jointly by the city and county, and the three lake parks. A fourth, Claudius Crozet, is privately-owned but open to the public.

Mint Springs Park
Crozet   (804) 974-3790

HOURS: Daily, Memorial Day–Labor Day

ADMISSION: $1 for children, $2 for adults (county residents); $2 for children, $3 for adults (non-county residents).
For a hiking trail map: Call County of Albemarle Parks and Rec at (804) 296-5844.

Mint Springs, nestled in the mountains above Crozet, offers swimming in a sand-bottom lake (Memorial Day–Labor Day), a bathhouse with vending in the summer, hiking trails, picnic shelters, and a small playground. Surrounded by mountains on three sides, Mint Springs is the prettiest of the county parks, and is very popular for family picnics and birthday parties.

SCHLEP FACTOR: Low for those in the Crozet area, but higher elsewhere. This is the only lake that has any significant shade near the beach.

DIRECTIONS: Take Route 250W to a right on Route 240W. At the stop sign in Crozet, make a left followed by an immediate right onto Route 788 (Railroad Avenue). At the fork, take a right onto Route 684 (Mint Springs Road). The park is 1/2 mile on the left.

Walnut Creek Park
Red Hill   (804) 979-0964 (bathhouse number)

HOURS: Daily, Memorial Day–Labor Day

ADMISSION: $1 for children, $2 for adults (county residents); $2 for children, $3 for adults (non-county residents). For a mountain bike trail map: Call County Parks and Rec at (804) 296-5844.

The largest and newest of the county parks, Walnut Creek offers swimming in a sand-bottom lake (Memorial Day–Labor Day), a bathhouse with snackbar in the summer, rugged mountain bike trails, and picnic shelters. Canoe rental is also available on the lake in the summer for $2 per hour. Nature trails, a children's playground, and better handicapped-accessibility are planned for the near future.

Schlep Factor: Low for those on the south side, but higher for everyone else. This is worth a visit in the summer (for the lake) or for families with older kids who are experienced mountain bikers.

Directions: Take the 250W Bypass which becomes Route 29S. Make a left on Route 708. Turn right on Route 631. Park is 1/2 mile on the left.

Chris Greene Lake Park

Earlysville   (804) 973-3790 (bathhouse number)

Hours: Daily, Memorial Day–Labor Day

Admission: $1 for children, $2 for adults (county residents); $2 for children, $3 for adults (non-county residents).

Just two minutes from the airport, Chris Greene Lake offers swimming in a sand-bottom lake (Memorial Day–Labor Day), bathhouse with snackbar in the summer, picnic areas and a small playground. The lake area here is especially good for toddlers, featuring a playground in the sand and a mushroom waterfall in the ankle-deep kiddie area. Canoe rental is available in the summer at $2 per hour. In the spring, Chris Greene is a popular spot for crappie fishing.

Schlep Factor: Low for those on the north side of town, higher elsewhere. Certainly worth a trip in the summer.

Directions: Take Route 29N to a left onto Airport Road. Go to the stop and turn right onto Route 606. Turn left on Chris Greene Lake Road (Route 850) and into the park.

Darden Towe Park

Route 20N, Charlottesville

Primarily an athletic field complex, Darden Towe also offers a small wooden playground, tennis courts, a small pond, a grassy trail by the Rivanna River, and picnic shelters. The shelter near the playground has restrooms and a water fountain and during summer baseball games also has a small snackbar. On weekends, Darden Towe can be flooded with people on hand to watch various athletic events, but the rest of the week the park is often empty. The parking lot and surrounding paved trails, therefore, are often a great place for rollerblading or beginner biking. The park also offers river access for small boats. The grassy trail that runs alongside the river makes up the initial section of the Rivanna Greenway.

Schlep Factor: Low for east end dwellers, higher elsewhere.

DIRECTIONS: Take the Route 250E Bypass over Free Bridge. At the next light turn left onto Route 20N. Take 20N about 1/2-mile to a left onto Elks Drive. The park is at the end of the road.

Claudius Crozet Park

Park Street, Crozet   (804) 924-5444

Just a bike ride from downtown Crozet, Claudius Crozet Park forms the hub of many Crozet activities and festivals. Here you will find a wonderful swimming pool (great for toddlers) with a snack bar, picnic facilities and a small playground. Each spring and fall, Claudius Crozet Park hosts the Crozet Arts and Crafts Festival, a great family event. The Fourth of July Fair is a great small town funky event, just right for kids.

SCHLEP FACTOR: Moderate, except for summer and during special events. The rest of the year there are few amenities to draw families from afar.

DIRECTIONS: Take Route 250W to the traffic light at Route 240 (Crozet Avenue). Turn right onto Crozet Avenue. Go about a mile to a right onto Tabor Street. Make the next right onto Park Street. Follow Park Street to the park on the left.

ALBEMARLE COUNTY SCHOOLS

Like the city, Albemarle County considers school playgrounds to be part of the public domain after school hours (and after any aftercare programs) and encourages families to use the playgrounds during these times. The playgrounds at county elementary schools are much better than those at the county parks listed above. Some also have paved walking trails. The county elementary schools include:

Agnor-Hurt Elementary
3201 Berkmar Drive, Charlottesville
Broadus Wood Elementary
185 Buck Mountain Road, Earlysville
Brownsville Elementary
5870 Rockfish Gap Turnpike, Crozet
Cale Elementary
1757 Avon Street Extended, Charlottesville
Crozet Elementary
1407 Crozet Avenue, Crozet
Greer Elementary
2055 Lambs Road, Charlottesville
Hollymead Elementary
2775 Powell Creek Drive, Charlottesville
Meriwether Lewis Elementary
1610 Owensville Road, Charlottesville
Murray Elementary
3251 Morgantown Road, Ivy
Red Hill Elementary
3901 Red Hill School Road, North Garden
Scottsville Elementary
7868 Scottsville Road, Scottsville
Stone-Robinson Elementary
958 N. Milton Road, Charlottesville
Stony Point Elementary
3893 Stony Point Road, Stony Point
Woodbrook Elementary
100 Woodbrook Drive, Charlottesville
Yancey Elementary
7625 Porters Road, Esmont

THE OUT-OF-TOWN-
BUT-WORTH-THE-DRIVE PARKS

Although many towns surrounding Charlottesville have wonderful little parks, we have only included here the out-of-town parks we would drive to as a destination (as opposed to dropping by when you are already in the area). If you are interested in visiting some of the smaller parks in neighboring towns, contact the town Department of Parks and Recreation. A few notable Departments of Parks and Rec include:

Culpeper, (540) 727-3412
Harrisonburg, (540) 433-9168
Staunton, (540) 332-3945
Waynesboro, (540) 942-6735
Richmond, (804) 780-6091

Ridgeview Park

Magnolia Drive, Waynesboro   (540) 942-6735 (Waynesboro
Department of Parks and Rec)

HOURS: Daily, daylight–dark

Charlottesville has no park that compares with Waynesboro's Ridgeview Park, so it is well worth the 45-minute drive. Like Tonsler Park, the play structure was built by the community and is massive (you can lose a kid in there if you aren't careful). From the parking lot, a long swinging bridge crosses the river to some nice hiking trails. In summer, a huge outdoor pool with three diving boards (two low, one that takes some courage) and a separate baby pool are open to the public for a nominal fee. Also in summer, a snack bar serves up several flavors of sno-cones and other snacks and is accessible from the park as well as the pool. Be sure to bring along bread to feed the ducks in the river.

SCHLEP FACTOR: Moderate. Certainly a longer drive than the Charlottesville parks, but there is enough to do at Ridgeview to make an afternoon of it. You will find restrooms, water fountains, and good parking. Although from the end of October until mid-April the water is shut off to most of the facilities in Ridgeview Park, the brick building next to the pool has restrooms and water fountains throughout the year. Most of the park is handicapped-accessible.

DIRECTIONS: Take I-64W over Afton Mountain to exit 94. Turn right off the ramp onto Rosser Avenue and go about 2 miles to the light at 13th Street (a large, iron-fenced cemetery will be on the right as you approach the light). Turn right onto 13th Street and go 2 blocks to Magnolia Street. Turn right onto Magnolia, which goes straight into the park.

Gypsy Hill Park

Staunton   (540) 332-3945 or (540) 332-3946

HOURS: Daily 6 AM–11 PM

In the early 1800s bands of gypsies set up camp outside of Staunton. They chose an area close to the natural springs they needed for cooking, drinking and watering their horses. Today, this 215-acre tract of land, now called Gypsy Hill Park, is Staunton's largest and finest municipal park. Here you will find (among other things) a pond, a large playground, basketball, volleyball and tennis courts, swimming and wading pools, a golf course and, new in 1997, a 4,000 square foot gymnasium. In the summer, The Stonewall Brigade Band, a Staunton instrumental band that has been around since the Civil War, gives free concerts (Monday nights at the bandstand, 8 PM). Summer Thursday nights bring Jazz In The Park, free family-oriented jazz performances. Also during the warmer months, kids can take a ride on a small train or feed ducks in the pond. Staunton is a happy little town that holds a festival at the drop of a hat, many of which are held here at Gypsy Hill Park.

SCHLEP FACTOR: Medium. Staunton is 45 minutes away, but Gypsy Hill has something to offer year-round. The park is huge, so plan on driving from one area of the park to the next. Constitution Drive encircles the park, and it is fine to park along this street for easier access to different areas. Restrooms are available in several locations and the entire park is handicapped-accessible. There is no vending available except at the pool snack bar during the summer.

DIRECTIONS: Take I-64W to I-81N. Take exit 222 to a right on Route 250W (Richmond Avenue). Pass the Frontier Museum on the left and continue west on Richmond Avenue. When you go down a hill and approach a large intersection with a prison on the left get into the right-hand lane. At the light make a right onto Greenville Avenue. Pass under a railroad bridge (where the street name changes to S. Coalter) and go through 1 stoplight. At the next block, turn left onto Frederick Street (between Woodrow Wilson's Birthplace and Mary Baldwin College). Go to the 3rd stoplight and turn right onto Augusta Street. At the 1st stoplight, turn left onto Churchville Avenue. Go approximately 2 blocks, then straight through the intersection to the main entrance.

HIKING AND CAMPING

Spectacular hiking and camping are easy to find in the Charlottesville area. Not all sites, however, are suitable for young children. According to Murphy's Law (Addendum 4, Section B), the probability of a 4-year-old announcing "I wanna go home!" ten minutes into a hike, is directly proportional to the amount of time it took to get to said hike. For this reason, we have selected hiking and camping sites carefully. We have picked trails with some kind of summit (a waterfall, a breathtaking view or a swimming hole) and campsites with enough amenities to keep the kids entertained. Our veteran hiking and camping families have also compiled a list of suggestions to help your excursions go smoothly. Happy trails!

HIKING

Here are a few tips to further improve your odds:

1   Bring plenty of water. A good rule is two quarts of water per person for a moderate hike in moderate weather. Never let your kids drink unpurified water no matter how pristine the source appears. To purify water on the trail, purchase an inexpensive water purifier or iodine tablets at an outdoor supply store.

2   Pack light snacks. Trail mix is the perennial favorite, but if your kids don't like it, try granola bars, fruit leather, rice cakes, energy bars or pretzels mixed with semi-sweet chocolate chips and dried fruits. Remember, even on short hikes, kids get hungry!

3   Bring comfortable walking shoes and layer clothing. Temperature changes dramatically throughout the day in the mountains. To stay comfortable, be sure you and your kids have several layers to add or peel depending on the temperature.

4   Take plenty of rests along the way.

5   A pair of binoculars or field glasses helps kids view wildlife up close (great for watching the hawk migration in the fall or baby deer in spring!).

6   Tuck a field guide or two into your backpack to identify birds, plants and other wildlife. The National Audubon Society and Scholastic Books have teamed up for a great new series of field guides for kids (available at local bookstores).

7   If you hike in the fall or winter, be aware of the possibility of hunters. Wear orange; be loud.

8   Don't forget your camera!

9   Pick up a free copy of *Blue Ridge Outdoors* at newsstands around town for up-to-date information on outdoor activities in the area. In-depth articles, an events calendar, advertisements for outdoor supplies and more can be found in this monthly publication. The want ads in the back are a great place to find used equipment, too.

For starters...

These are great spots to get your family's feet wet (sometimes literally) if you are new to hiking. But seasoned hikers should consider these as well. Often the most rewarding hikes are the ones that are easy to get to and don't require so much of your stamina that you can't enjoy your surroundings.

Thomas Jefferson Parkway Trail
Thomas Jefferson Parkway (Route 53), Charlottesville

When the much anticipated Thomas Jefferson Parkway Trail opens sometime in 2000, residents and visitors will find a spectacular addition to the hiking and biking around Charlottesville. This trail, which will begin at the new parking lot near the intersection of Routes 20 and 53, will wind 2.4 miles up the mountain to the entrance of Monticello. Along the way, hikers and bikers will cross Carter Mountain, pass Michie Tavern, and be treated to dramatic mountain views. Since the trail (amazingly enough) will only slope five degrees amd will be gravel and boardwalk, the entire hike will be handicapped-accessible.

SCHLEP FACTOR: Should be low, although we will have to reserve final judgment for opening day. At nearly five miles round-trip, the trail will be too long for families with young children to hike in its entirety.

DIRECTIONS: Take I-64 to exit 121A (Route 20S). Go through one light to a left on Thomas Jefferson Parkway. The trail begins at the parking lot on the right.

Ivy Creek Natural Area
Hydraulic Road, Charlottesville

One hundred years ago, Ivy Creek was a dairy farm and the land was almost entirely open pasture. These pastures, growing undisturbed for over 70 years, are now more than halfway through their transformation to a mature forest. The land is now jointly run by the city and the county parks and recreation departments. If you have never tried hiking with your kids, Ivy Creek is a great place to start. Pick up a trail map as you enter and within minutes you will have completely forgotten you are just minutes from downtown Charlottesville.

A short paved trail that starts at the parking lot is accessible to wheelchairs and strollers and is great for a ten-minute nature break with a toddler. One trail favored by the Ivy Creek guides is the red reservoir trail which leads visitors over a stream and past the reservoir. The Peninsula trail is too long for small children, but beavers are often spotted out in the water and can put on quite a show for hikers.

The barn (a remnant of the dairy farm) is open Monday, Wednesday and Friday from 10 AM to noon. Inside you will find all kinds of bones, nests and other interesting specimens. The barn is also the site of special programs sponsored by the Ivy Creek Foundation, many of which are great for families. To find out more about the Foundation's programs, check *The Daily Progress* or join the foundation to receive its quarterly newsletter.

SCHLEP FACTOR: Virtually zilch! With water and restrooms on site and close proximity to Charlottesville, Ivy Creek should be on your "visit often" list. Some handicapped- and stroller-accessibility.

DIRECTIONS: From Route 29N turn left on Hydraulic Road, go to the light at the Rock Store (Route 676) and turn left. Ivy Creek is on the left before you reach the Rivanna Reservoir.

Sugar Hollow Reservoir —Moormans River Trails

White Hall, Albemarle County

Although not fully recovered from the devastating flood of 1995, the Sugar Hollow area is still a favorite warm weather hiking spot. It is more rugged than Ivy Creek but still a short drive from Charlottesville. To get to one of the favorite trails, the South Fork Trail, you must first cross the river on foot. This is usually not nearly as hard as it sounds; in summer you can often walk across without even getting your feet wet. The first portion of this trail is wide and shady, but before you reach Blue Hole, an icy-cold swimming hole, the trail gets much steeper. Families with young children should skip the swimming hole and instead leave time to double back on the trail and cool off in the river. A second trail, the North Fork Trail, snakes alongside the river, with plenty of great spots for kids to cool off along the way. This trail is actually just a continuation of the road going into Sugar Hollow.

One note: In summer, you may be tempted to walk the creek bed from the parking area down to the banks of a beautiful crystalline lake— where you immediately sink knee-deep in smelly muck. Impromptu mudslinging (of the literal kind) may follow. Kids find this little adjunct highly amusing. Many parents do not.

Be sure to bring water shoes/sandals for Sugar Hollow hiking, as the river bed is all rocks. Drinking water, towels and a change of clothes or swimwear are also recommended.

SCHLEP FACTOR: Moderate. Getting to Sugar Hollow is not hard, despite the twists and turns, but parking near the trail can occasionally be a problem on weekends. No restroom facilities are available, so this is a great opportunity to teach the kids the fine art of "using the woods".
Note: The trails at Sugar Hollow are not marked, so carefully note your route! If the water in the Moormans is very high (not typical, but possible) do not attempt to cross the river bed.

DIRECTIONS: Take Barracks Road west (becomes Garth Road) to White Hall. At Garrison's Grocery, instead of following the paved road where it turns sharply to the right, go straight onto Sugar Hollow Road. Follow this road for more than 4 miles past the Sugar Hollow Dam. Continue past the dam for about a mile to a clearing on the left where you may park. The South Fork trail begins just across the river and up the bank. The North Fork is the road you just came in on. Park and continue up the road on foot.

A RIDE AND A HIKE...
CHAIR LIFT RIDES UP MASSANUTTEN AND WINTERGREEN MOUNTAINS

Massanutten
HOURS: Mondays and Wednesdays 10 AM–2 PM May–early September, Wednesdays only for rest of September, and Wednesdays and Sundays in October. Call for exact schedule.
ADMISSION: $3 for children under 12, $5 for adults.

Wintergreen
HOURS: Daily 10 AM–4 PM Fourth of July weekend, Labor Day weekend, weekends in October.
ADMISSION: $4 for children, $5 for adults.

During the off-season, kids will love a hike combined with a chair lift ride at one of our local ski resorts. One lift is in operation on limited days at each resort. Our favorite chair lift/hike can be found at Massanutten resort, where guests begin at the ski lodge, then ride up to a 1,000-foot elevation. Pack along a picnic, enjoy the view, then hike back down—no uphill hiking required. At Wintergreen, the chair lift takes guests down the mountain. After enjoying a picnic on the wide, grassy slopes, guests can choose to either hike back up to the ski lodge or ride the ski lifts back up. Both resorts offer all-day passes, and tickets can be purchased at the lift.

SCHLEP FACTOR: Moderate. Each resort is a 45-minute drive from Charlottesville, and the chair lift rides are offered only during limited months and days. The experience for families with children 4 and up is memorable. Since there is nothing more than a metal bar restraining riders from a long fall from the lifts, this trip should not be attempted by families with squirmy toddlers. Each resort also offers other activities and dining opportunities.

DIRECTIONS: Follow directions to Massanutten or Wintergreen ski areas in our Skiing listing.

Gems along Skyline Drive...

Skyline Drive, the only public road along this section of the Shenandoah National Forest, weaves 105 miles from Front Royal to Rockfish Gap. Along the way, families will find lots of great family hikes. These are a few of our favorites, but don't stop here. The next time you enter Skyline Drive, ask at the gatehouse to purchase ($1) a copy of *Short Hikes in Shenandoah National Park*, a 16-page guide by the Shenandoah Natural History Association. The guide can also be purchased by calling the Association directly at (540) 999-3582.

ADMISSION: The fee to enter Skyline Drive is $10 per car for a seven-day pass or $20 for an annual pass. Since Skyline Drive offers many wonderful family hikes, we suggest local families purchase the annual pass. There is no fee for the Blue Ridge Parkway.

Dark Hollow Falls
Mile marker 50.7, Skyline Drive

Located just off Skyline Drive in the Shenandoah National Park, Dark Hollow Falls is a perfect hike for families with young children: a quick hike in and out with rewards of spectacular views of water cascading down dark, moss-covered rocks. The round trip hike is nearly 1-1/2 miles, but the head of the falls is only 1/2-mile from the parking lot. Once you reach the head of the falls, if your kids are still game, complete the hike by continuing along the trail to the bottom of the falls.

SCHLEP FACTOR: Moderate. This trail is very popular during tourist season, so you may want to time your visit midweek or during the off-season. Allow about 1-1/2 hours to complete the full hike. Dark Hollow Falls is right across the street from Byrd Visitor Center which features exhibits about the mountain folk who once made their home in the park. It is also very close to Big Meadows Lodge, where you can stop in for a snack or a Ranger Show.

DIRECTIONS: Take Route 29N to Ruckersville. At the main intersection in Ruckersville, turn left onto Route 33W. Go 15 miles on Route 33 to a right into the Swift Run Gap entrance to Skyline Drive. Turn left onto Skyline Drive and go north to Byrd Visitor Center.

Little Calf Mountain
Mile marker 99.5, Skyline Drive

Only a mile to the spectacular summit, Little Calf Mountain is one of our all-time favorite hikes for families with young children. On the way up, you'll pass through open fields where the tasty remnants of an old apple orchard remain, and an old pine forest before reaching a plateau. A trail joins the plateau on the left and will take you to the summit of Little Calf Mountain. The open, grassy summit is the perfect spot for a picnic, and since there are no precipitous drop-offs, kids can run unbridled without worry. Bring along binoculars for watching wildlife, particularly in the fall when the hawks are migrating.

SCHLEP FACTOR: Low. The trail is about 45 minutes from town with parking at the base. On weekdays, you will often have the trail to yourselves. Bring along a backpack for babies, but kids 2 and up can typically handle this hike if you don't mind occasional rests or piggybacking along the way.

DIRECTIONS: Take I-64W to the Rockfish Gap entrance to Skyline Drive on Afton Mountain. Go north on Skyline Drive for about 5 miles to milepost 99.5.

Stony Man Nature Trail at Skyland
Mile marker 41.5, Skyline Drive

If you are visiting Skyland Lodge for dinner, horseback riding or lodging, don't miss this 1-1/2 mile hike to a great view. You can pick up a box lunch at Skyland Lodge or bring your own picnic to enjoy at the summit. The parking area for the nature trail is just inside Skyland's north entrance. From the parking lot, follow the Appalachian Trail (blazed white) for about 1/2 mile to a trail crossing. At this point, the Appalachian Trail is at its highest point in the park, so leave time for each kid to stand on the trail crossing and chant, "I am the highest! I am the highest!" (If your children are 6 or under, allow all day for this.) Continue straight on the trail (the Appalachian Trail branches off to the right). At the next trail crossing, choose either path; the end of the trail is circular and this is where the trail meets itself. Ahead are the remains of an old copper mine and spectacular views of the valley. Any spot along this section is a good place for a picnic.

SCHLEP FACTOR: Moderate. Even though this is a beautiful hike, Skyland is more than an hour's drive from Charlottesville, so if you're just looking for a hike, do something closer. If you want to fill a day or a weekend with outdoor activities, Skyland is a wonderful destination.

DIRECTIONS: Take Route 29N to Ruckersville. At the main intersection in Ruckersville, turn left onto Route 33W. Go 15 miles to a right into the Swift Run Gap entrance; Stony Man Nature Trail is just inside the north entrance to Skyland.

TWO GREAT HIKES
ALONG THE BLUE RIDGE PARKWAY

The Blue Ridge Parkway begins where Skyline Drive ends at Rockfish Gap and continues south for 469 miles to Cherokee, North Carolina. Unlike Skyline Drive, there is no fee to enter the Parkway. There are plenty of scenic overlooks along the way, but no gas stations or restaurants, so plan accordingly. These are two of our favorite Parkway hikes close to Charlottesville.

Mountain Farm Trail
Blue Ridge Parkway, Humpback Visitor Center   (540) 943-4716
HOURS: Daily 9 AM–5 PM, staffed 10 AM–4 PM

This short (1/4 mile) flat trail is a perfect introduction to "hiking" along the Parkway for preschoolers and is an educational stop for kids of all ages. The self-guided trail leads visitors through a typical mountain farm found in the Blue Ridge in the late 1800s. Here you will find a log cabin home, chicken coops, a garden, a springhouse and other farm buildings that encourage kids to imagine what life was like in the Blue Ridge before modern amenities and conveniences. During summer and early fall, guides in period costume host demonstrations of farm life on Sunday afternoons. For families with older kids, when you complete the tour, follow the trail to the end, through the gate and across the highway to the trailhead for Humpback Rocks. For families with younger kids, pack a picnic and have lunch in the grassy field adjacent to the Visitor Center.

SCHLEP FACTOR: Very low. The Humpback Visitor Center (adjacent to the Mountain Farm parking lot) has drinking fountains and restrooms and the trail is easy to negotiate, even for families with strollers. The trail and Visitor Center are handicapped-accessible.

DIRECTIONS: Take I-64W to exit 99 on Afton Mountain. Take a right turn onto the Blue Ridge Parkway and go south for 5.8 miles to the Humpback Rocks Visitor Center parking lot.

Humpback Rocks
Blue Ridge Parkway

Just across the highway from the end of the Mountain Farm trail, you will find the trailhead for Humpback Rocks. From the bottom of the trail, you can see the summit of Humpback, a huge rock outcropping that pops out of the trees far above. Triumphant hikers standing atop the rocks look like tiny specks to those below. Point the summit out to your kids before you start the trek up because the summit immediately becomes obscured by the trees. The hike starts out easy enough, but as you near the top becomes rocky and more difficult. Just as the kids start to grumble and talk about turning back, the outcropping soars from seemingly nowhere, leading hikers to a breathtaking view of the surrounding countryside.

SCHLEP FACTOR: Fairly high for families with young children (although you will see plenty of preschoolers along the trail); lower for older kids. Most families can complete the hike within 1-1/2 hours or less. Parking is available at the base, or park in the Mountain Farm lot, which has a visitor center with restrooms and water and is a short walk to the trailhead. The trail is mostly shaded with benches along the way for rests, but bring plenty of water for the hike up.

DIRECTIONS: Follow directions to the Mountain Farm Trail. Either park in the Humpback Rocks Visitor Center parking lot at the Mountain Farm, or continue south to the base of Humpback and the parking lot on the left.

GEORGE WASHINGTON NATIONAL FOREST FAVORITES...

Saint Mary's Wilderness Area
Augusta County (near Stuarts Draft)

At nearly 10,000 acres, Saint Mary's is Virginia's largest federal wilderness area. Families visiting in the spring will be treated to massive rhododendrons and mountain laurel blooming along the trail. The trail follows the Saint Mary's River, with waterfalls and swimming holes along the way. Begin at the trailhead and hike in for one mile until the trail forks. Take the left fork to reach a nearly 20-foot high waterfall cascading into a cool, clear swimming hole. For the adventurous (and energetic) there are more waterfalls and pools above the main falls. For families with older children, Saint Mary's offers some of the best backpacking in our area.

SCHLEP FACTOR: Moderate. Saint Mary's is an hour drive from Charlottesville, but the spectacular scenery and numerous swimming holes makes this a great hike for kids.

DIRECTIONS: Take I-64W to I-81S near Staunton. At interchange #54 (Raphine exit), turn left onto Route 56 towards Steele's Tavern. Turn left onto Route 608 then right onto Route 41 to the trailhead.

Crabtree Falls

Nelson County (in George Washington National Forest in the Blue Ridge Mountains)

Reportedly the highest waterfalls in the eastern United States, Crabtree Falls rewards hikers with spectacular views. And since the falls (like so many waterfalls in the east) cascade down in a series of drops rather than in one long plunge, families can enjoy the view from many different points along the hike. The first overlook is a mere 700 feet from the lower parking lot, but once your kids get their first glimpse of the water rushing down the mountain, they'll want to forge ahead to the next overlook, and the next…just remind them that what goes up (them) must also come down. Luckily, the descent is much faster than the ascent. The peak time for viewing the falls is winter through spring, when the water is high, but the trail remains popular year-round.

Two words of caution: First, if you visit in the winter, <u>ice on the trail can make this hike treacherous.</u> Second, it is imperative that you and your family <u>stay on the trail. Do not climb rocks at the overlooks or wade into the stream, which is very slippery. Several hikers who have not heeded this advice have been swept over the falls and killed.</u>

SCHLEP FACTOR: Fairly high. The road to Crabtree Falls is a narrow, winding highway (follow directions carefully) and nearly an hour from Charlottesville. Don't visit on holidays (particularly the Fourth of July, Memorial Day and Labor Day) when the parking lot fills to capacity early in the day, leaving cars lined up a mile down Route 56. The hike is steep, so is best suited to kids 7 and up. Younger kids can easily walk to the first overlook or two (it's less than a mile to the second overlook) and will enjoy the 110-foot wooden bridge that crosses the Tye River at the entrance. The entire hike is nearly six miles round trip, so don't plan on hiking the entire way with children! Water and restrooms are available at the base.

DIRECTIONS: Follow Route 29S to Route 56W (note that 56E intersects 29S several miles before 56W). Take Route 56W about 10 miles to Massies Mill. The trail will be just 9.5 miles beyond Massies Mill on the left.

THE ICONS...

Just as Monticello and Ash Lawn-Highland have become icons of Charlottesville history, so have Whiteoak Canyon and Old Rag Mountain become synonymous with hiking in our area. No self-respecting guide to hikes around Charlottesville could leave them out. They are not, however, typical family hikes. Both are long and strenuous and only physically fit families with middle grade kids or older should attempt to hike them in their entirety. But there's no rule saying you can't go part of the way up, then head back down. For these hikes, we have suggested several reasonable stopping points along the way where families with younger children might consider turning back.

Also note that to prevent overuse, there is now a $5 fee for anyone over age 17 to hike Old Rag and Whiteoak Canyon. Either a Park Ranger or an honor box will be at the trailhead to collect the fee.

Old Rag Mountain

The complete circuit is 7 miles; allow six or more hours. Reaching the overlooks of the valley will require about a four-mile round-trip hike.

Old Rag Mountain is instantly recognizable from overlooks along Skyline Drive. While most peaks in the Blue Ridge are covered with greenery right up to their summit, Old Rag is bare, its ancient granite crown rising out of the greenery that surrounds it. While this is one of the most challenging hikes in the area, it is also one of the most rewarding. From the trailhead, take the upward trail heading off to the left. The first two miles of this trail is a series of switchbacks (that's hiking lingo meaning the trail zigzags up the mountain rather than heading straight up). In this switchback area the trail passes by a spring and through a hardwood forest until finally reaching a ridge with several nice overlooks of the Shenandoah Valley. Beyond the ridge, the trail becomes rocky and steep. Families with younger children should have lunch or a snack and let the kids scramble about the boulders for a while before heading back down. Families with older kids may want to continue on another mile to the summit. Be warned, however, that from this point hikers will not so much hike as rock-scramble their way to the summit. This section of the hike is filled with crevices and fissures and has an other-worldly feel that really plays to the imagination of children. A series of false summits teases hikers into thinking they have reached the top, only to find one more climb to reach the real summit. The real summit has a cement trail post indicating the elevation. Here, families can enjoy a spring, and panoramic views. After leaving the summit, hikers should take the switchback trail around the back side of Old Rag, past a stone camping shelter, and down the mountain. When you come to the fire service roads intersection, take the hard right (Important! If you keep going straight here you will not return to your car!) and continue for two miles to the parking lot. Celebrate!

SCHLEP FACTOR: High. As we said, this one is not for the weak of heart. You will find porta-potties at the trailhead and pit toilets at Old Rag Shelter on the trail. The trail is popular on weekends, and parking may be difficult as cars generally park by the road near the trailhead. An overflow parking lot 3/4 mile down the road is clearly marked (but will add 1-1/2 miles to your hike). The summit can be breezy and cold so be sure to bring along at least a light windproof jacket.

DIRECTIONS: Take Route 29N to a left onto Route 231 in Madison. Continue on Route 231 through Banco and Etlan. Near Sperryville, turn left onto Route 602 (at the brown "Old Rag Mountain" sign) and follow Route 602 for 3.4 miles to the trailhead.

Whiteoak Canyon

The complete hike is 7.5 miles; allow six or more hours.
The hike to the first falls is less than three miles round trip and requires about two hours of hiking. Allow more time for swimming and rock scrambling.

Whiteoak Canyon, boasting six waterfalls over 50 feet and ancient hemlocks along the trail, is one of the most popular hikes along Skyline Drive, and is included in almost every guide to hikes in the area. Lucky for us, nearly every one of these guides tells hikers to access the upper section of the trail from Skyland on Skyline Drive, leaving the lower trailhead near Syria much less crowded. Park near the trailhead and follow the trail to the camping registration kiosk. Bear right and follow the blue-blazed trail that follows the river. This trail, which crosses two bridges, runs through a small creek bed, and winds through a grove of giant hemlocks, starts out relatively flat with tempting swimming holes along the way. Try to keep the kids on task until you reach the first waterfall, about a 45-minute hike at a child's pace. As you near the falls the trail grows a bit steeper and rockier, then the falls appear, taking a breathtaking drop from the rock face into a crystalline pool below. This is a perfect stopping point for families with younger children. While swimming in the pools is allowed, <u>be sure to stay off the slippery rocks.</u> After a picnic and swim, follow the trail back the way you came, leaving enough time for boulder-scrambling and swimming in some of the pools you bypassed on the way up. Families with older children can continue up the trail where more falls appear at regular intervals. The top of the falls, roughly three miles from the trailhead, has a nice flat rock for picnicking and looking out over the falls. At this point, hikers can retrace their steps to complete the six-mile hike. Families looking for a still longer hike can take the bridge over the river to the left and stay on this fire trail until it intersects Cedar Run trail. A left onto Cedar Run trail will bring hikers back to the parking lot to complete the seven-mile-plus loop.

SCHLEP FACTOR: Moderate. White Oak Canyon is easier than Old Rag, mostly because the swimming holes that follow the trail make it easy to stop at any point along the hike. The trail to the first waterfall is not excessively steep, making the hike to the first falls do-able for children as young as 4.

Although the trail is spectacular from the upper entrance at Skyland, we highly recommend that families follow our directions to the lower trailhead. This entrance is closer, less crowded, and since the trail begins with the ascent (the trail begins with the descent from Skyland) tired children will be able to end their day with a downhill hike rather than an uphill one. Bring along a swimsuit and towel or change of clothes. There is a porta-potty at the trailhead.

DIRECTIONS: Take Route 29N to a left onto Route 231 in Madison. Stay on Route 231 for about 5 miles to the town of Banco, then turn left onto Route 670. In Syria, take a right on Route 643/600. The road forks twice; bear to the left at each fork, then continue for 3.5 miles past the second fork to the parking area on the left. Note: brown signs guide the way from Syria.

CAMPING

So you have mastered hiking with your kids and are ready to embark on an all-night adventure. If you have never camped with kids before, there is one thing you need to know: it is the schleppiest thing you will ever voluntarily do. Because of this, we have selected campgrounds that 1) are close enough so you won't feel you have crawled to the ends of the earth to get there, and 2) have enough facilities and amenities so you will be able to relax once you arrive. Our families who camp regularly offer the following camping tips to help your trip go smoothly:

Camp in your yard on your first night out, especially if you have kids under four. Some toddlers zonk right out in a tent after a day full of activities. Others become live wires and will be bouncing off the tent 'til the wee hours of the morning. Coming from the parent of a toddler who has done the latter, you will want to know which you have before you leave home.

Go easy on the caffeine and sugar. Many camping traditions (s'mores, roasted marshmallows, and hot chocolate) contain one or both. Not a problem for most adults, but sugar and caffeine coursing through the veins of a child at bedtime can mean a wakeful night for all of you.

Foods in individual packaging, while not environmentally-friendly enough to use every day, are helpful for camping, especially for your first trips out when you don't want to invest in a camp stove. Instant soups in cups, juice boxes and small boxes of cereal all pack well.

If possible, camp midweek or at least avoid holiday weekends. Also, call the campground ahead of time and ask if any special activities are planned for the time you wish to visit. A large event can swamp campgrounds with visitors, making your stay seem more like a flashback to Woodstock than a family back-to-nature experience.

Need to rent equipment? Blue Ridge Mountain Sports in the Barracks Road Shopping Center (804) 977-4400 rents tents, backpacks, sleeping bags (adult sizes only) and child carriers. Deposits are required and reservations should be made in advance.

Not sure what to bring? Pick up a backpacker's or car camper's checklist at Blue Ridge Mountain Sports.

GROUP CAMPING SITES

Camp Albemarle

Free Union Road (Route 601), Free Union
Reservation: minimum is 15, maximum is 100. Can be made as much as a year in advance, but short notice requests can often be accommodated. Call Elly Tucker (804) 293-3500

ADMISSION: $3 per person for day use, $5 per person for overnight use.

Tucked away off Free Union Road, 17-acre Camp Albemarle was built by the Civilian Conservation Corps in the 1940s. Generations of families have cooled off in the Moormans River which runs alongside the camp, explored the nature trails, run through the grassy fields, and communed by the campfire or in the huge mess hall. Those who have not fully embraced the "great outdoors" philosophy will take comfort in cabins with bunks, bathhouses with warm showers and the full kitchen in the mess hall.

Sure, you'll need to gather 15 of your closest friends and reserve the camp in advance (Camp Albemarle is a group camping facility), but sharing cooking and clean-up responsibilities with several other families leaves more time for the fun stuff, too. And since only one group at a time is allowed at the camp, you and your friends will have the place to yourselves. The full kitchen and cabins mean you can bring less stuff, but if you do find you've forgotten something crucial to survival, the camp is only a ten-minute drive to Barracks Road Shopping Center or less than a mile to Maupins Store in Free Union.

SCHLEP FACTOR: Fairly low. You'll have to organize some friends and call in advance, but after that it's all downhill. Restrooms provide flush toilets, sinks and warm showers.

DIRECTIONS: Take Barracks Road west to a right at the Hunt Country Store (just past Foxfield) onto Free Union Road (Route 601). Camp Albemarle is 3 miles ahead on the left. The entrance is easy to miss, so look for the 4-H Way street sign just before the second bridge.

TENT CAMPING

Big Meadows
Milemarker 51.2, Skyline Drive
Information: (540) 999-3231/*Reservations:* (800) 365-2267
WEBSITE: http://www.visitshenandoah.com
HOURS: Daily April–November
ADMISSION: $17 per site per night (there are over 200 sites)
Reservations: Required for a certain number of campsites, the rest are first come/first served although they fill quickly.
Lodge reservations: Call (800) 999-4714 several months in advance of your planned stay.
Byrd Visitor Center is open daily 9 AM–5 PM April–mid-November. There is a fee to enter Skyline Drive.

The only Shenandoah National Park campground for which campsites may be reserved, Big Meadows is one of the most popular campgrounds in the Park. Weekends (especially holidays) fill quickly and campsites are assigned. We suggest midweek camping here to avoid the crowds. Still, Big Meadows has much to offer families. Byrd Visitor Center, one of the two Visitor Centers in the park, is located here. Inside, families can see exhibits about the park's history, attend special programs, and browse through the extensive collection of children's nature books. The Junior Ranger Program for kids is also offered at Byrd during the summer. Kids pick up a free packet in the Center and complete a number of nature activities including a guided walk with a park ranger to earn Junior Ranger Badges (way cool for elementary-age kids). Also fun for families are the park rangers' Birds of Prey show and Ranger Talks held at the amphitheater in the morning and evening, respectively.

Restrooms and cold water sinks are sprinkled throughout the campground. On site, guests will also find a coin-operated warm shower/laundry facility and a small camp store. Big Meadows Lodge, less than a mile away, has a playground, restaurant, large camp store and gas station. If you're not up for a true camping experience, the lodge offers more refined accommodations.

DIRECTIONS: Take Route 29N to a left on Route 33W at the main intersection in Ruckersville. Follow Route 33W up the mountain to the Swift Run Gap entrance to Skyline Drive. Go north (right) on Skyline Drive almost 15 miles to Big Meadows.

Loft Mountain

Mile marker 79.8, Skyline Drive

WEBSITE: http://www.visitshenandoah.com

HOURS: April–October for over 220 campsites.

ADMISSION: $14 per campsite.

There is a fee to enter Skyline Drive.

Families looking for a bit quieter and more secluded (albeit slightly more rugged) camping experience will enjoy Loft Mountain Campground. Much less crowded than Big Meadows, Loft Mountain offers spectacular scenery and plenty of great family hiking. Ranger Talks, guided hikes, and campfire programs are offered in the summer. The Junior Ranger Program is also available here during the warmer months. Laundry facilities, warm showers, a small restaurant, camp store and gas station are all located on site as well.

SCHLEP FACTOR: Pretty low, especially for families with kids elementary age and older. There are fewer "extras" here (no playground, Visitor Center, or huge restaurant), making camping with preschoolers a bit more difficult. Arrive early, especially on weekends and holidays, to secure a campsite.

DIRECTIONS: Take I-64W to the top of Afton Mountain. Enter Skyline Drive at the Rockfish Gap entrance on Afton and head north (right) on Skyline Drive. Go about 20 miles to Loft Mountain at mile marker 79.5.

Sherando Lake

HOURS: Campsites are open with full service from April 1–October 31. The campsites are open outside this period, weather permitting, with no running water (and no fee).

ADMISSION: For day visitors, $8 per carload ($6 for couples, $4 for individuals). For camping, $15 for sites without electricity, $20 for sites with electricity.

Campsites tend to fill up early on summer weekends, so arrive early in the day on Friday or by Thursday morning on holiday weekends to avoid disappointment.

The Sherando Lake Recreation Area, fourteen miles south of Waynesboro, is a wonderful spot for family camping. Two lakes, a lower one for swimming, boating and fishing, and an upper one reserved for fishing and boating, form the core of the park's activities. Miles of hiking trails are accessible from the camping areas, as well. The lower swimming lake, which has sandy beaches, a shaded, grassy area, and a bathhouse with warm showers, also makes a great spot for a day visit.

Three family camping areas are available on a first come/first served basis. Most families prefer the A and B loop sites which have flush toilets and warm showers and are located on an open grassy area. The C loop is more wooded and elevated and provides flush toilets but no showers. A separate group camping area that can accommodate up to 125 people must be reserved in advance through the Pedlar Ranger District office at (540) 291-2188.

SCHLEP FACTOR: Relatively low for camping (don't forget the marshmallows). Plenty of convenient facilities and a short 35- to 45-minute drive from Charlottesville. Handicapped parking is available.

DIRECTIONS: Take I-64W over Afton Mountain to the Lyndhurst exit. Turn left at the exit and follow this road (Route 664) several miles to Sherando Lake on the left.

Misty Mountain Camp Resort
Greenwood   (888) 647-8900

WEBSITE: http://www.mistycamp.com

HOURS: Daily year-round, activities only April–October.

ADMISSION: Overnight fee from $18.95 per couple for a primitive tent site–$26.95 per couple for a water and 50 amp electric site. Additional family members: Children under 3 for free, $2.75 for children, $4 for adults. *Rustic cabins:* $39 per couple per night, additional family members are $2.75 children, $4 adults.

Day use includes use of swimming pool, playgrounds and sporting equipment and is available Sunday–Thursday for children under 3 for free, $2.75 for children, $4 for adults.

Reservations: Required, so make two weeks or more in advance for campsites, a month or more for the cabins.

Afraid your kids will be bored stiff with nothing but the woods and wildlife for entertainment? Bring them to Misty Mountain Camp Resort, a mere 15-minute drive from Charlottesville, where the entertainment is built into the camping experience. Kids love the swimming pool with a kids-only sliding board, two playgrounds (one just for toddlers), a game room with billiards, air hockey, pinball and video games, and the sports field with a variety of equipment kids can borrow. Families camping over the weekend will find tons of family programs, including movies, games in the Rec Hall, and visits from the camp mascots (adults in critter suits). In addition, the camp has a different theme each weekend, ranging from Christmas in July to Carnival Weekend, with activities themed around the event.

Most campsites are in open areas and offer little privacy, although some secluded sites are available. The management tries to accommodate special requests regarding campsite assignments. Rustic cabins and a group camping site are also available. Hot water showers and flush toilets can be found in the bathhouses.

SCHLEP FACTOR: Pretty low. The camp is very close to Charlottesville, and although it is definitely not the place to go for a secluded back-to-nature experience, it is a good campsite for families who aren't quite ready to leave entertainment behind. The camp is open during the week for day use, so your family can try out some of the amenities before committing to an overnight trip. An on-site camp store sells sodas, ice cream, souvenirs and camping supplies.

DIRECTIONS: Take Route 250W 1/2 mile past I-64 to the camp on the left. From I-64W, take exit 107 (Crozet) and follow Route 250W as above.

FOR THE TENT-CAMPING IMPAIRED...

Skyland Lodge Cabins

Milemarker 41.7, Skyline Drive

Reservations: (800) 999-4714, Monday–Friday 8 AM–5 PM.
Reservations for the lodge and cabins are taken beginning June 1 for the following year. They fill quickly, but it is sometimes possible to snag a midweek reservation on less notice.

WEBSITE: http://www.visitshenandoah.com

HOURS: The lodge April–November, cabins May–October
All amenities (including the dining room) at Skyland follow the lodge schedule and close from December–March.

ADMISSION: There is a fee to enter Skyline Drive (see Gems along Skyline Drive).

Although not technically "camping," the cabins at Skyland are rustic enough to make kids feel like they are roughing it, with the convenience of blueberry ice cream pie next door! Managed by the National Park Service, Skyland is perfect for families not ready to commit to a full-blown camping trip. Cabins have one or two double beds, bathrooms with warm showers, and full linens. Skyland also has a lodge, but choose the cabins for a more camp-like experience. On the grounds you will also find a playground, a restaurant (with the legendary pie), and horseback and pony rides. The lodge also has a variety of Ranger Talks scheduled, where park rangers present a wide variety of nature topics for families and a junior ranger program for kids.

SCHLEP FACTOR: Fairly high, considering you will need to make reservations well in advance. Once you're there, Skyland is a breeze. Even if you miss lodging reservations, this is well worth a day trip. If you prefer a lodge a bit closer to home, try Big Meadows (although our families prefer Skyland for the views and horseback riding).

DIRECTIONS: Take Route 29N to Ruckersville. At the main intersection in Ruckersville, turn left onto Route 33W. Go 15 miles on Route 33 to a right into the Swift Run Gap entrance to Skyline Drive. Turn left onto Skyline Drive and go north 23 miles to Skyland Lodge.

FAMILY CAMPS

Camp Friendship

Palmyra   (800) 873-3223 or (804) 589-8950

WEBSITE: http://www.campfriendship.com

HOURS: Family camps last week of August and Labor Day Weekend.

ADMISSION: $53 for children, $58 for adults per day, $1100 for a full week for a family of 4 or more.

Minimum stay: Three nights.

Minimum age: No minimum age for children during family camps; planned activities, however, are for children ages 3 and up.

Reservations: In January or February as family camps fill early.

You grew up, got a job, had a family, but each year when summer comes around you still get a hankering for bug juice and campfire sing-alongs. Here's your chance to go back to summer camp and relive it all—this time with your family. Twice each summer, Camp Friendship in Palmyra opens its doors to families. The full range of camp activities is offered, including (but not limited to) archery, arts and crafts, horseback riding, pool and lake swimming, and nature programs. Those craving excitement will be happy to find a high ropes course, water ski and canoe clinics, and rock climbing and caving trips. Planned activities for children 3 and up assure that Mom and Dad have time to explore the camp offerings on their own.

SCHLEP FACTOR: High. Be sure to make reservations well in advance. Each family is assigned a private cabin, but tent campers can be accommodated. All meals are included and are served camp-style in the cafeteria.

DIRECTIONS: Take I-64E to exit 136 (Zion's Crossroads). Turn right and go south on Route 15 for 7-1/2 miles to the camp on the right.

GUIDED TRIPS

Overnight Trips from Graves Mountain Lodge Stables

Syria   (540) 923-5071 or (540) 786-7403

WEBSITE: http://www.gravesmountain.com

HOURS: Daily, mid-March–Thanksgiving.

ADMISSION: Start at $125 per person per night, family rates available.

Reservations: Necessary, and should be made as far in advance as possible.

Minimum age: At least 8 years old for overnight trips, no horseback experience necessary (although slightly younger children with riding experience will be considered).

Tom and Patricia Seay offer all sorts of horseback rides from the Graves Mountain Lodge Stables, but if you really want to see the Seay's shine, book an overnight trip. When it comes to personal service and attention to detail, these folks rival the Ritz Carlton. Before your visit, the Seay's send you saddlebags to pack. You pack the bags, throw the family in the car and drive to the lodge. The Seay's take care of the rest. You choose how much horseback riding you want to do, what type of scenery you would like to see and where you want to spend the night. Guests can choose to sleep in an old log cabin, an authentic teepee, or in the lodge. After your ride, sit back while the crew starts the campfire and prepares a full meal selected to please your family's tastebuds. While you're at your campsite, you'll have the opportunity to try out the full range of camping activities. Hiking? They know the trails. Fishing? They'll have the gear. Whittling. Guitar-strumming. Whatever you want to do. The next morning you can ride your horse back to the barn. Or even better, stay for more than one night. You'll be glad you did.

SCHLEP FACTOR: Pretty low. The $125 per person fee might seem steep, but it is actually a good value considering it includes guides, horses, all equipment, meals and snacks. These folks really know how to take care of their guests.

DIRECTIONS: Take Route 29N to a left onto Route 231 in Madison. Follow Route 231 through Madison to the fork in the road. Take the left fork and continue on Route 231 toward Sperryville. Go about 5 miles to the town of Banco and take a left on Route 670. Go 4 miles to Graves Mountain Lodge. The stables are across from the lodge.

Backpacking and Canoeing Trips with Outdoor Insights

6370 Midway Road, Crozet   (540) 456-8742

WEBSITE: No website, but e-mail sziemer@cstone.net

HOURS: Trips available year-round.

ADMISSION: Varies widely depending on length of trip, destination and number of people.

Minimum age: At least 10 years old to participate.

Reservations: Required, and should be made three weeks in advance.

Even families with little or no backpacking or canoeing experience can enjoy our wilderness areas with Scott Ziemer's custom trips. Families choose where they want to go—Saint Mary's Wilderness Area is a popular choice for backpacking, and the James River popular for canoeing—and how long they want to stay. Families then work with Scott to develop an itinerary and camp menu. Scott does all the food buying and provides all the other necessities (except for backpacks and sleeping bags, which the client must provide), making this a great choice for families with little time or know-how for backpacking. Families can feel confident knowing Scott has 25 years experience in backpacking and canoeing and also has his Wilderness First Responder certificate (one step down from being an EMT). He is also really knowledgeable about our environment and wilderness ecosystems, making this memorable trip educational as well.

Outdoor Insights also offers eco-trips, rockclimbing instruction and a summer day camp for kids ages 11–14 that focuses on hiking, mountain biking and canoeing.

SCHLEP FACTOR: Low, for backpacking, since Scott provides almost all the necessities. If you enjoy camping and hiking but not the prep work, this could be your ticket back to the wilderness!

DIRECTIONS: Scott will arrange a meeting place depending on where you are going.

NATURE

Kids have a natural curiosity about the world around them, so getting them excited about one of these activities should be easy. Since most of these pursuits are hands-on (not to mention eyes, teeth, and feet-on), be sure to read the passages carefully so you will arrive prepared!

ANIMALS

SPCA Shelter

2075 Woodburn Road, Charlottesville　　(804) 973-5959

WEBSITE: http://www.cvillespca.org.
http://www.webweaving.com/spca
The second website has pictures and histories of animals available for adoption.

HOURS: Monday–Saturday 9 AM–4 PM, Sundays noon–4 PM

ADMISSION: Free, but donations appreciated.

In years past, the SPCA has served as not only a temporary home for stray animals in our area, but also as a permanent home for a variety of farm animals, many of whom were disabled. In anticipation of losing much of their property to VDOT, the facility has had to scale back the petting farm, but guests can still visit with a number of geese, an old donkey and the many animals (dogs, cats and rabbits) who wind up at the facility. Some of our families bring along a box of Milkbones to feed the dogs, and all love visiting "Kitty City", the separate room where kittens brought into the SPCA roam freely.

Seeing dogs in cages is sad, but provides a great opportunity to talk to your kids about responsible pet ownership. And of course, if you're in need of a great pet, young or old, check out the SPCA for adoptions.

In the summer months, the SPCA has an almost daily need to transport injured or orphaned animals to the Wildlife Center in Waynesboro. If you and your family would like to volunteer, even on an occasional basis, contact the SPCA.

SCHLEP FACTOR: Practically none. Kids 6 and under are especially thrilled, although animal lovers of all ages will enjoy a trip here. Be advised that some young children are frightened by the barking dogs, and that all children need to keep their hands out of the cages. The facility has a public restroom and is handicapped-accessible.

DIRECTIONS: Take Route 29N to a left at Hydraulic Road. Go through 1 traffic light to a right onto Woodburn Road. Follow Woodburn for 1/2 mile to a right into the shelter.

Luray Reptile Center
Route 211W, Luray   (540) 743-4113

WEBSITE: http://www.lurayzoo.com

HOURS: Daily 10 AM–5 PM April–June, 10 AM–6 PM July–August, 10 AM–5 PM September–October, closed rest of year.

ADMISSION: $4 for children, $5 for adults, $4.50 for seniors. Group rates available.

Massive pythons, Indian cobras, lizards and alligators await visitors at the Luray Reptile Center. Kids and adults alike will enjoy a fun and educational trip to this park. The reptile center is all indoors—great for a rainy day—and is exceptionally well-maintained. Outside there is a large petting zoo with tame deer, llamas, goats and other small animals. Bring along quarters for the goat food machine and goats will nibble the food from the palm of your hand. There are also several life-sized dinosaur reproductions that will give kids a feel for how large these animals really were. A nice museum store rounds out the Reptile Center's offerings.

SCHLEP FACTOR: High, considering this is a one hour-and-10-minute drive from Charlottesville. One combination our families swear by, especially on a rainy day, is to first visit Luray Caverns, then pop down the street to Mindi's Mexican Restaurant for lunch (located halfway between the caverns and the Reptile Park; open Tuesday–Sunday). Afterwards, head over to the Reptile Center for the afternoon. The kids have a great time and snooze on the way home. Unfortunately, the park offers only a porta-potty, and no drinking fountains or vending. The park is handicapped- and stroller-accessible.

DIRECTIONS: Take Route 29N to a left on Route 33W at the light in Ruckersville. Follow Route 33W to Elkton and take Route 340N to Luray (very well marked). In Luray, take Route 211 to the Reptile Center (about 1-1/2 miles past Luray Caverns).

★ Natural Bridge Petting Zoo
Natural Bridge   (540) 291-2420

HOURS: Daily 9 AM–6 PM before Thanksgiving, after Thanksgiving open weekends only, weather permitting, closed holidays.

ADMISSION: Free for children under 3, $4.50 for children, $6.50 for adults; rates lower in cold weather and for groups.

The five-acre Natural Bridge Zoo boasts the largest collection of animals in Virginia. Llamas, donkeys, deer, flamingos and pygmy goats roam free, while other animals such as giraffes are penned but close enough for kids to pet. Dangerous animals such as alligators, bears and tigers are at a safe viewing distance but close enough for children to gain an appreciation for their size and beauty. In all, more than 400 species of reptiles, birds and mammals make their home at the zoo, including an elephant that kids can ride (separate fee). Buy a bag of food at the entrance and let the kids feed many of the animals by hand.

SCHLEP FACTOR: Fairly high because of the 1-1/4 hour drive. Still, this makes a great day trip for families with kids under 12, especially when combined with one of the other Natural Bridge attractions. Restrooms, a covered picnic area and small snack bar (with a few lunch items like grilled cheese and fries) are available. The zoo is stroller- and handicapped-accessible but paths are gravel, which makes pushing a bit difficult.

DIRECTIONS: Take I-64W to I-81S (near Staunton). Follow I-81S to exit 180A (Route 11S). Take Route 11S 3-1/2 miles to the zoo on the right.

Graves Mountain Lodge Cattle Drives
Syria   (540) 923-5071 or (540) 786-7403

HOURS: Drives held on Fridays, approximately every two weeks early April–early November. Call for specific dates.

ADMISSION: $50 for half day, $90 for full day, and $125 for overnight. Prices include meals and snacks. Family rates available.
Reservations: Necessary, and can be made two weeks in advance.
Minimum age: Riders should be at least 8 years old.

Ready for something totally different? Every two weeks from spring to fall, Graves Mountain Lodge hosts a rodeo-style event featuring the lodge's cattle. Beforehand, somebody has to ride horses up into the hills and drive all the cattle down for the event. Those somebodies could be you and your family. Spend a half-day, a full day or an overnight trip riding up into the mountains and corralling cattle (stopping, of course, for some delicious home-cooked meals along the way). Since no fast or fancy horseback maneuvers are required, kids eight and over are welcome to participate, even if they have had no prior riding experience. Think of it as a chance to use those video game skills they've been perfecting all these years.

SCHLEP FACTOR: Very low. Tom and Patricia Seay are in a league of their own when it comes to taking care of all the little details. Call for a reservation and they handle the rest.

DIRECTIONS: Take Route 29N to a left on Route 231 in Madison. Go about 5 miles to the town of Banco. Turn left on Route 670 in Banco and go 4 miles to Graves Mountain Lodge. The stables are across from the lodge.

On The Wild Side Zoological Park

Madison   (540) 948-4000

HOURS: Daily 9 AM–5 PM May 4–Memorial Day, 9 AM–7:30 PM Memorial Day–Labor Day, 10 AM–5 PM Labor Day–Christmas Eve; closed rest of the year

ADMISSION: Free for children under 3, $4 for children 3–12, $6 for adults. Group rates available.

Practically in our own backyard, On The Wild Side Zoo offers guests a close-up look at a variety of imported and native animals. Monkeys, camels, llamas and exotic cats are but a few of the animals kids will encounter here. Bring along quarters for the animal food dispensers sprinkled throughout the park. Kids especially enjoy feeding and petting the pygmy goats enclosed in a very accessible rink. A separate reptile exhibit with snakes and exotic lizards is popular and a good way for kids to learn how to identify poisonous Virginia snakes from a safe distance.

Despite its small size—or maybe because of it—kids five and under seem to enjoy visiting again and again. The zoo can be easily seen in an hour, with a good mix of indoor and outdoor exhibits. Since it is so close to Charlottesville, On The Wild Side makes an easy afternoon outing.

SCHLEP FACTOR: Low. The closest zoo to Charlottesville, On The Wild Side is located on 29N and is only about 20 minutes from Charlottesville. Restrooms and limited vending are available, and the park is stroller- and handicapped-accessible.

DIRECTIONS: Take Route 29N to Madison. On The Wild Side is on the left across from Madison High School.

ARBORETUMS AND BOTANICAL GARDENS

JMU ARBORETUM AND BOTANICAL GARDEN

Harrisonburg   (540) 568-6340 or (540) 568-6225

WEBSITE: http://www.jmu.edu/external/arb
HOURS: Daily, dawn to dusk year-round.
ADMISSION: Free.

Nature-loving families will enjoy a trip to the 125-acre JMU Arboretum. Miles of wide, well-marked trails lead to habitats ranging from bog gardens to forests to rock and herb gardens. A pond with fish, ducks, turtles and other wildlife is popular with children, as is a suspension bridge in the middle of one of the gardens. The arboretum is especially beautiful in the spring when bulb gardens are in bloom and in the fall when foliage peaks, but is worth an afternoon of family hiking and exploration any time of the year.

SCHLEP FACTOR: Fairly high, since the arboretum is an hour away, but consider trying out one of the other Harrisonburg attractions, then bring a picnic to the arboretum. There are porta-potties along the trails and the paths are stroller- and handicapped-accessible.

DIRECTIONS: Take Route 29N to a left onto Route 33 at the main intersection in Ruckersville. Follow Route 33 over the mountain and into Harrisonburg. Stay on Route 33 when it crosses under I-81 then go about a mile to the fork in the road. Bear left at the fork onto Market Street East. Go less than a mile to a left onto Main Street South. Go about 1-1/2 miles to a left onto Port Republic Road. Cross over I-81, then make a left at the Texaco station. Take the next left which becomes University Boulevard. Stay on University Boulevard past the Convocation Center to the Arboretum entrance on the right.

PLANETARIUMS AND OBSERVATORIES

Eastern Mennonite University Planetarium and Hostetter Museum of Natural History

1200 Park Road, Harrisonburg   (540) 432-4400

WEBSITE: http://www.emu.edu

HOURS: Certain Sunday afternoons at 2 PM, October–March. Call ahead to find out on which dates they offer shows.

The adjacent Hostetter Museum hours: 2 PM–3:30 PM on the same Sundays as Planetarium shows.

ADMISSION: Free for families, but contribution appreciated.

Visitors to the EMU Planetarium will be treated to half hour of "sky watching" on the 30-foot planetarium dome. A projector presents the sun, moon, major planets and over 1200 stars. Other celestial phenomena are presented with help from special-effect projectors. The planetarium show themes change periodically, making repeat trips worthwhile. Afterwards, pop in next door to the Museum of Natural History to see more than 6,000 items, including anthropological artifacts, botanical specimens, fossils, gems, crystals, rocks and mounted heads of mammals.

SCHLEP FACTOR: High for families driving from Charlottesville. Be sure to call ahead for dates, as the planetarium and museum are open only select Sundays, October through March. Arrive at 2 PM when the building opens so your family can browse the museum before and after the planetarium show.

DIRECTIONS: Take Route 29N to a left onto Route 33W at the main intersection in Ruckersville. Follow Route 33 over the mountain. In Harrisonburg, turn right onto Vine Street. Stay on Vine to Route 11 when the name changes to Mount Clinton Pike. Continue on Mount Clinton Pike to a right onto Park Road. Go to the first EMU classroom building, Suter Science Center, which will be on the right. The Museum and Planetarium are inside the Science Center.

McCormick Observatory

McCormick Road, Charlottesville   (804) 924-7494

WEBSITE: http://www.astro.virginia.edu

HOURS 1st and 3rd Fridays of each month, 9 PM–11 PM (Daylight Savings Time), 8 PM–10 PM (Standard Time), closed when preempted by Fan Mountain Observatory open house.

ADMISSION Free.

The McCormick Observatory, a research facility for the U.Va. Astronomy Department, is open to the public twice monthly. Three telescopes, including one 26" 'scope, are available for star-and-planet-gazing (we saw Jupiter and four of its moons the night we were there). Astronomy Department staff are on hand to explain how to use the equipment and to fill in details about what you are viewing. Afterwards, check out the small Astronomy Museum that displays a replica of Thomas Jefferson's telescope, a collection of historic optical pieces, and pictures of famous comets and nebulae. One or two slide shows are also offered each night. The night we visited there were two: one about the birth and death of stars and one about how the Observatory works. The shows, well-done and informative, are interesting for kids and adults alike.

SCHLEP FACTOR Fairly high, especially during Daylight Savings Time when the Observatory doesn't open 'til 9 PM, but definitely worth keeping kids ages 8 and up awake for. Once you are there, parking is easy and staff members are friendly and helpful. Try to avoid visiting on weekends when there are popular U.Va. events scheduled (e.g., Homecoming, Parents' Weekend and graduation) or you may face uncommonly long waits for a turn at the 'scopes. Bring along a small flashlight for moving around outdoors and a jacket if it is cool out. Also, take a peek at the sky before you head up to the Observatory. If it's overcast, you won't be able to see much through the telescopes.

DIRECTIONS: Take Route 29S to a right on McCormick (in the University area). When McCormick seems to fork, take the left fork uphill. At the stop sign, turn right and continue up the hill until you see the domed Observatory. Park alongside the driveway or on the grass on the left.

Fan Mountain Observatory

Covesville   (804) 924-7494

WEBSITE: http://www.astro.virginia.edu.

HOURS: Open one Friday evening in April, one Friday evening in October.

ADMISSION Free, but advance tickets required and can be obtained by calling U.Va. Astronomy Department at the above number.

As far as schleppiness goes, this is about as bad as it gets: waiting for six months for an open house, applying for advance tickets, driving all the way to Covesville to stand in line—maybe for hours—for a glimpse at the stars through some telescopes. And if the weather is bad, you won't be able to see anything. If you're still reading this, shrugging your shoulders and saying, "So?", Fan Mountain Observatory is for you. For dyed-in-the-wool stargazers and stargazers-to-be, there's simply no place else to be on these two Friday evenings.

Sometime in early April or October, call the U.Va. Astronomy Department for free tickets and instructions. Your family will be given a tour group number when you arrive at the mountain. While you wait for your group to be called, you can watch the ongoing slide show and talk given by the Department or enjoy viewing the sky through smaller telescopes brought up by local amateur astronomers. When your group is called, you will be brought to the observatory for a chance to look through the 'scopes (one measuring a hefty 40"). Astronomers are on hand to fill in details about what you are viewing and to help with equipment.

One of our families who visited said that although getting to Fan Mountain was a huge effort, once they were there, "looking upward and hearing from astronomers about this great universe we are so fortunate to live in, life's day-to-day hassles sure paled in the starlight."

SCHLEP FACTOR   Very high. Have your family visit McCormick Observatory first. If they want more try Fan Mountain, following these tips:

1) Leave kids under age 12 at home, unless they are enthusiastic amateur astronomers. This trip is absolutely not suitable for young children.

2) Dress warmly. You will be outside most of the time, and it is cooler and breezier up on the mountain than in Charlottesville.

3) Bring along a small flashlight and a thermos of hot cocoa to keep the kids fueled and warm.

4) Plan to arrive early rather than late, especially with children. Although it is difficult to see much before 7:30 PM, arriving much later assures you a long wait. One of our families arrived at 8:45 PM and was assigned to group #19. At 10 PM, group #8 was called. You get the picture.

On the upside, they do have restrooms!

DIRECTIONS: Directions will be given when you receive your tickets.

GEOLOGY

Visit a sampling of area caverns and you will find they have two things in common. One, many were discovered by some variation of two adventurous boys, a partially-obscured hole in the ground leading to the vast cavern, and a hapless, unsuspecting dog. Second, the management of each cave will go to great lengths to attract visitors and distinguish their cave as the best entertainment value. Herein lies the secret to great family entertainment. Although children may not be impressed with the subtle geologic variations that distinguish each cave, they will delight in the "add-ons" designed to lure customers. With this in mind, at the end of each listing we have included the "extras" you will find that make that cavern unique (to kids, not geologists).

We have chosen to review only the caves that are great for families; although Endless Caverns is a beautiful cave and an easy drive from Charlottesville, the tour relies heavily on geologic details and at 75 minutes is truly endless for young children. Save that one for an adult excursion.

Remember, the temperature in all caverns is about 56 degrees year-round, so be sure to bring a jacket. Also, before heading into any of the caverns, be sure your kids are fed and have gone to the bathroom, because although you will see formations that look like bacon, castles and Cinderella, none of them will look like McDonald's or a restroom.

Grand Caverns
Grottoes   (540) 249-5705

Hours: Daily 9 AM–5 PM April 1–October 31 and weekends in March, closed rest of year.

Admission: Children under 3 for free, $7 for children, $11 for adults.

Grand Caverns is America's oldest show cave and also happens to be the closest cave for Charlottesville residents. Discovered in 1804, Grand Caverns is home to the second largest stalagmite in the U.S., and was visited by "Stonewall" Jackson's troops during the Civil War. The hundreds of shield formations found here have mystified geologists since the cave's discovery. During the hour-long tour, guides provide a good mix of geologic information and fantasy (pointing out formations that look like zoo animals, Cinderella, cheese pizza, etc.) The tour is generally well-suited to kids.

Special because: It is so close to Charlottesville, meaning that your kids are less likely to step out of the car with that this-better-be-good look on their faces. Also, there is a large park around the caverns which includes a picnic area, hiking, miniature golf and a huge swimming pool (some separate fees apply).

**SCHLEP
FACTOR:** Pretty low. Be advised that after you park you will have to climb a fairly long, steep hill (by kid standards) to the cavern entrance. Restrooms, a drinking fountain and vending are available on site, as is a gift shop. Just in case you forgot, jackets are available to borrow.

DIRECTIONS: Take I-64W to the exit for Route 340 in Waynesboro. Turn north (right) onto Route 340 and go about 17 miles to the caverns on the left. Signs will assist you.

Luray Caverns
Route 211W, Luray   (540) 743-6551
WEBSITE: http://wwwluraycaverns.com
HOURS: Daily, including all holidays.
Tours: First tour is at 9 AM. Closing time varies seasonally, so call ahead for exact hours.
ADMISSION: Children under 7 for free, $6 for children ages 7–13, $13 for adults, $11 for seniors. Admission fee includes admission to both the caverns and the Historic Car and Carriage Museum.

Luray Caverns, the most visited caverns in the east, is the most professional local cavern. The one-hour tour is both educational and entertaining, and the knowledgeable guides patiently answer all questions. The rooms in Luray are enormous—some with ceilings more than ten stories high. A highlight for kids is listening to the world's only "stalacpipe" organ. Kids also get a kick out of rubbing the "fried eggs" for good luck on the way out.
Special because: The cavern's "stalacpipe" organ and the Historic Car & Carriage Museum, located next door. The museum boasts "a collection of antique cars, carriages, coaches and costumes dating back to 1725." Kids will love the 1892 Benz (one of the oldest still-running cars in the country) and the Conestoga wagon.

**SCHLEP
FACTOR:** High, since Luray is an hour-and-ten-minute drive from Charlottesville. Once you arrive, the caverns are easy. You'll find clean restrooms with a baby-changing area, a restaurant, a country store and a picnic area.
      One combination our families swear by (particularly on a rainy day) is visiting Luray in the morning, then stopping by Mindi's Mexican Restaurant for lunch. After lunch, head down the road to the Luray Reptile Center (see our listing under Animals). The restaurant is located on Route 211W, halfway between the Caverns and the Reptile Center, and is open Tuesday–Sunday.

DIRECTIONS: Take Route 29N to a left on Route 33W at the light in Ruckersville. Follow Route 33W to Elkton and take Route 340N to Luray (very well marked). In Luray, take Route 211 to the caverns. (There are probably 15 signs. You can't miss it.)

Natural Bridge Caverns

Natural Bridge   (800) 533-1410 or (540) 291-2121 (Hotel number, they will transfer your call)

WEBSITE: http://www.naturalbridgeva.com

HOURS: Daily 10 AM–5 PM, March–mid-November, closed rest of year

ADMISSION: Children 5 and under for free, $3.50 for children, $7 for adults. Combination tickets for the Caverns, Natural Bridge and the Natural Bridge Wax Museum are available.

Right down the street from Natural Bridge is Natural Bridge Caverns, supposedly the deepest caverns on the East Coast. You can purchase your tickets at the cavern entrance or at the Natural Bridge Visitor Center for a 45-minute tour. As with almost all caverns in the area, strollers aren't permitted inside and there are a good many steps, so families with young children may not want to tour both Natural Bridge and the cavern on the same day.

Special because of: The other Natural Bridge attractions located just a stone's throw away. One more perk: the cavern is said to be haunted. The mournful wails of a woman have been heard in the caverns since 1889, when workers fled, leaving behind their tools and refusing to return. Their equipment was found in 1978. The ghost was documented for the last time (so far) in 1988, when she wailed through a tour guide's presentation (or maybe it was just a howling 3-year-old). Maybe your group will be the latest witnesses.

SCHLEP FACTOR: Moderate, considering the drive of over an hour, but bump that up if your kids are already tired and cranky from a day of hiking! No wheelchair or stroller access.

DIRECTIONS: Take I-64W to I-81S (near Staunton) to exit 180A. From the exit, follow Route 11S about 2 miles to the Caverns on the left.

Shenandoah Caverns

Shenandoah   (540) 477-3115

Hours: Daily, including holidays, 9 AM–closing time, varies seasonally so call ahead for exact hours.

Admission: Children under 5 for free, $5.50 for children ages 5–14, $12 for adults, $10.50 for seniors. Admission fee includes the hour-long tour of the caverns and the Celebrations On Parade exhibit.

Despite the 1-1/4 hour drive from Charlottesville, Shenandoah Caverns is probably the best cavern for young children. First, your descent (and, more important, your ascent) is by elevator, so there are no steps on the tour and you can bring a stroller! Wheelchairs are also permitted in the cavern; 70% of the tour is handicapped-accessible, although there is one portion of the tour where strollers and wheelchairs must be parked. Thanks to skillful lighting and low ceilings in some areas (adults have to duck down for some parts), Shenandoah feels more like a real cave. Although natural-colored lighting is used for most of the tour, colored lights are used in a few areas, prompting "ooohs" and "ahhhs" from kids of all ages.

Special because: Celebrations on Parade, a funky "museum" that will take you on a tour of animated window displays from the 1920s, '30s, and '40s. Little kids love the four 22-foot animated bears once used in the Rose Bowl Parade.

Schlep Factor: Moderate, considering the drive from Charlottesville, but easy once you're there. A coffee shop, open June–August, offers sandwiches, fries, sodas and milkshakes, and the large gift shop is kiddie heaven.
After your visit, consider stopping by one of the Harrisonburg attractions. PJ's Arcade and Pizzeria or The Bull Pen are nice complements to this outing.

Directions: Take I-64W to I-81N to Exit 269. Follow the signs to the caverns.

Morefield Gem Mine

Amelia   (804) 561-3399

HOURS: Tuesday–Saturday, 9 AM–4:30 PM in summer; Thursday–Saturday 9 AM–4:30 PM in spring and fall. Closed Christmas Day–early March. Group reservations available Tuesday and Wednesday in spring and fall.

ADMISSION: Free for children under 3, $6 for children 4–12, $8 for adults. Buckets and shovels provided.

All it takes is an adventurous spirit and a willingness to get your hands dirty to discover a true hidden gem on the backroads of Amelia County. The Morefield Gem Mine, a working recreational mine in operation since 1929, offers guests the opportunity to unearth and carry home any of over 70 types of minerals, including amethyst, amazonite, garnet and topaz. Smithsonian Institution and university researchers will work the mine in hopes of finding new minerals, but the bulk of visitors are families looking for an entertaining day of panning for gems.

After a 20-minute briefing, guests enter a 1-acre roped-off area just outside the mine entrance where they fill buckets with dirt and pour it through screens at the spring-fed sluice. The dirt washes away, leaving gems behind. Guests may pan for minerals until closing time, and everyone leaves with gems. Also, if you make a request during the briefing, the owners will take families to the top of the mine to peek into the mine shaft.

Inside, a small museum displays minerals from the mine and from around the world. The gift shop offers such items as gem jewelry, rock identification guide books, rock tumblers and polishing grit. Morefield has become such a popular birthday party destination that party packages may soon be added.

SCHLEP FACTOR: High. The mine is almost 2 hours from Charlottesville and can be tricky to find, but our families rate this a must-see attraction. On your way, be sure to watch road numbers carefully! Expect kids to get dirty— REALLY dirty if it has been raining. Bring along a change of clothes (including shoes). Hoses are available outside the Gift Shop. Rubber boots, a large plastic bag for muddy shoes and clothes, and a supply of large ziplock bags for storing gems are also recommended. Picnic tables and drink and snack vending are available. The mine is stroller- and handicapped-accessible. Families looking for more fun in the area will find a zoo 11 miles from the mine on Route 360, and Richmond is just a 1/2 hour away.

DIRECTIONS: Take I-64E to Gum Spring in Goochland County. Take the exit for Route 522 and at the bottom of the ramp turn right (south) onto Route 522. Turn left onto Route 6/522 and go to Goochland Courthouse. About 1-1/2 miles past the Courthouse turn right onto Route 522. Immediately cross the James River and go to the stoplight at Route 60. Continue straight through the light and Route 522 merges into Route 13. Continue south on Route 13 for 2-1/2 miles to a left on Route 609. Follow Route 609 until it dead-ends into Gemito Road. Turn left and go 1000 feet to the transformer station, and turn right onto Route 609. Follow Route 609 for about 9 miles to a left onto Route 360. Follow Route 360 for about 2-1/2 miles. When you pass McDonald's, look for a brown Morefield Mine sign and take the next right onto Route 628. Go about a mile to the mine on the left. For the zoo, continue straight on Route 360 for 11 miles past the turn-off for the mine.

Natural Bridge

Natural Bridge   (800) 533-1410 or (540) 291-2121 (Hotel number, they will transfer your call)

WEBSITE: http://www.naturalbridgeva.com

HOURS: Daily, but hours change seasonally so call ahead.

ADMISSION: Children under 5 for free, $4 for children, $8 for adults
Combination tickets for the Bridge, the Natural Bridge Caverns and the Natural Bridge Wax Museum are available.

When you arrive at the Natural Bridge Visitor Center, flanked by an immense hotel and a wax museum, it is easy to wonder if perhaps the scenic wonder will pale in comparison to the man-made one. As you begin the descent into the canyon, however, a gentle waterfall flowing beside a trail lined with 1600-year-old arborvitae trees, you realize you are about to encounter something unique. Just around the bend the bridge rises from the landscape, inspiring awe in young and old alike, deservedly one of the Seven Wonders of the Natural World. A young George Washington surveyed the bridge and his initials, carved into the tunnel walls, can still be seen today.

The wide, shady trail that winds beneath the bridge continues for almost a mile with several interesting sites along the way. After the initial steps down into the canyon, the trail is perfect for strollers or wheelchairs (a shuttle bus can bypass the steps if needed). Do bring a stroller for little ones. It is only a short walk to the bridge, but the trail is so inviting and interesting you will want to keep going.

After your hike, grab a table by Cedar Creek at the Summer House Cafe (open Easter through October) and cool off with an ice cream or cold drink. Kids can feed the trout in the creek or watch the swans.

SCHLEP FACTOR: Moderately low. Natural Bridge is a little over an hour from Charlottesville, but is an easy drive (mostly interstate) and has plenty of parking, dining options, and restrooms.

DIRECTIONS: Take I-64W to I-81S (near Staunton). Follow I-81S to exit 180A. From the exit follow Route 11S about 3 miles to the Natural Bridge Visitor Center.

PICK-YOUR-OWN-FRUIT-
AND-VEGETABLE-PATCHES

One of our favorite things about Charlottesville is the plethora of mom-and-pop farms and orchards, where visitors are invited to drop in and fill a bag with apples, peaches and the like. These are a few locations that offer a pick-your-own opportunity, but don't stop here! If you are wandering along backroads during the growing season, keep your eyes open for other farms and orchards. Many nail up handwritten signs at the end of the drive inviting guests, and one may become your family's best-kept secret!

The Berry Patch
Free Union   (804) 963-0659

HOURS: Monday–Friday 8 AM–noon and 5 PM–dark, Saturdays 8 AM–6 PM, closed Sundays.
Berry season is typically the entire month of June.
Call ahead for picking conditions.

If you've never made it out to this Free Union gem during berry season, you have missed one of the real pleasures of summer. Fill your bucket with raspberries, blueberries and blackberries to the whisper of water rushing down the river at the back of the property. Be warned, though, berry picking is as addictive as gambling, albeit not nearly as expensive. A gallon of berries will run you less than the gallon of ice cream you'll need to pick up on the way home to go with it. And the snacking your kids will invariably do out in the field is on the house.

SCHLEP FACTOR: Fairly low for west-side dwellers, but higher for those of the east side of town. Compare the price of these home-picked berries to those in the grocery store, and you'll willingly make the drive. Containers are provided. The best picking (fullest bushes) is generally found before the weekend rush. Call ahead to find out what's ripe!

DIRECTIONS: Take Barracks Road west past Foxfield to the Hunt Country Store. Turn right at the store onto Route 601, Free Union Road. Follow Route 601 about 4 miles into the village of Free Union past the Free Union Country School. At the doctor's office in Free Union, take a sharp left (which will still be Route 601) to a second, almost immediate left onto Millington Road. Bear to the right at the fork in the road onto Wesley Chapel Road. Follow Wesley Chapel Road 3 miles and look for signs to the Berry Patch.

Carter Mountain Orchard

Thomas Jefferson Parkway (Route 53), Charlottesville
(804) 977-1833

HOURS: Daily 9 AM–6 PM, July 1–Thanksgiving, then weekends (weather permitting) until Christmas.

With sweeping views of the county (and beyond), a bakery that sells fresh-made apple products, a craft store and more, Carter Mountain Orchard is one of the most popular orchards in the area. Many people, however, don't realize that the orchard is also open in the summer for peach and nectarine picking. The bakery sells peach products and peach ice cream and you still get the same fabulous views. Apple picking begins in early September and continues until the end of October. For two weekends in October, the orchard holds an apple harvest festival with live music, hayrides and lots of apple pickers. Whenever you choose to visit, bring a picnic and your camera. Backpacks for babies are a good idea (the orchard is not suitable for strollers), and if you have a pair of binoculars, kids enjoy trying to identify buildings in downtown Charlottesville from the observation deck (they may even be able to find home!).

SCHLEP FACTOR: Surprisingly low. Carter Mountain, right down the street from Monticello and Ash Lawn-Highland, is convenient to I-64 and just minutes from downtown. You'll find plenty of parking, restrooms (not just porta-potties) and refreshments on site, although a sign says the water is not suitable for drinking. We suggest long pants tucked into socks, with shoes, to avoid poison ivy.

DIRECTIONS: Take I-64 to exit 121A (Route 20S). Take Route 20S through one light and turn left onto Thomas Jefferson Parkway (Route 53). Carter Mountain Orchard is on the right.

Critzer Farm & Nursery

Route 151 Afton   (540) 456-7250

HOURS: Strawberry picking Monday–Saturday 9 AM–6 PM, Sunday 10 AM–5 PM, mid-May–early June. Pumpkin picking weekends only in October. Pumpkin pickers are required to ride the hayride to the pumpkin patch, so call ahead for hayride schedule.

Nestled at the foot of the Blue Ridge Mountains in a rustic, country-store atmosphere, Critzer Farm and Nursery is a beautiful spot for strawberry and pumpkin picking. Kids will enjoy the goats (new this fall) and a variety of fowl such as geese, ducks, and herons, who make their home on the farm's pond. In the late spring, Critzer is hard to beat for strawberry picking. The ten acres of strawberries assure a long-lasting harvest of the juicy fruit, yet since visitors are allowed to drive out to the fields, tired children won't have to walk back to the farm when they are finished picking. On weekends in October, the farm offers hayrides to the pumpkin patch. The Fall Festival, held one weekend in mid-October, is especially fun with draft horse demonstrations, other animals and lots of kid's games and contests.

SCHLEP FACTOR: Fairly low. Critzer is an easy 25-minute drive from Charlottesville. A soda machine, water fountains and porta-potty restrooms are available, and the farm is bus, handicapped- and stroller-accessible. Gardeners will find a large line of premium bedding plants, native perennials and mums for sale as well as fresh vegetables and local sweet corn in the summer. In the near future, look for Critzers to add to their family-friendly activities and special events.

DIRECTIONS: Take Route 250W for about 16 miles to a left on Route 151. The farm is 1 mile ahead on the right.

Double B Farm

28200 Constitution Highway, Rhodesville   (540) 854-4277

HOURS: *Strawberry picking:* Monday–Saturday 9 AM–6 PM, Sunday 10 AM–5 PM early June–mid-July. Blackberry picking July–August. Monday–Saturday 9 AM–6 PM, Sunday 10 AM–5 PM.
Pumpkin picking: Saturdays 9 AM–6 PM, Sunday 10 AM–5 PM, open for weekends in October.
Reservations: Required for groups to pick pumpkins during the week.

Despite the 45-minute drive from Charlottesville, Double B Farm is a fantastic spot for strawberry and blackberry picking in the early summer and pumpkin picking in the fall. The farm is very family-friendly and worth a trip during any of the pick-your-own seasons, but they really shine during weekends in October. Hayrides to the pumpkin patch, a petting farm, a hay maze, and free refreshments, all await visitors during this time. Take one look at the place during pumpkin season and you can tell that the owner, Bob Schwartz, is still a kid at heart.

SCHLEP FACTOR: Fairly high because of the drive. Since the strawberry season is so late at Double B, however, this may be the only place where you will be able to pick strawberries in July! Strawberry and blackberry seasons vary annually, so call ahead to be sure fruit is ready for picking. The farm has picnic areas, vending, porta-potty restrooms, and is handicapped- and stroller-accessible.
Tip: Consider combining a trip here with a visit to Montpelier, about 15 miles away.

DIRECTIONS: Take Route 29N to a right on Route 33 in Ruckersville. Take Route 33 7 miles to a left on Route 20N. Follow Route 20N about 12 miles to the town of Orange. In Orange, continue on Route 20N (watch carefully for the signs as the road makes 2 turns in town). Go about 13 miles beyond Orange on 20N to the farm on the right.

MORE OUTDOOR ADVENTURES

Whether you are looking for an exhilarating afternoon of grass skiing or a kick-your-shoes-off day of fishing, Central Virginia is the place to be for outdoor activities. Families looking for even more high-octane outdoor excitement will be happy to hear there are no fewer than six amusement and water parks that are a do-able day trip from Charlottesville. You'll find those listings in our Richmond and Northern Virginia chapters.

BATTING CAGES

Planet Fun

3005 Berkmar Drive, Charlottesville   (804) 975-4386

HOURS: Daily, year-round, weather permitting. Call ahead for current operating schedule. Open extended hours in the summer.

ADMISSION: $1 for 15 pitches.

Aspiring sluggers will appreciate the seven batting cages at Planet Fun, with speeds ranging from faster-than-a-speeding-bicycle (35 mph) to faster-than-a-speeding-minivan (70 mph). Players don a helmet and select the speed and type of ball (baseball or softball), then shimmy up to the plate for fifteen pitches. Only one person at a time is allowed in the cages, so Mom or Dad will have to coach from the sidelines. Afterward, pop over to some of the other attractions at the amusement center (bumper boats, go-carts, mini-golf or the arcade).

SCHLEP FACTOR: Low. Planet Fun is convenient to Route 29N and, except for weekends, is rarely overcrowded.

DIRECTIONS: Take Route 29N to a left onto Rio Road. At the next light turn right onto Berkmar Drive. Follow Berkmar through 1 traffic light to Planet Fun on the right.

The Bull Pen

Deyerle Avenue, Harrisonburg   (540) 433-2243

HOURS: Daily, March–mid-November, weather permitting. Call ahead for a current operating schedule. Extended hours in the summer.

ADMISSION: $1 for 14 pitches.

The Bull Pen in Harrisonburg, similar to Charlottesville's Planet Fun, offers seven batting cages. Slow, medium and fast baseball and softball cages are available with speeds ranging from 35–85 mph. Parents are allowed inside the slow pitch cages to help beginners. Visitors to the Bull Pen will also find two tracks of go-carts, miniature golf and a handful of arcade games.

SCHLEP FACTOR: Holy smokes! You weren't really considering driving all the way to Harrisonburg for batting cages, were you? Good. But if you're in the area and need a fun diversion for your family, drop by! You'll also find restrooms and vending on site, and right down the street is PJ's Family Amusement.

DIRECTIONS: Take Route 29N to a left on Route 33 in Ruckersville. Follow Route 33 over the mountain and into Harrisonburg. Just past the Valley Mall, turn left onto University Boulevard (the Kroger plaza will be on the right). Turn left on Deyerle Avenue. The Bull Pen is just ahead on the right.

BICYCLING

Thomas Jefferson Parkway Trail
Thomas Jefferson Parkway (Route 53), Charlottesville

When the much anticipated Thomas Jefferson Parkway Trail opens sometime in 2000, residents and visitors will find a spectacular addition to the hiking and biking around Charlottesville. This trail, which will begin at the new parking lot near the intersection of Routes 20 and 53, will wind 2.4 miles up the mountain to the entrance of Monticello. Along the way, hikers and bikers will cross Carter Mountain, pass Michie Tavern, and be treated to dramatic mountain views. Since the trail (amazingly enough) will only slope five degrees amd will be gravel and boardwalk, the entire hike will be handicapped-accessible.

SCHLEP FACTOR: Should be low, although since the trail won't be completed until 2000, we have to reserve judgment for opening day.

DIRECTIONS: Take I-64 to exit 121A (Route 20S). Go through 1 traffic light on Route 20S, then turn left onto Thomas Jefferson Parkway. The trail head parking lot is on the right.

Rivanna Greenbelt Trail
Chesapeake Street, Charlottesville
HOURS: Daily, 7 AM–dark
ADMISSION: Free

This walking trail, with wide, flat trails weaving through woods and beside the Rivanna River, is one of the best trails for young or beginner mountain bikers in the city. The trail, accessed through Riverview Park, is 1.3 miles and is heavily used by bikers and joggers.

SCHLEP FACTOR: Low. Just toss the bikes in the back of the car and go!

DIRECTIONS Take 250E Bypass to a right on High Street just before Free Bridge. Bear left onto Meade Avenue at the fork and turn left onto Chesapeake Street at Meade Park. Follow Chesapeake Street to the end and Riverview Park will be right in front of you.

Walnut Creek Park Trails
Red Hill

HOURS: Daily, Memorial Day–Labor Day

ADMISSION: $1 for children, $2 for adults (county residents); $2 for children, $3 for adults (non-county residents).

For a mountain bike trail map, call County Parks and Rec at (804) 296-5844.

Albemarle County's newest and largest lake park offers miles of mountain bike trails divided into three categories: green, blue and black. The green trails are grassy and wide enough for bicyclists to ride through single-file. Although there are a few hills on the green trails, there are no obstacles, making them do-able by kids who are already adept at biking but may be new to mountain biking. The blue trails are intermediate with obstacles such as logs and rocks. The black trails are the most rugged and should be left to very experienced riders.

SCHLEP FACTOR: Moderate. A trail map is posted on the bulletin board by the parking lot.

DIRECTIONS: Take the 250W Bypass which becomes Route 29S. Make a left on Route 708. Turn right on Route 631. Park is 1/2 mile on the left.

BOATING, CANOEING, TUBING AND SUCH

THE PROFESSIONALS ON THE JAMES RIVER

Folks often confuse the two rafting companies on the James. Be sure to follow directions closely to avoid showing up at one location only to find out you had reservations at the other.

James River Runners
10082 Hatton Ferry Road, Scottsville   (804) 286-2338

WEBSITE: http://www.jamesriver.com

HOURS: Daily, May–October

Shuttle service: 8 AM–6 PM

Reservations: Required, 24 hours for weekday and 2–3 days for weekends, more for large groups.

Minimum ages/requirements: 4 years old for rafting, 6 years for tubing, 10 years for canoeing, and 12 years for kayaking. All participants must be able to swim.

Jeff and Christie Schmick and their crew at the Hatton Ferry might be as effective as psychotherapists in taming those tempers that flare on hot summer days. For 20 years the James River Runners have been hauling folks up the James River to tube, raft, canoe or kayak back down. Along the way, guests will find mild Class I and II rapids, islands that beg for a picnic, and plentiful wildlife both above and under the water.

Safety is the primary focus of this company, but with the private entry and exit stations that make getting in and out of the river a snap, we guess that relaxation is near the top of their list as well. Wear your swimsuit and a hat, bring along lunch and drinks in a cooler, and plenty of sunscreen. A change of clothes and a towel should be left in the car. The James River is known for its small-mouth bass population, so consider bringing along fishing gear or a mask and snorkel (depending on your intentions). The River Runners provide all equipment, equipment instruction, and a shuttle service up the river, along with secure parking and primitive camping. Be sure to call ahead for reservations, and visit their website for comprehensive pricing and other details.

SCHLEP FACTOR: Moderately high, when you consider the packing, advance reservations and the drive, but on a sweltering day it's well worth the effort. Once you're on the river, allow at least 2 hours for tubing, or 3 to 4 hours for the standard rafting/canoeing/kayaking trip (longer trips are available). Note that right across the parking lot from the James River Runners is the historic Hatton Ferry, one of two poled ferries left in the U.S. The ferry is a quick visit, so hop over after your trip down the river.

DIRECTIONS: Take I-64 to Exit 121A (Route 20S). Follow Route 20S for 17-1/2 miles (the road narrows). Fifty feet after you pass the "Welcome To Scottsville" sign, turn right on Route 726. Go 1 block to the stop sign, then continue straight for 1/4 mile to a second stop sign and turn right (you will still be on Route 726). Go 3 miles to a left on Route 625. Take Route 625 2 miles to the James River Runners' property.

James River Reeling & Rafting

265 Ferry Street, Scottsville   (804) 286-4386

WEBSITE: http://www.reelingandrafting.com

HOURS: Daily, late April–mid-October.

Shuttle service: On the half-hour 10:30 AM–2:30 PM.

Reservations: Required, one to two weeks for canoes and kayaks, one week for tubing, two to three days for rafting.

Rafting is available only in the spring and fall when water levels are high.

Minimum ages: 6 years for tubing, canoeing and rafting, 12 years for kayaking

Long known as the Other Guys on the James, James River Reeling & Rafting have collected twelve years of experience and is now a serious contender for the tubing dollar. As with the River Runners, equipment, equipment instruction and the shuttle service are included in the fee. You bring your swimsuit, lunch and drinks in a cooler, and lots of sunscreen. Toss in a mask and snorkel for a fish eye's view of wildlife, or fishing equipment if you'd rather reel them in. Separate guided fishing trips are available for fishing enthusiasts. Also bring along a towel and change of clothes to leave in your car.

The Reeling & Rafting trip is along a different section of the James from the River Runners', so take a trip with both companies and pick your favorite. Check out their website for pricing and other specifics.

SCHLEP FACTOR: As with River Runners, moderate but worth it. Allow 3–3-1/2 hours for tubing, 3–5 hours for canoeing and kayaking (longer trips available). The private take-out ramp is adjacent to the public boat ramp and offers secure parking and primitive camping.

DIRECTIONS: Take I-64 to exit 121A (Route 20S). Follow Route 20S into Scottsville. Turn left on Main Street (at the Citgo gas station). Go 2 blocks to the corner of Main and Ferry Streets. James River Reeling & Rafting will be on your right.

CANOE RENTALS AT THE LAKES

In the summer, Chris Greene Lake in Earlysville and Walnut Creek Lake in Red Hill rent canoes at the bathhouse for $2 per hour. In addition, you will have to pay a parking fee to enter the park during summer months. Both lakes are available for boating during other seasons as well, but you will need to provide your own non-fuel-powered boat.

DO-IT-YOURSELF BOATING LOCATIONS

You'll need your own boat to explore the waters of these local lakes and rivers. Note that many of these locations supply the drinking water for communities in our area. No swimming is allowed and trash should be kept out of the water. No schlep factor has been given here; we figure anybody willing to load a boat onto their car really doesn't care.

Beaver Creek Lake
Route 680, Crozet   (804) 296-5844

Beaver Creek Lake is run by the Albemarle County Parks and Recreation Department and is the water supply for the Crozet area. At 104 acres, this is the largest fishing lake in the county. Only non-fuel-powered boats are allowed. Boat launch and restrooms are available.

DIRECTIONS: Take Route 250W toward Crozet. At the fork, bear right onto Route 240 and immediately look for a brown recreation sign and take a hard right onto Route 680. Beaver Creek Lake is 3–4 miles ahead on Route 680.

Totier Creek Lake
Route 726, Scottsville   (804) 296-5844

This 66-acre lake, run by the Albemarle County Parks and Recreation Department, is the water supply for Scottsville. Only non-fuel-powered boats are allowed. Boat launch and restrooms are available.

DIRECTIONS: Take I-64 to exit 121A (Route 20S). Follow Route 20S to a right on Route 726. Turn left on Route 845 and the lake is at the end of the road (brown recreation signs will guide you).

Lake Albemarle
Garth Road, Charlottesville   (804) 296-4731

Lake Albemarle is run by the Department of Game and Inland Fisheries. Only non-fuel-powered boats can be used on the lake. You will find a boat launch but no restrooms here.

DIRECTIONS: Take Barracks Road west (becomes Garth Road) about 5 miles past the Hunt Country Corner store. Turn left onto Lake Albemarle Road and follow this road about 2.5 miles to the lake.

Rivanna Reservoir
Woodlands Road, Charlottesville

The Rivanna Reservoir, run by the Rivanna Water and Sewer Authority, is the main water impoundment for the City of Charlottesville. Only non-fuel-powered boats are allowed. A boat launch (but no restroom) is available on-site. Note that at this time there is no contact number for recreational use of the reservoir. Please do not call the Rivanna Water and Sewer Authority with recreational questions.

DIRECTIONS: Take Hydraulic Road to a left at the Rock Store onto Route 676. Go about 1 mile to the reservoir. A boat ramp is available next to the bridge, on the left.

Rivanna River

Darden Towe Park, Charlottesville   (804) 296-5844

The Rivanna River can be accessed through Darden Towe Park. Only non-fuel-powered boats or boats with electric motors are allowed on the river.

DIRECTIONS: Take Route 250E Bypass over Free Bridge. Turn left at the light onto Route 20N. Follow Route 20N for approximately 1/2 mile to a left on Elk Drive. Follow Elk Drive into the park.

DRIVE-IN THEATERS

Fork Union Drive-In

Route 612, Fork Union   (804) 842-3624

HOURS: Friday, Saturday and Sunday evenings, May–October. Two shows nightly. The first, generally best for families, begins at dusk. Gates open at 7 PM.

ADMISSION: Free for children 5 and under, $3 for children 6–10, $6 for adults. Call for nightly schedule. Monthly schedules are posted around town.

For a little blast-from-the-past, throw pajamas on the kids and hop over to the Fork Union Drive-In for family movies you can watch from the car. Actually, most folks bring chairs and blankets and sit outside on the grass—the perfect solution for kids who get antsy midway through a flick. A large grassy area in front of the movie screen provides more room for kids to run off steam. Pack a late-dinner picnic or pick up popcorn and drinks at the snack bar, then tune in the movie through your car radio (for kids, that trick alone catapults parents up to wizard status). Most of the kid flicks tend to be shown in July and August, but you will often find family-friendly films during other months as well.

SCHLEP FACTOR: Moderate, since the theater is a 45-minute drive from Charlottesville (but after running pell-mell through the field, kids will probably sleep on the way home). Once you're there, relaxing is easy. The snack bar provides light snacks and restrooms.

DIRECTIONS: Take I-64E to exit 136 (Route 15, Zion's Crossroads). Take Route 15S. When you reach Fork Union, make a right on Route 612. The Drive-In will be on the left.

FISHING

Rose River Vineyard and Trout Farm

Route 648, Syria   (540) 923-4050

HOURS: Daily, 9 AM–5 PM March–October, but closes if drought or high temperatures stress the fish. Call ahead to be sure they are open.
Wine tastings and tours: Saturdays and Sundays 11 AM–5 PM.

ADMISSION: Free, but there is a $3 fee for fishing poles, and fish caught are $3 per pound. Bait and fish-cleaning are available for a separate fee.

Take the scenic drive up to Syria for an afternoon of trout fishing in Rose River's two stocked ponds. Visitors are invited to rent a pole, bait up with corn bait and see what they can catch. All the trout are raised on the premises (large lanes filled with fish intrigue kids), and you only pay for what you catch. For the squeamish, fish-cleaning is available for a separate fee. Right down the street, the farm also operates a vineyard with tours and wine-tastings, so one parent can take the kids fishing while the other tours the wine-making facilities. Rose River borders Shenandoah National Park and offers plenty of hiking and picnic spots, too.

SCHLEP FACTOR: Moderate. Although Rose River Farm is a 45-minute ride from Charlottesville, the drive is scenic and you don't have to bring any fishing equipment. The farm has a juice machine and usually sandwiches are for sale if you forgot your picnic. The farm is stroller- and handicapped-accessible and there are porta-potty restrooms. Afterwards, head a mile down the street to Graves Mountain Lodge for dinner (be sure to call in advance for reservations at (540) 923-4231.)

DIRECTIONS: Take Route 29N to left on Route 231 in Madison. Go through Madison, bear left at the fork and continue on Route 231 toward Sperryville. Go about 5 miles to the town of Banco and turn left onto Route 670. Follow Route 670 for about 5 miles (you will pass Graves Mountain Lodge), then turn left onto Route 648. The entrance to Rose River Vineyards is on the right, the entrance to the trout farm just beyond on the right.

DO-IT-YOURSELF FISHING LOCATIONS

Fishing is available at these Albemarle County locations. Keep in mind that everyone 16 and older needs a fishing license. Call the Department of Game and Inland Fisheries at (804) 296-4731 for details.

Beaver Creek (see Boating)
Totier Creek (see Boating)
Lake Albemarle (see Boating)
Rivanna Reservoir (see Boating)
Rivanna River (see Boating)
Chris Greene Lake (see Parks)
Mint Springs Lake (see Parks)
Walnut Creek Lake (see Parks)
Sugar Hollow Reservoir (see Hiking/Camping for directions). No boats. Only shoreline fishing is allowed.

GO-CARTS

Planet Fun

Berkmar Drive, Charlottesville   (804) 975-4386

HOURS: Daily, April–late October, weather permitting, Friday–Sunday when area schools are in session. Call ahead for current operating schedule.

ADMISSION: Young children ride free with a paying adult, $1 for passengers for a 5-minute ride, $4 for drivers. Thursday (Family Day) go-carts (as well as many other attractions) are $2.

Minimum requirements/age: Children must be 60" tall to drive and must be at least 16 years old with a valid driver's license to carry a passenger.

Can't wait for that rite of passage when you finally turn over the car keys to your kids? Experience it now, along with the gray hairs that inevitably accompany the experience, at the Planet Fun Raceway. Any kid over five feet can take a car for a fast and furious five-minute spin around the oval track. Smaller kids can ride in the car with a licensed adult. While you're there, check out some of the other Planet Fun offerings.

SCHLEP FACTOR: Low. Since the go-carts are open on an erratic schedule, we suggest that visitors call ahead to avoid disappointment.

DIRECTIONS: Take Route 29N to a left onto E. Rio Road. Go to the first light and turn right onto Berkmar. Follow Berkmar through 1 traffic light to Planet Fun on the right.

The Bull Pen

Deyerle Avenue, Harrisonburg   (540) 433-2243

HOURS: Daily, March–mid-November, weather permitting. Call ahead for current operating schedule; extended hours in the summer.

ADMISSION: $4 for the Indy track, $5 for the NASCAR track. Both rides are 5 minutes.

Minimum requirements/age: Drivers must be at least 10 years old and 58" tall to drive on the Indy track, 14 years old and 62" for the NASCAR track, and must be 16 or older with a valid driver's license to carry a passenger (Indy track only). Passengers must be at least 4 years old.

Visitors to the Bull Pen in Harrisonburg can choose from two go-cart tracks. One, the Indy track, is best suited for families. This course snakes around an 890-foot track with lots of twists and turns (go ahead and make that appointment with your chiropractor before you visit). The cars on this track go 18 mph, and single and double cars are available. The second course is the mini-NASCAR track. The cars here (singles only) zip around the oval track at 25 mph. After your ride, check out some of the other attractions at the Bull Pen, such as batting cages, mini-golf and a small arcade.

SCHLEP FACTOR: High. Don't even think of driving all the way to Harrisonburg for a 5-minute go-cart ride, but if you're visiting other Harrisonburg attractions be sure to stop by.

DIRECTIONS: Take Route 29N to a left onto Route 33 in Ruckersville (the main intersection). Follow Route 33 over the mountain and into Harrisonburg. Just past Valley Mall turn left at the light onto University Boulevard (the Kroger plaza will be on the right). Turn left onto Deyerle Avenue. The Bull Pen will be just ahead on the right.

GOLF

Golf is a difficult game for adults to master, let alone kids. Our golfing families suggest that kids take lots of trips to the Highlands Practice Range before hitting the courses. Although it is tempting to take advantage of Meadowcreek and McIntire, the local public golf courses, these aren't the best courses for young golfers. McIntire has greens which are difficult for kids to play. Meadowcreek is a better bet, but take your kids on an afternoon to avoid crowds. One favorite course for kids is the Swannanoa Golf Course on Afton Mountain (540) 943-8864. That course is shorter and the atmosphere more casual.

Highlands Practice Range

Route 29, Ruckersville   (804) 985-2765

No website, but e-mail: highlands' golf@juno.com

HOURS: Daily, year-round. Daylight Savings Time (April–October): Monday–Thursday 7:30 AM–9:30 PM, Friday and Saturday 7:30 AM–10:30 PM, Sunday 7:30 AM–6:30 PM; Standard Time. (October–April): Monday–Sunday noon–8 PM. Closed some holidays.

ADMISSION: Use of the mat tees and a bucket of 100+ balls costs $8.75, $1 off for kids and 10% discount for seniors. Many specials and combination prices available. Group discounts available.

Equipment rental: Free for children, but fee for adults; putters are free for everyone.

Anne Marie and Peter Scheuermann, owners of the Highlands Practice Range, encourage kids to come practice at their Ruckersville facility. The nearly-new operation has plenty of space to stretch out and even provides heaters during the winter months. Covered tees are available year-round so kids can play in any weather. The Highlands also has a short game practice area for chipping and putting. The putting green is artificial but great fun for kids. New at the Highlands is the Putt-A-Round course, an 18-hole putting course designed to allow even non-golfing members to enjoy the Highlands. It offers a real putting surface, not miniature course quality.

SCHLEP FACTOR: Low. Golf is a difficult sport to master, but the Highlands makes the practice, practice, practice part fun, fun, fun. Conveniently located and meticulously maintained with restrooms, vending, and a covered patio on-site, the facility is handicapped- and stroller-accessible.

DIRECTIONS: Take Route 29N to Ruckersville. From the main intersection in Ruckersville (at Routes 29 and 33) go less than a mile to the 3rd cross-over on Route 29N. Turn left into the cross-over and go straight across to the Highlands parking lot.

HORSEBACK RIDING

In case you didn't notice, we are smack-dab in horse country. There are many wonderful stables in our area that offer lessons and boarding, and a fair number that run trail rides as well. We couldn't include all of them, so we chose a few popular stables that offer trail rides to those with no prior riding experience.

Skyland Stables

Skyline Drive   (540) 999-2210

HOURS: Daily, April–late November, closed rest of the year.

ADMISSION: Horseback riding:1 hour trail ride $20 per person Monday–Friday, $22 weekends; 2-1/2 hour trail ride (summers only) $42 per person; pony rides $3 per child for 15 minutes, $6 for a 1/2 hour. Skyline Drive Admission $10 per vehicle for a seven-day pass or $20 for access.
Reservations: Required for horseback riding and may be made one day in advance (weekends book quickly); no reservations for pony rides.
Minimum requirements: Horseback riders must be at least 58" tall, no age restrictions; pony riders should be under 58" tall.

If your family needs a change of pace from hiking on Skyline Drive, cruise over to Skyland Stables and see the park on horseback! Never been on a horse before? No problem. Ninety percent of the stable's guests are never-evers, and the rides are geared to beginners. A one-hour group ride into the park leaves four times a day (more often during the summer). Your guide will tell you about the wildlife and point out sites along the way. You'll pass an old apple orchard, a homestead foundation and trees that are over 600 years old. At one point you'll cross a bridge where you can see waterfalls that feed into Whiteoak Canyon. During the summer, the stable also offers a 2-1/2 hour ride to Whiteoak Falls that leaves at 8:15 AM.

If your kids are under 58" tall they can ride a pony around the stable (parents walk beside the pony). It's a fun adjunct to a day of hiking for kids, and dirt cheap, too.

For all rides, wear long pants and tennis shoes (no sandals). You also may want to bring along water for the longer trail ride, although you will have to carry it yourself in a backpack.

SCHLEP FACTOR: Moderate. Skyland is nearly a 1-1/2 hour drive from Charlottesville, so consider coming up for the day. There is lots to do here—hiking, camping, even a restaurant—so make those horseback reservations for a morning ride and make a day of it. The stables have restrooms and vending (water bottles are available at vending) and they can accommodate some disabilities (call ahead for information).

DIRECTIONS: Take Route 29N to Ruckersville. At the main intersection in Ruckersville, turn left onto Route 33W. Go 15 miles on Route 33 to a right into the Swift Run Gap entrance to Skyline Drive. Turn left onto Skyline Drive and go north 23 miles to Skyland Lodge.

Graves Mountain Lodge
Syria   (540) 923-5071

WEBSITE: www.gravesmountain.com

HOURS: Daily, mid-March–Thanksgiving

ADMISSION: 1-1/2 hour trail ride $20 per person; 1/2 day ride $50 per person (includes snacks); full day rides $90 per person (includes lunch); overnights $125 per person (includes all meals). Family rates available.
Reservations: Required, and should be made as far in advance as possible, especially for overnight trips.
Minimum age: Horseback riders should be at least 8 years old, although they will consider experienced riders as young as 6.

There is no such thing as a typical trail ride at Graves Mountain Lodge, because Tom and Patricia Seay see to it that each customer gets a custom-tailored tour of the area. You tell them what you want to see. Skyline Drive? Hoover camp? Water? Mountains? No problem. For longer rides, snacks and meals are included and—you guessed it—no standard-issue box lunches. They fix what you like to eat. If you really want to see these folks shine, book them for an overnight trip (see Camping) or for something truly unique, try a cattle drive (see Animals). None of their rides requires prior riding or camping experience, either. For personal service and attention to detail, we really can't say enough about these folks. You'll want to do this one again and again.

SCHLEP FACTOR: Very low despite the 45-minute drive. Here's the game plan: you call for reservations. You throw the family in the car and drive to Madison. You get out of your car and onto your horses. No problem. No stuff to schlep.

DIRECTIONS: Take Route 29N to a left on Route 231 in Madison. Go through Madison and bear left at the fork and continue on Route 231 toward Sperryville. Go about 5 miles to the town of Banco and take a left onto Route 670. Take Route 670 about 4 miles to Graves Mountain Lodge. The stable is just across from the lodge.

Rodes Farm Stable at Wintergreen Resort

Nelson County   (804) 325-8260

WEBSITE: www.wintergreenresort.com

HOURS: Daily, mid-March–November, except Wednesdays; closed rest of the year.

ADMISSION: Horseback riding: 1 hour trail ride $30 per person Monday–Friday, $35 weekends and holidays; 15-minute pony rides $12 per child. Rates lower for resort guests and subject to change.

Reservations: Required for all equestrian activities and should be made two days to one week in advance.

Minimum age: Trail riders must be at least 11, younger kids can take miniature horse rides or lessons.

Riding lessons: Call for more information.

One of Wintergreen's best-kept secrets is Rodes Farm Stables. Upon your arrival, you will likely be greeted by a flock of geese and Petunia, a huge pot-bellied pig. Reserve a one-hour trail ride in advance for a close-up view of deer, birds and an occasional fox. Your guide will lead your group through woods and fields and past a small lake. If you have never been on a horse before, you're in good company; the majority of visitors to the stable have never ridden.

For younger children, the stable offers "pony" rides on one of their two miniature horses. Parents lead the miniature horse around the ring for fifteen minutes. The stable is especially good at coordinating activities to assure that every member of your family has some equestrian exposure. For example, one parent and an older child can go on a trail ride while the other parent and younger child take a lesson or do pony rides.

Holidays are especially fun at the stable. On the Fourth of July, the stable hosts a visit from Uncle Sam, and other family activities. On Easter, visitors are treated to egg hunts with prizes such as free riding lessons for finding the golden egg. Halloween brings a miniature haunted house, stable hands in costume, a costume contest, games and prizes. Call the stable for details.

SCHLEP FACTOR: Surprisingly low. Rodes Farm is only a 25-minute drive from Charlottesville. The crew at the stable are especially helpful and go out of their way to make sure everyone is enjoying themselves. The barn is stroller- and handicapped-accessible and has restrooms, water, and vending.

DIRECTIONS: For families traveling from the south end of town, take Route 29S to a right on Route 6 at Walton's Market. Take Route 6 for 6 miles to a stop. Take a left at the stop onto Route 151. Go 1 mile to a right onto Rodes Farm Drive at the Wintergreen/Rodes Farm Stable sign. Go less than 1 mile to the green-and-white barn.

For families driving from the north or west end of Charlottesville, take Route 250W to a left on Route 151. Follow Route 151 to a right onto Rodes Farm Drive. Go less than 1 mile to the stable.

Shenandoah Acres Resort

Stuarts Draft   (540) 337-1911

WEBSITE: http://www.shenacres.com

HOURS: Daily, 10 AM–5 PM (drop-in trail rides Memorial Day–Labor Day); after Labor Day, trail rides are available on a reservation basis only.

ADMISSION: $9 per person for the short (25-minute) ride or $16 for the long (1-hour) ride.

Minimum age: Children 6 and older may ride alone; children under 6 can ride for half-price with a paying adult.

Dress recommendations: Close-toed shoes, pants

Trail rides at Shenandoah Acres are super easy during the summer; all you have to do is show up at the beachhouse, plunk down the fee and hop on a horse. No reservations needed, and, since little ones can ride on the same horse as a parent, no need to leave preschoolers home with a sitter. The rides leave from the corral next to the beachhouse and are announced over the PA system to bathers on the beach. Riders follow the trails on the Shenandoah Acres property—mostly woods with one stream crossing. If you are spending the day at the Shenandoah Acres lake (see Lake Swimming), throw shoes and shorts in the car so you can take advantage of this easy add-on to a fun day.

SCHLEP FACTOR: Pretty low since the resort offers drop-in rides during the summer. Don't plan on coming just for the trail rides; Shenandoah Acres offers enough activities to fill a day or more.

DIRECTIONS: Take I-64W over Afton Mountain to Exit 94. Turn left onto Route 340S. Go 5 miles to the 5th traffic light and turn left onto Route 608/610. Follow Route 608 to Route 610 (it's the same road, only the number changes) for 1.8 miles to a left onto Lake Road and into the park.

HOT AIR BALLOONING

If you've ever chanced upon a hot air balloon drifting over the Charlottesville countryside, you may well have experienced balloon fever. Your heart races. You find yourself ignoring appointments and street signs in order to chase the balloon to its dramatic landing. There's no doubt about it, hot air balloons bring out the kid in all of us. Unfortunately, ballooning is an expensive proposition, running $150 per person for a morning of flying. The Charlottesville balloon operators are a friendly lot, though, and are more than happy to allow anyone willing to rise early enough to watch as the balloons are filled and launched (most balloons leave at sunrise, although afternoon flights are sometimes offered, weather depending). Call one of the professional operators below to find out where to meet to watch the launch, or to splurge on a flight. Children five and older are welcome to fly.

Bear Balloon Company
(the familiar Boar's Head balloon)
contact Rick Behr at (804) 971-1757
This is the largest balloon operator in town. Rick has an eight-person basket and therefore can offer group and stand-by rates.

Bonaire Charters
contact Scott Cohrs at (804) 293-3561

MINIATURE GOLF

You will find a miniature golf course or two in many of the towns surrounding Charlottesville, but since we have several right here, we have chosen to review only the courses in our immediate area. Although Little Links at Kegler's closed in 1998, perhaps new ownership will breathe new life into this fun course.

Planet Fun

Berkmar Drive, Charlottesville   (804) 975-4386

HOURS: Daily, year-round. Hours vary seasonally so call ahead for operating hours. Open extended hours in the summer.

ADMISSION: Children 3 and under play for free, $4 for everyone else. On Thursdays or after 5 PM on Sundays, the fee is $2 for kids and accompanying adults.

The miniature golf course at Planet Fun offers interesting twists, turns, complications and water. Lots of water! Playing this course with a toddler in tow quickly breaks down into a water-slinging event. The challenging features and interesting landscaping of this course, however, make it a favorite with grade-schoolers. Guests will also find an air-conditioned arcade, a snack bar, and several other outdoor attractions to entertain beyond the golf course.

SCHLEP FACTOR: Fairly low. The great thing about Planet Fun, the variety of attractions, can also be a problem. It is hard to bring a child to play miniature golf without trying some of the other offerings! The course also has a special handicapped-accessible section.

DIRECTIONS: Take Route 29N to a left at the light at Rio Road. At the next light turn right onto Berkmar Drive. Follow Berkmar through 1 traffic light to Planet Fun on the right.

Putt Putt

Rio Road, Charlottesville   (804) 973-5509

HOURS: Daily, mid-March–Thanksgiving, 9 AM–midnight during summer, afternoons until 9 PM when school is in session.

ADMISSION: $1 for kids 4 and under, $4 per game for everyone over 4.

In operation at its Rio Road location for 30 years, Putt Putt is still the favorite miniature golf course for families with very young children. The big jungle animals, a Putt Putt icon, make this a thrill even for kids too young to know which end of the club to hold. Putt Putt has two courses to choose from and you will find fewer–okay, we'll say it–serious miniature golfers (never thought you would hear those words used together, did you?) than at the other miniature golf courses. Tiny plastic clubs for toddlers are available, as are birthday party packages. A hole-in-one still wins a discounted game.

SCHLEP FACTOR: None. This is a great spur-of-the-moment stop. Canned drinks and restrooms are available.

DIRECTIONS: Take Route 29N to a right onto Rio Road at the Fashion Square Mall. Putt Putt is less than 1/2 mile ahead on the left. (Hint: it's the only joint with a giraffe on the roof.)

Putt-A-Round at the Highlands Golf Center
Ruckersville   (804) 985-2765

HOURS: Daily, year-round. Daylight Savings Time (April–October): Monday–Thursday 7:30 AM–9:30 PM, Friday and Saturday 7:30 AM–10:30 PM, Sunday 7:30 AM–6:30 PM; Standard Time. (October–April): Monday–Sunday noon–8 PM. Closed some holidays.

ADMISSION: $5 per round per person.

Non-golfing families need not be intimidated by this professional-looking golf center. The owners of the Highlands are particularly family-friendly and have recently opened this putting area so non-golfers can enjoy the Highlands, too. The course here is the only one of its kind in Virginia: a real putting green surface on a miniature golf-style course. Don't expect to find any windmills or giraffes on the course; instead, attractive landscaping is meant to soothe and calm players. Maybe this is the right place to get your toddler to slow down....

SCHLEP FACTOR: Low. This is a great stop for all families with kids 5 and up. If you have a golfer or budding golfer, they can enjoy the practice range while the rest of the family tries out the putting course. A covered patio, vending and restrooms round out the offerings here.

DIRECTIONS: Take Route 29N to the main intersection in Ruckersville (Routes 29 and 33). Continue on Route 29N for about a mile to the third cross-over on Route 29. Turn left into the cross-over and the Highlands will be straight across Route 29.

CLIMBING AND RAPPELLING

The Plunge at Wintergreen

Wintergreen   (540) 325-2200

Hours: Saturdays, May–October

Reservations: Call ahead for specific instructions.

Admission: $35 per person for 2 hours rappelling, $30 per person for 1-1/2 hours.

Minimum age: None, but kids under 18 must be accompanied by an adult.

If your kids have mastered climbing at the indoor gyms and are ready for a taste of the real thing, plan a Saturday at Wintergreen's climbing/rappelling program. Experienced instructors take a small group to The Plunge, Wintergreen's natural rock face, for an experience kids (and adults) are guaranteed to be talking about for years to come. All equipment is provided and the instructors are very patient and helpful. Although Wintergreen has no age restriction, due to the physical maturity and concentration necessary for these activities (not to mention the cost involved), we recommend this for kids eight and up.

Schlep Factor: Moderate. Wintergreen is 45 minutes to an hour away, but this is a must-do for outdoorsy families with middle graders and older.

Directions: Take Route 250W to a left on Route 151S. Follow Route 151S for 14 miles to a right on Route 664. Go 4-1/2 miles to Wintergreen on the right.

Outdoor Insights

Crozet   (804) 456-8742

Hours: Trips available daily, year-round.

Admission: $50 for kids 12–16, $65 for kids over 16, $95 for adults.

Reservations: Call 10 days in advance.

Minimum age: 12 years old.

Scott Ziemer of Outdoor Insights will spend a day on the Parkway with your family teaching you the basics of rock climbing and rappelling. Raven's Roost or Twenty-Minute Cliff are two of his favorite spots for beginner climbing and offer gorgeous views as well. Scott provides all of the equipment; you bring just lunch and a camera. One nice perk: Scott has his Wilderness First Responder certificate, which is one step below EMT (not that you'll need it).

Schlep Factor: Fairly low since Scott takes care of most of the essentials.

Directions: Site will be arranged with Scott when you make your reservation.

GRASS SKIING

Bryce Resort

Basye   (800) 821-1444

HOURS: www.bryceresort.com
Sundays and Wednesdays, 10:30 AM–1 PM early July–August, and
Sundays 11 AM–2 PM in October. Call ahead for exact schedule.

ADMISSION: $26 for lesson, rental and lift ticket.
Minimum age/requirements: 12 years old and in good physical
condition.

No, that wasn't a typo. Grass skiing originated in Europe as a training
method for skiers. Now visitors at Bryce Resort (age twelve and up) can
don the short, tread-like skis and ski the green hills of Bryce in the off-
season. Just as in snow skiing, the ski-lifts bring participants back to the
top of the mountain. Grass skiing is fun but it isn't easy, so consider your
family's strength and agility before making the trek.

After working up a sweat on the slopes, take a dip in the pool or lake
($3 for each). Paddleboat and canoe rentals are available on the lake, and
for the boundlessly energetic, windsurfing lessons can be arranged (24
hours in advance, (540) 856-2121). The resort also offers horseback and
pony rides, miniature golf and several restaurants.

SCHLEP FACTOR: High, because of the 1-1/2+ hour drive from Charlottesville, but there is
plenty to do at Bryce to fill an afternoon or a weekend.

DIRECTIONS: Take Route 29N to a left on Route 33 in Ruckersville. Follow Route 33
over the mountain into Harrisonburg. In Harrisonburg, take I-81N to
Exit 273 (Mount Jackson). Turn right onto Route 292, and go a short
distance to a right on Route 11. Go 3-4 miles through the town of Mount
Jackson, then turn right on Route 263. Go 11 miles on Route 263 to
Bryce Resort on the right.

OUTDOOR GAMES

Splathouse

946 Grady Avenue, Charlottesville   (804) 977-5287

WEBSITE: http://www.splathouse.com

HOURS: Daily, year-round

ADMISSION: Varies, but typically is $45 for a five-hour outdoor session.
Minimum group size for outdoor fields is 12; families who do not meet the minimum will be combined with another group.
Reservations: Required, and should be made two weeks in advance, although shorter notice can often be accommodated. Call for availability, but no walk-ins accepted.
Minimum age: 12, 11-year-olds okay if accompanied by an adult.

In addition to the indoor facility at the old Monticello Dairy, Splathouse also offers outdoor paintball in a 45-acre wooded setting. Five fields with varying terrain and obstacles, such as underbrush-and-vine pathways, provide a thrilling backdrop for an afternoon of suspense-filled strategy games. For the uninitiated, paintballs are small bath bead-like pellets filled with non-staining dye. They are shot from a gun. The balls sting a bit on contact, so the game is only appropriate for kids age 12 and up. For adrenaline junkies who love to be outside, outdoor paintball at Splathouse hits the spot (literally).

SCHLEP FACTOR: High. Since paintball requires advance reservations and a large chunk of an afternoon, it is more of an event than simply an attraction. Save this one for families with teens.

DIRECTIONS: (To Splathouse. Guests will carpool to the nearby fields.) Take Route 29S to a left onto Barracks Road at the shopping center. Go 1 mile through 2 stoplights to the flashing yellow light and turn right onto 10th Street. Go about 20 feet to the next stop light and turn left onto Grady Avenue; the Splathouse is just ahead on the right.

The Marvelous Maize Maze

McGaheysville   (540) 289-5377 (Jerry Mundy)

HOURS: Daily, 10 AM–dusk mid-July–October. The Haunted Maze, open select days in October, is open 7 PM–11 PM, closed rest of the year.

ADMISSION: Free for children under 3, $3 for kids 3–12, $5 for adults.

From the if-you-build-it-they-will-come school of thought comes Jerry Mundy, a Massanutten-area dairy farmer who each summer carves an intricate maze into his cornfield. Tourists come from miles around to work their way through the 3-1/2 acre maze, most stumbling out of the end within a half-hour. Along the way, visual clues ranging from an igloo and an "earthquake bridge" give guests hints on finding the exit. To keep things interesting, the Mundys carve a different maze each year. Last year, during his inaugural run, the maze spelled MILK. The admission fee includes a hayride tour of the dairy farm and farm animals as well as access to the maze. Near Halloween, older kids will get a kick out of the Haunted Maze, where creatures lurking in the corn jump out at visitors.

SCHLEP FACTOR: High if you are driving all the way to Massanutten just for the maze, but still a unique experience for families. Combine a trip here with one of the other Massanutten or Harrisonburg attractions for a fun summer afternoon. Milk and juice are available for sale and there are porta-potty restrooms on site. The maze is do-able with strollers and wheelchairs, although both will have to be lifted over some obstacles. Electric wheelchairs are not recommended.

DIRECTIONS: Take Route 29N to a left on Route 33 at the main intersection in Ruckersville. Follow Route 33 over the mountain. When you pass the Massanutten Resort entrance in McGaheysville, continue on Route 33 for another 4–5 miles. At the 7-Eleven and Exxon station, turn left on Route 655. Go 2-1/2 miles to a right on Route 672. Go about 1 mile to a left on Route 658. Go about 1 mile to the maze on the right.

ROPES COURSES

Pull together several families for a challenging day on one of these local ropes courses. Families can choose from either a high ropes course, which focuses on the development of confidence and self-reliance of the individual, or a low ropes course which focuses on team-building. For the high ropes courses, participants are required to wear spotting belts and other safety equipment, making for a safe and memorable day. Low ropes courses typically require little or no climbing from participants and are safe even for young children.

Falls River Course in Batesville

Batesville   (804) 971-8599

WEBSITE: http://www.fallsrivercenter.com

HOURS: Daily, year-round, starting times are flexible.

Minimum age: High ropes 13 years, low ropes 10 years.

Minimum number participants: Seven to eight, possibly down to five to six if children, but prefer larger group.

Reservations: Required, and should be made three weeks or more in advance, farther ahead during the summer.

ADMISSION: $40 per person for a 4-hour low ropes and $60 per person for a 4-hour high ropes.

Falls River Center, long known for their quality work with corporate groups, is now branching out to include more youth groups. The 80-acre Falls River Center, fronting on the Mechums River, has peaceful waterfalls, hardwoods and meadows that belie the high-energy outing ahead. Falls River has more than a dozen local facilitators to choose from, some of whom came from the nationally-acclaimed Outward Bound program. Each group will have a facilitator handpicked to meet the specific needs and dynamics of the group.

For the high ropes course, participants climb a cargo net to the course, which is suspended 30-40 feet in the air. Rather than climbing back down between events, participants stay in the treetops for the afternoon, working their way through a series of challenging events. The low ropes course includes activities such as a spider's web, where a team must get through a rope web without touching the rope.

SCHLEP FACTOR: Fairly high because of the reservations and number of participants required.

DIRECTIONS: Directions will be given when reservations are made.

Poplar Ridge Ropes Course at U.Va.

University of Virginia Campus, Charlottesville   (804) 924-3791

Website: http://www.virginia.edu/~imurals/poplar'ridge

Hours: Daily, year-round to groups of 6 or more.

Admission: Per person, the half-day program is $15 for low ropes, $20 for a combination low and high ropes and $30 for high ropes.
Minimum age: High ropes 12 years, low ropes approximately 8 years.
Reservations: Required, and should be made two weeks in advance, one month in advance for appointments in late August, September and October.

Right on Mr. Jefferson's Grounds there is a 30-foot telephone pole. And sitting on top of that pole is a teensy-weensy round disk. And perched atop of that teensy-weensy round disk—could be you and your loved ones. Sound scary? That's what Jay Roberts and the rest of the Poplar Ridge crew are shooting for at U.Va.'s high ropes course, since confronting our fears and pushing ourselves beyond what we believe we can do supposedly leads to greater self-confidence and self-reliance. A variety of activities normally reserved for winged animals awaits visitors to the course, or if your kids (yeah, that's it...it's the kids) aren't quite up for swinging 20–60 feet through the trees, try out the low ropes or a combination course. The low course focuses on team-building, and the combination is a kind of ropes course smorgasbord offering a little bit of everything.

Schlep Factor: Fairly high because of the reservations and number of participants required.

Directions: Sorry, can't divulge the secret location. You have to make reservations, then Jay will tell your group how to get there.

Camp Friendship Course

Palmyra   (804) 589-8950 or (800) 873-3223

Hours: Daily, September–May by appointment only, to groups of 8 or more.

Admission: $17 per person for a half-day, includes instruction and use of the course.
Minimum age: 12 years old for high ropes, all ages for low ropes.

The popular and extensive ropes course at Camp Friendship in Palmyra is reserved for campers during the summer, but during the off-season, the course opens to groups of all ages. School, scouting and church groups have all tried their hands at this course, but it is open to any group of eight or more persons. Camp Friendship, believing that children are never too young to begin learning trust and cooperation, offers their low ropes course to children as young as preschool-age. The high ropes course, reserved for older children, offers activities such as climbing up to a 40-foot high platform for a zip-line ride back down to terra firma. Sounds like kid stuff, doesn't it?

SCHLEP FACTOR: Fairly high because of the reservations and number of participants required.

DIRECTIONS: Take I-64E to exit 136 (Zion's Crossroads). Turn right on Route 15 and go south for 7-1/2 miles to the camp on the right.

SKATEBOARDING AND IN-LINE SKATING

Need equipment? Freestyle at Rio Hill offers a large selection of rollerblades and skateboards for sale or rent, or pick up used equipment at their October ski swap.

Massanutten Resort Skate Park

McGaheysville   (540) 289-4954

HOURS: 10 AM–dark April–October, but hours vary so call ahead.

ADMISSION: Based upon time usage, but starts at $5 for park access and $12 for park access plus rental.

The Massanutten Resort Skate Park, once reserved for resort owners, opened for public use in 1998. Kids of all ages give the half-acre park high marks for the 15–20 obstacles, including ramps, rails, half-pipes and pyramids. Since the family-oriented park is closely supervised, even tots who can barely skate are able to co-exist safely with experienced teens. Call ahead for special events such as demonstrations by professional skateboarders, and skateboard competitions.

SCHLEP FACTOR: Fairly low, despite the 45-minute drive to the resort. Skateboards and in-line skates from child's size 6 to adult sizes can be rented at the on-site pro shop. Helmets (required) and pads can also be rented. While at the resort, also enjoy a round of miniature golf at the shady, unique course located behind the swimming pool. The resort has one restaurant, and snacks can be purchased at the resort's General Store.

DIRECTIONS: Take Route 29N to a left on Route 33 in Ruckersville (the major intersection). Follow Route 33 over the mountain to a right on Route 644 at the Massanutten sign. Proceed through the gatehouse and follow Massanutten Drive to the ski area.

SNOW SKIING AND SNOWBOARDING

Charlottesville residents are lucky to have two very nice ski areas (by East Coast standards) within an hour's drive. Which is better, Massanutten or Wintergreen? Actually, neither, although families usually prefer one over the other. Both are worth a visit to decide for yourself.

1   If you can swing it, visit midweek when the lines are short, the parking easier and the tickets less expensive.

2   If midweek isn't an option, consider Sunday afternoons when the resort crowds thin out. Also, call both resorts to find out if any big events are planned for the day you want to attend. If there is an event at one resort, go to the other one.

3   Be sure to bring waterproof pants and jacket, gloves or mittens, a hat, thick knee socks and additional layers depending on the temperature. Remember, both resorts are always at least ten degrees colder than Charlottesville and can be very windy!

4   Above all, remember this: rumor has it the word "schlep" is actually an old Yiddish word meaning "to haul ski equipment." Whichever resort you choose, bring your wallet and your patience. You will need both. It takes a few visits to get the routine down, but skiing families will tell you it is well worth the effort!

Need equipment? Massanutten and Wintergreen offer on-site rentals. In addition, Freestyle at Berkmar Crossing offers seasonal rentals and sells a wide variety of ski and snowboard equipment. If you want to buy used equipment, Freestyle hosts a ski swap in late October and another in late November with great bargains on both adult- and child-size equipment for those who arrive early. Play It Again Sports at Rio Hill also offers lots of reasonably priced used and new equipment.

Both Massanutten and Wintergreen offer *adaptive ski programs* to help those with disabilities learn to ski. Call the resort for details.

Massanutten Resort

McGaheysville   (540) 289-9441

WEBSITE: http://www.massresort.com

HOURS: Daily, 9 AM–4:30 PM; Twilight 12:30 PM–10 PM, Extended Day 9 AM–10 PM, Half Day 9 AM– 12:30 PM, or Monday–Friday (only non-holidays) 12:30 PM–4:30 PM, Night 5 PM–10PM.

ADMISSION: Varies widely, but goes up particularly on holidays and weekends.

The Massanutten ski lodge lacks the sparkle of Wintergreen's ritzy lodge and is trickier for young families to negotiate, although a rumored lodge renovation could close that gap. As of 1999, the lodge offers only one cafeteria-style restaurant within walking distance to the slopes; it can get crowded and smoky and there are too many steps for a child in ski boots. Teens, however, give Massanutten high marks for the awesome snowboard park and more efficient lifts, including one quad lift. Thanks to their extraordinary snowmaking, Massanutten often has the longest ski season of any Virginia resort. Another coup for Massanutten was the opening of their tubing park in 1997, a one-of-a-kind for this area (see our listing under Snow Sledding and Tubing).

Despite the functional problems of Massanutten, the Ski-Wee program for kids four and up is excellent, and the slopes are well-maintained. Weekends and holidays are crowded, so a midweek visit is a must for beginners. Kids five and under receive complimentary lift tickets every day with a paid adult ticket.

SCHLEP FACTOR: High. Parking is difficult and dining is a problem. Also note that since Massanutten is primarily a time-share resort, some amenities such as the indoor pool are not open to resort day visitors.

DIRECTIONS: Take Route 29N to a left on Route 33 in Ruckersville (the major intersection). Follow Route 33 over the mountain to a right on Route 644 at the Massanutten sign. Proceed through the gatehouse and follow Massanutten Drive to the ski area.

Wintergreen Resort
Wintergreen   (804) 325-2200

WEBSITE: http://www.wintergreenresort.com for seasonal information.

HOURS: Daily 9 AM–4:30 PM; Nightly Sunday–Thursday 5 PM–10PM, Friday and Saturday 6 PM–11 PM; Twilight daily 12:30 PM–closing.

ADMISSION: Varies widely, but goes up particularly on holidays and weekends.

Wintergreen is easier for young families to negotiate thanks in part to a central courtyard with ski-in, ski-out access from the beginner slopes. A beautiful ski lodge with a half-dozen shops, equipment rentals, several dining spots and the Treehouse, Wintergreen's children's program area, are all conveniently located on this courtyard. If you need a lesson for your child, reserve it a day in advance by calling the Treehouse (804)-325-8170 for half or full-day programs or the ski school (804)-325-8065 for hour-long private or group lessons. The lessons here are a blast for kids. Beginners are taught in their own kids-only "terrain garden" with specially trained instructors.

Weekends and holidays during ski season are very crowded and can be intimidating to a child just learning to negotiate the slopes and lifts. Instead, try to plan a midweek visit. Kids under five receive complimentary lift tickets every day with a paid adult lift ticket. Wednesday is family day; kids 17 and under ski free with a parent. Rentals are extra for both programs.

Right off the slopes you will find cafeteria-style dining, an outdoor grill (great for hot chocolate runs) and a couple of fancier albeit still family-friendly restaurants.

If the slopes don't tire them out, head farther up the mountain to the Wintergarden spa, which has an airy indoor pool with hot tubs (kids love to dash to the outdoor tubs in the snow) and a restaurant.

SCHLEP FACTOR: Pretty high. Parking is easier than at Massanutten, but still plan on arriving early for a good spot. Arriving a half-hour before the slopes open is a good idea. Once you are ticketed and suited up, the rest of the day is all downhill.

DIRECTIONS: Take Route 250W to a left on Route 151S. Follow Route 151S for 14.2 miles to a right on Route 664. Go 4.5 miles and bear right at the fork to the Wintergreen gatehouse. Follow Wintergreen Drive up the mountain to the ski area parking.

SNOW SLEDDING AND TUBING

Massanutten Resort
McGaheysville   (540) 289-9441

WEBSITE: http://www.massresort.com

HOURS: Daily, during ski season: sledding sessions are two hours long; the first session begins 9 AM, the last begins 7 PM.

ADMISSION: $10 per person per session. Children under 44" pay half price but must be accompanied by a paying adult.

Massanutten was the first Virginia resort to offer snow tubing, a great ski-alternative for kids and adults. Tubers (lingo for those riding tubes, not members of the potato family) pick up a tube in one of three sizes (kid, adult, or a double for a kid and an adult) and ride one of two handle-tow lifts to the top of the 900-foot hill. The rest comes as natural as a snowball fight. Massanutten's strict enforcement of their Snow Tubing Policy help keep this a fun and safe activity for the whole family, but the sport, like skiing, is not without risks. The policy is: (1) Tubers under 44" must be accompanied by a paying adult, (2) only one rider under 44" is allowed on each tube and, (3) no ski boots are allowed on the tubing runs. We recommend dressing as you would for skiing, but be certain you have a waterproof outer layer (including gloves and boots) as tubers have more contact with the snow.

SCHLEP FACTOR: Moderate. Not as schleppy as skiing, but still, whenever you mix kids and lots of layers of clothing, you have a high-maintenance event. For younger kids who are exhausted after one hike to the top of a sledding hill, the tow lifts makes this the best way to enjoy an afternoon of tubing. The Snow Tubing Park at Massanutten is very popular. Tickets for all sessions go on sale at 8:30 AM to the general public and a day in advance for Massanutten owners and overnight guests. Many sessions, especially on holidays and weekends, sell out early—sometimes before the ticket window opens for the day. Call (540) 289-5032 up to 9 PM the night before your planned visit to find out which sessions are unavailable for the next day and plan on arriving before 8 AM to snag tickets.

DIRECTIONS: Take Route 29N to a left on Route 33 in Ruckersville (the main intersection). Follow Route 33 over the mountain to a right onto Route 644 at the Massanutten sign. Turn left onto Massanutten Drive and proceed through the gatehouse. Follow Massanutten Drive to the ski area.

McIntire Park
Charlottesville
Daily, until dusk.

You won't find any lifts to the top of the hills at McIntire Park, no steaming cups of hot chocolate (or even an open restroom), but families flock to McIntire on snowy days to take advantage of some of the best sledding hills around...and it's free! Bring along a thermos of hot chocolate and lots of waterproof clothes (especially gloves) and remember what it was like to be a kid on a wintry afternoon.

SCHLEP FACTOR: Pretty high. The location is good and the parking plentiful but once you have lugged a 30-pound toddler to the top of a hill a bunch of times, we guarantee you won't be thinking about location or parking.

DIRECTIONS: Take the 250E Bypass to the McIntire Park exit. Turn left at the stop and follow the road into McIntire Park.

SPELUNKING

Highland Adventures

Monterey   (540) 468-2722

HOURS: Daily, year-round.

ADMISSION: $30 per person per day for groups of six or more; smaller groups pay more per person.

Minimum age: 5 years.

Reservations: Necessary, and should be made up to three months in advance, although trips on shorter notice sometimes can be accommodated.

For families who find touring commercial caves too tame, Rick Lambert at Highland Adventures will show you the darker and less touristy side of caving. Rick, who has been caving for nearly 40 years and has his EMT certificate, outfits groups with headlamps and other safety gear, then guides them into any of ten caves in a ten-county area. A big chunk of Rick's business is families, consequently he knows the secrets of successful trips with kids. For starters, Rick advises bringing more than one child. "One five-year old will complain," he says with a laugh, "but two will compete."

Although Rick provides most of the equipment, families will need to bring their own meals and snacks. Other family adventures are available and include mountain biking, rock climbing and foraging. Overnight trips are available and may combine any of the adventures.

SCHLEP FACTOR: Fairly high since most of the caves are a 2-hour drive from Charlottesville; however, Rick conducts tours at any time of day (or night), in any weather, and at any time of the year. Rick is very safety-conscious and makes this potentially risky sport accessible to and safe for families.

DIRECTIONS: A meeting place will be arranged at the time of your reservation.

OUTDOOR SWIMMING POOLS

McIntire Park Wading Pool
Forest Hills Park Wading Pool
McIntire   (804) 295-9072/*Forest Hills*   (804) 296-1444

HOURS: Monday–Friday 10:30 AM–5:30 PM, weekends noon–5 PM. Pools open when city schools close for the summer and close when city schools reopen. Both continue weekend operation until Labor Day weekend.

ADMISSION: Free at Forest Hills, 25¢ per person at McIntire.

These public wading pools, run by the Charlottesville Department of Recreation and Leisure Services, offer little ones a chance to cool off without the danger of wading into deeper water. Both are close to playgrounds, making it easy to play and swim. These are great fun for five-and-unders, but older kids may find them a bit of a yawn.

SCHLEP FACTOR: Pretty low, especially for the McIntire Pool, which is right off the 250 Bypass. Forest Hills is more difficult to negotiate, mainly because there is no parking directly adjacent to the wading pools. Despite the shallow water and lifeguards, these pools can get crowded, so a vigilant eye is still necessary for non-swimmers. All city pools require a parent to be in the water with children ages 8 and under. Bathhouses with restrooms and changing areas are available at both locations. Arm flotation devices are discouraged and all babies must wear swim diapers.

DIRECTIONS: *McIntire Park:* Take the 250E Bypass to a left into the lower playground parking lot at McIntire Park. Note: during peak traffic hours motorists are not allowed to turn left into the park, making a U–turn further down the Bypass necessary.
Forest Hills: Take Cherry Avenue to 9th Street. Go south (left) on 9th Street to Forest Hills Avenue. The park is at the intersection of Forest Hills Avenue, Prospect Avenue and 9th Street, right behind Buford Middle School.

Onesty Pool at Meade Park
Washington Park Pool
Onesty   (804) 295-7532/*Washington Park*   (804) 977-2607

HOURS: Weekdays noon–6 PM , weekends noon–5 PM. Starting the last Friday in June, both pools are open each Friday from 6 PM–8 PM and on weekends from 5 PM–8 PM for free swimming. Pools offer daily operation when the city schools close for the summer until schools re-open in the fall. Both pools continue to operate on weekends through Labor Day, and Washington Park Pool opens on weekends from

Memorial Day until schools dismiss for the summer.

75¢ for children, $3 for adults (city residents); $1.75 for children, $4.50 for adults (non-city residents). Seniors and disabled rates available as are pool passes for multiple visits. Swim lessons: Available at both pools through the Department of Recreation and Leisure Services.

Charlottesville's two public pools can be found at Meade and Washington Parks, although you can bet that on hot summer days they can be heard for miles around. Onesty pool is a Z–shape with a one-meter diving board and a separate fenced wading pool. A nice, shady playground is immediately adjacent to the pool as is a bathhouse with snack machines. Although the pool is old, Onesty is very popular during the summer months.

If you haven't been to the recently remodeled Washington Park pool, you're missing one of the best cooling-off spots in the area. This pool boasts a huge shallow area with a 92-foot beach entry and a mushroom waterfall. The pool slopes gently into the deeper section which is less than seven feet at its deepest point. A bathhouse and drink machines round out the offerings. In the near future, a waterslide and a snacks stand will be added, making this the Charlottesville gathering spot on sultry, summer afternoons.

SCHLEP FACTOR: Moderate. Although both have adequate lifeguards, the city pools can become crowded, making parental supervision necessary, especially for non-swimmers. All city pools require parents of children 8 and under to be in the water with their child, unless the child has passed a swim test. For non-swimmers, arm flotation devices are discouraged and all babies must wear swim diapers. Both pools have good handicapped accessibility via lifts or plastic wheelchairs.

Note: Be advised that both pools have a maximum bathing capacity and when that number is reached, the pools close. On hot summer days, this capacity is often reached within a couple of hours of opening time, so arrive early to avoid disappointment.

DIRECTIONS: *For Onesty Pool:* Take the 250E Bypass to a right on High Street just before Free Bridge. Bear left onto Meade Avenue at the fork and go a short distance to the parking lot on the left.

For Washington Park Pool: Take Route 29S to a left onto Barracks Road at the shopping center. Go one mile through 2 stoplights to the flashing yellow light. Turn left onto 10th Street and the parking lot is at the end of 10th Street.

Claudius Crozet Park Pool

Claudius Crozet Park, Crozet   (804) 977-0406 (info)

HOURS: Daily, 11 AM–8 PM June and July, 11 AM–7 PM August, closed during the week if school is in session.

ADMISSION: Free for children under 6, $3 for children ages 6–12, $4 for everyone 13 years and up.
Family Season passes: $225

The new Crozet pool is so thoughtfully designed, so progressive and fun, you would swear it is one of those pricey private pools. It is, in fact, open to anyone willing to plop down the admission fee. Apparently the word hasn't gotten out, because the crowds never seem to be overwhelming. One section of the pool is sloped in like a beach. In the middle, a mushroom waterfall showers toddlers. A sharp L-turn separates this shallow area from the deep, making it hard for a small child to accidentally drift into deep water. In addition, a separate fenced baby pool safely corrals little ones.

Other amenities include umbrella-shaded picnic tables, a well-stocked, snack bar, and well-maintained restrooms. Claudius Crozet Park also has a play structure, although it is not in the pool area.

SCHLEP FACTOR: Moderate. For many families, Crozet is a bit of a drive, but perhaps that has helped keep the crowds down. For families with young children, this is a great public pool. Bring a picnic and plan to spend the day.

DIRECTIONS: Take Route 250W to a right on Route 240 (seems like a fork in the road). Follow 240 into Crozet. At the stop, turn left onto Crozet Avenue. Go a short distance to a left onto Tabor Street. Take the next right onto Park Road and follow it to the park on the left.

Ridgeview Park Pool

Ridgeview Park, Waynesboro   (540) 942-6767

HOURS: Monday–Saturday 10 AM–6 PM, Sunday, Memorial Day–Labor Day 1 PM–6 PM; Weekday hours are curtailed if school opens before Labor Day. Waynesboro residents swim free daily from 6 PM–7:30 PM.

ADMISSION: $1 for children under 15 years, $2.50 for 15 years and up.
Family season passes: $90

The pool at Ridgeview Park is a hit with families of all ages. In an age when diving boards have become as rare as a buffalo nickel, older kids will be thrilled to find three diving boards at Ridgeview: one low, one medium and one that takes a little courage. For younger kids, there is an enormous fenced wading pool. A great snack bar (sno-cones are the big draw here) will keep everyone happy. Start your day at the huge wooden climbing structure in the park, then hop over to the pool when the temperature soars.

SCHLEP FACTOR: Moderate. For area families living on the far west side of town, the Ridgeview Park pool may be closer than many of the City of Charlottesville pools. The facilities here are wonderful, and the city does a super job of maintaining the pool. This one is a great value and definitely worth the drive. The pool and park are handicapped-accessible.

DIRECTIONS: Take I-64W over Afton Mountain to Exit 96. Turn right off the ramp and go 2 miles to the light at 13th Street. Turn right onto 13th Street. Go 2 blocks to a right on Magnolia and straight into the park.

The Wintergarden at Wintergreen Resort

Wintergreen   (804) 325-2200
http://www.wintergreenresort.com

HOURS: Sunday–Thursday, 10 AM–8 PM, Friday–Saturday, Memorial Day–Labor Day, 10 AM–10 PM.

ADMISSION: Free for children under 5, $9 for children 6–12, $12 for anyone over age 12. Admission fee allows access to the outdoor and indoor pools, hot tubs, steam rooms and fitness center.

For a change of pace on those stifling days of August, cruise over to Wintergreen for a dip in the 25-meter outdoor pool at the Wintergarden Spa. The temperature is always about ten degrees cooler on the mountain and the scenery on the way up is spectacular. The unique dumbbell-shaped pool offers a large shallow area as well as lap swimming lanes. The pool area also has several hot tubs, a toddler pool and lots of room to relax. Although the admission fee is steep, it includes admission to all the amenities in the Wintergarden and makes for a fun day for kids of all ages. One outing our families enjoy is eating Sunday brunch (a huge spread) at the Copper Mine, then heading up to the Wintergarden for a swim.

SCHLEP FACTOR: High because of the drive and fee. Once you're there, the pool is easy. A pro shop sells anything you may have forgotten and there is vending and a changing room with restrooms and showers. Be advised that there are many steps from the parking lot to the building. Some families may want to use the circular drive that allows drop-off at the building entrance.

DIRECTIONS: Take Route 250W to a left onto Route 151S. Go about 14 miles through the town of Nellysford and turn right on Route 664. Go 4.5 miles then bear right at the fork into the resort (Wintergreen Drive). Pass through the gatehouse and follow Wintergreen Drive for about 3 miles (you will pass the Mountain Inn) to the intersection with Blue Ridge Drive. The Wintergarden is the large building on the hill. Park in the lower lot.

LAKE SWIMMING

Albemarle County Public Swimming Lakes

Mint Springs Lake, Crozet   (804) 823-5889
Chris Greene Lake, Earlysville   (804) 973-3790
Walnut Creek Lake, Red Hill   (804) 979-0960

HOURS: Daily, Memorial Day–Labor Day, when area schools are on break, weekends only when schools are in session.

ADMISSION: $1 for children, $2 for adults (county residents); $2 for children, $3 for adults (non-county residents).

Season passes: Available, free passes for Albemarle county seniors.

Albemarle County's public lakes are popular cooling-off spots for area families. All have sand-bottom lakes with full bathhouses and lifeguards. Snack bars are available at Chris Greene and Walnut Creek, while Mint Springs offers vending only. Chris Greene has gained popularity with the toddler set with the recent addition of a playground in the sand and a mushroom waterfall. Surrounded by mountains on three sides, Mint Springs is the only one of the three lakes to offer any significant shade and is therefore the best beach if you have a baby in tow. Walnut Creek, the largest and newest lake, has a playground planned for the near future. For information on additional activities at these lakes, see our chapter on Parks.

SCHLEP FACTOR: Moderately high. Lake water. Sand. Lots of kids. You get the picture. Be sure to pack in lots of sand toys and prepare for the tedious process of de-sanding tired kids before returning to your car. Still, lots of fun for the kids.

DIRECTIONS: See our listing under Parks.

Shenandoah Acres Resort Lake

Stuarts Draft   (540) 337-1911 or (800) 654-1714

WEBSITE: http://wwwshenacres.com
HOURS: Daily, 10 AM–7 PM Memorial Day–Labor Day.
ADMISSION: Free for children under 5, $4.75 for children 6–11, $6.50 for adults.

The lake at Shenandoah Acres Resort can best be described as one part water park to two parts Huck Finn swimmin' hole. Metal slides ranging from tame to terrifying empty into the lake along with merry-go-rounds and Clyde the Slide, a small dinosaur water slide for toddlers. The centerpiece is a two-story tower with a zip-line down to the water (a hit with kids ten and up). The whole lake is encircled by a sandy beach, with shade available for babies.

Right off the beach you'll find spacious locker rooms with showers, an ice cream stand, snack bar, necessity shop and arcade (great for kids four and up when the sun becomes overbearing).

Shenandoah Acres also boasts horseback rides, miniature golf, tennis, hiking and picnic areas—enough to occupy the entire family for days. If you do decide to stay overnight, there are 150 tent-camping sites as well as condos, cottages and even a motel.

SCHLEP FACTOR: Pretty low, because there is so much to do once you get there. Route 608/610 is a winding road that changes numbers, so watch carefully to be sure you are on the right road. Thanks to the locker rooms, shop (if you forget the sunscreen or sand toys) and snack bar, once you are there getting in and out is easy—considering you are mixing sand, ice cream and kids all in one place.

DIRECTIONS: Take I-64W to exit 94. Turn left off the ramp onto Route 340S. Go 5 miles to the fifth traffic light and turn left onto Route 608/610. Follow Route 608 to Route 610 (same road, only the number changes) for 1.8 miles to a right onto Lake Road and into the resort.

Sherando Lake

Waynesboro   (540) 291-2188

Website:
Hours: Daily, sunrise to dusk, mid-April–October, exact operating schedule depends on the weather.
Admission: $8 per carload, $6 for couples, $4 for individuals per day for entire recreation area.

Sherando Lake is popular for camping and hiking, but many people don't realize the recreation area is also great for day use. There are two lakes at Sherando, but only the lower, larger lake is available for swimmers. Here, visitors will find a sandy beach with roped-off swimming area and a bathhouse with warm showers and flush toilets. In the summer, the bathhouse also has snack and soda vending machines. Hiking trails and a picnic area are available as well. Since most area lakes are only open from Memorial Day–Labor Day, Sherando provides families with an extended swimming season.

Schlep Factor: Moderate. Sherando is a bit farther than most area lakes and no lifeguards are on duty, but during our Indian summers, Sherando is the only lake still open for swimming.

Directions: Take I-64W over Afton Mountain to the Lyndhurst Exit. Turn left at the exit and follow this road (Route 664) several miles to Sherando Lake on the left.

TRAINS, PLANES AND SUCH

Dillwyn Train

Buckingham Branch Railroad Station (Route 15), Dillwyn
(800) 451-6318

Website: http://www.odcnrhs.org
Hours: Select Saturdays in October for the Autumn Leaf Rambler, the spring for the James River Rambler: 9:30 AM–1 PM and 1:30 PM–5 PM: December for the Santa Train, five 45-minute trips daily, the first at 9:45 AM and the last at 2:15 PM.
Admission: Free for children under 2, $9 for children 2–12, $16 for adults.
Admission for Santa Train: Free for children under 2, $7 for all others. Other shorter trips are occasionally available.
Reservations: Required, and fill quickly, so call well in advance (up to two months).

Clattering over a long bridge, through a rock quarry and past miles of Virginia hillsides ablaze in fall colors, the Old Dominion Railway is a great way to view fall foliage with kids in tow. The fall ride is 3-1/2 hours long, but roaming about is permitted, if not the best part of the ride for kids. The four-car diesel train offers restored coaches from the 1920s and 1950s and is an amazing piece of history.

The James River Rambler trip runs the same 3-1/2 hour course, but this time features the Virginia countryside dressed in soft spring colors. In December, the Santa Train thrills kids with a 45-minute ride with the Jolly Old Elf himself, who visits with children and passes out candy canes.

SCHLEP FACTOR: Moderate, but our families rate this as a must-do seasonal attraction. The drive to Dillwyn takes 45 minutes to an hour. Porta-potties are available at the station and there is a restroom on the train. The train runs rain or shine and seating is on a first-come, first-served basis. If you'd like to snare inside seats, arrive at least a half-hour early. There is more room in the covered, outside cars and on crisp fall days the breeze is refreshing, if not downright hypnotic for little ones who tend to conk out in the fresh air. For the longer rides, pack a picnic or arrange in advance to buy a box lunch on the train for $6 per person.

DIRECTIONS: Take I-64 to Exit 121A (Route 20S). Stay on Route 20S to Dillwyn. Turn left (north) on Route 15 in Dillwyn and the train station will be on the left. Signs for parking are clearly marked.

The Flying Circus
Bealton   (540) 439-8661
WEBSITE: http://www.flyingcircusair.com
HOURS: Sundays, doors open 11 AM, show time is 2:30 PM, May–October.
ADMISSION: Free for children under 3, $3 for children 3–12, $10 for adults.
Open cockpit biplane rides are available before and after the show.

On a 200-acre site outside of Warrenton, the Flying Circus delights visitors with an old-fashioned air show that really makes flying—in all its forms—accessible to kids. The Daredevil Wing walkers are a special thrill, but the hot-air balloons and parachutists rank high as well. The old-fashioned biplanes, brightly painted and decorated, seem to take on distinct personalities and kids will often pick their favorites. After the show, kids can take a bi-plane ride (for an additional fee) or get pilots' autographs. On the grounds you will also find a gift shop and a hangar full of antique military and stunt planes.

SCHLEP FACTOR: High, because of the hour-plus drive, but still a lot of fun. A snack stand sells hot dogs, barbecue, soft drinks, candy and ice cream. Spectators may choose to sit in bleachers or bring lawn chairs and a blanket for a picnic. The facility is stroller- and handicapped-accessible.

DIRECTIONS: Take Route 29N to a right on Route 17 towards Fredericksburg. Follow Route 17 until it crosses Route 28 and then continue on Route 17 for 3-1/2 miles to a left on Route 644. The Flying Circus is just off Route 644. Signs from Route 17 guide you.

INDOOR ADVENTURES

Whoever stoically declared, "Into every life some rain must fall," must have never been locked in a house with a five-year-old during the rainy season. Admittedly, Charlottesville is easier to negotiate when skies are fair, but our searching unearthed enough indoor diversions to keep a wide array of ages and interests entertained when the weather doesn't cooperate. And don't forget that our Museums, Nature, Richmond, and Northern Virginia chapters offer more great indoor adventures, too.

ARCADES

Planet Fun

3005 Berkmar Drive, Charlottesville   (804) 975-4386

HOURS: Daily, year-round, hours vary seasonally so call ahead.

Dozens of arcade games from old-fashioned skee-ball to high-tech virtual-reality fill every nook and cranny of the ground floor at Planet Fun. The arcade may be popular with preteens, but preschoolers will find many amusements scaled just for them. Prices range from one token for simple games to four for the high-tech multi-dimensional stuff (a token costs a quarter). Many of the games dispense tickets that kids can redeem for prizes, so bring along a large zip-lock bag for each child to stash their tickets.

Besides the arcade, Planet Fun also boasts go-carts, batting cages, bumper boats, miniature golf and an indoor ball pit with sky tubes. The upstairs is reserved for birthday parties.

SCHLEP FACTOR: Fairly low, although there is so much to do at Planet Fun, you might have a hard time dragging the kids out of the place! Bring along lots of dollar bills, the tokens disappear quickly. There are restrooms with a changing table, water fountains and a snack bar. Limited handicapped and stroller accessibility.

DIRECTIONS: Take Route 29N to a left onto Rio Road. At the next light turn right onto Berkmar Drive. Planet Fun is about a mile ahead on the right.

BASKETBALL

Covenant Church Family Night Basketball

1025 E. Rio Road, Charlottesville   (804) 973-5536

HOURS: Thursdays, 8:30 PM–10 PM year-round.

ADMISSION: Free

Head over to Covenant Church on Thursday evenings to shoot hoops in their new, regulation-sized gymnasium. When the kids tire of basketball, a free game room overlooking the court offers video games, billiards and air hockey. Drop by a bit earlier and enjoy roller skating in the gym before the basketball session begins (see Roller Skating, below). Basketballs are provided and families are invited to participate; no church affiliation is necessary.

SCHLEP FACTOR: Low. The church is conveniently located with plenty of parking. Occasionally a snack stand is open during Family Night and offers sodas, chips and candy. Otherwise guests will find water fountains and soda vending. The main floor of the gymnasium is handicapped-accessible, however the upstairs game room is not.

DIRECTIONS: Take Route 29N to a right onto Rio Road at Fashion Square Mall. Follow Rio Road until it becomes 2 lanes, cross a bridge and the church will be on the immediate left. The gymnasium is in the back.

Downtown Recreation Center

800 E. Market Street, Charlottesville   (804) 296-0772

HOURS: Monday–Friday, 2 PM–9 PM, Saturday 1 PM–6 PM.
Classes or special events close gym floor so call ahead to verify.

ADMISSION: Admission and equipment are free.

The Downtown Recreation Center, operated by the Charlottesville Recreation and Leisure Services Department, is a great spot for families looking to shoot a few hoops together. The center offers a supervised court with six backboards and plenty of balls, including light, easy-to-handle balls for the little ones. The center also has a weight room in the back, and upstairs families will find a game room with ping pong, billiards, cards, checkers and computers. A variety of children's classes from gymnastics to basketball to arts and crafts are offered at the center, too, so pick up a current brochure while you're there.

The building, once the National Guard Armory, is slated for a major facelift. After the renovation families can look forward to new heating and air systems, a brand new gym floor, and remodeled restrooms and entryway.

SCHLEP FACTOR: Low, thanks to generous operating hours and easy parking in the Market Street Parking Garage less than a block away. Be sure to call ahead since classes and special events have priority for use of the gym floor. Vending in the lobby provides candy, crackers and drinks. Note that the upstairs is not handicapped-accessible.

DIRECTIONS: Take the 250E Bypass to a right at the light at McIntire Road. Follow McIntire Road to the light at Preston Avenue and turn left on to Market Street. Park in the Market Street Parking Garage (on the right) and walk the short way to the Center.

BOOKS

THE JEFFERSON-MADISON REGIONAL LIBRARY

The Charlottesville area is one of the most well-read areas of the country, boasting a public library use 42% greater than the national average. Long-range plans for our local library system, the Jefferson-Madison Regional Library (J-MRL), call for the addition of two more branches to fill our ever-expanding appetite for books. To date, there are nine branches, and all have children's book sections. Each branch, except for the bookmobile, offers storytimes and other children's programs. The following branches are favorites of Free Union Country School families because of amenities, convenience or just overall ambiance, but through the interlibrary loan system, any book can be delivered to your branch from other branches, making for a truly integrated library system. Ask your librarian for details. Library cards are free and are a great way to instill a sense of responsibility in older children.

The Bookmobile

The Bookmobile schedule is subject to change. Current schedules are available at the information desk of any of the J-MRL branches.

This big blue library-on-wheels is a fun twist for kids. Although you won't find storytimes in the bookmobile, kids love visiting Mr. Frye, the driver/librarian, and picking out a story or two from the shelves. Although anyone can browse the shelves and read stories on the bus, a library card is necessary to check out books. Ask Mr. Frye how he keeps the books from spilling as he drives!

SCHLEP FACTOR: Moderate. Unless you have a schedule of stops, this Roving Literary Machine can be as slippery to catch as a wet toddler. There is only one bookmobile; it visits communities not served by a nearby library branch twice each month for anywhere from 1/2-hour to an hour at a time. Consider picking one location and marking it on your calendar so you won't forget.

Central Branch

201 E. Market Street, Charlottesville   (804) 979-7151

HOURS: Monday–Thursday 9 AM–9 PM , Friday–Saturday 9 AM–5 PM year-round, also open Sunday 1 PM–5 PM; Labor day–Memorial Day, closed holidays.

Central, the main library branch in the J-MRL system, feels like an old-fashioned library. Housed in the old court house, Central has more amenities than you will find at other branches. Movies, computers and a huge selection of books occupy the children's section. Older kids feel like detectives as they browse the stacks downstairs. Upstairs, kids love the cavernous storyhour room. Central library hosts many special events, including a First Night Virginia performance on New Year's Eve.

SCHLEP FACTOR: Low; although parking in this area can be difficult, your best bet may be to park in the Market Street Parking Garage and walk over. The Librarian at the check-out desk will validate your parking receipt for two-hours free parking. Central has the longest hours of any branch in the system. For stroller and handicapped accessibility, there is a ramp outside and elevators inside, but restrooms are not handicapped-accessible.

DIRECTIONS: Take the 250E Bypass to a right at the light at McIntire Road. Follow McIntire to the light at Preston Avenue and turn left onto Market Street. The Central Library will be about a mile ahead on the left, although you may wish to continue on Market for another couple of blocks to a right into the Market Street Parking Garage.

Gordon Avenue Branch

1500 Gordon Avenue, Charlottesville   (804) 296-5544

HOURS: Monday 9 AM–9 PM, Tuesday 9 AM–6 PM, Wednesday noon–9 PM, Thursday–Saturday 10 AM–6 PM, closed Sundays and holidays.

The Gordon Avenue Library, located on a shady, tree-lined street, feels like an intimate neighborhood library. The library is a quick walk down sidewalked streets from The Lawn at U.Va.. On one of our glorious fall days, consider packing a picnic, and after a trip to the library, stroll over to The Lawn for lunch. Gordon Avenue Library is known for its huge African-American book collection and also as the site of the annual Friends of the Library Book Sale, held each spring.

SCHLEP FACTOR: Low. Although parking anywhere around the University can be a nightmare, the Gordon Avenue Library has its own adjacent parking lot. Although you normally won't have any problem finding a space in the lot, in the past there have been problems with students leaving their cars in the lot all day. The library cracked down and started towing nonlibrary users, so be sure to be in the library if you park in the lot. If you do plan to walk over to The Lawn, find a streetside space instead.

DIRECTIONS: Take Route 29S toward the University. Turn left onto University Avenue at the light. At the next light turn left onto Rugby Road. Turn right onto Gordon Avenue and the library will be on the right.

Northside Branch

Albemarle Shopping Center, Charlottesville   (804) 973-7893

HOURS: Monday–Tuesday noon–9 PM, Wednesday–Thursday 10 AM–6 PM, Friday–Saturday 10 AM–5 PM, closed Sundays and holidays.

The only J-MRL branch housed in a shopping center, the Northside branch is a boon to parents on a tight schedule. The location is convenient and the parking is easy. The children's area, though not as comprehensive as Central's, is nevertheless inviting, with a central arena for cuddling up with a story and cubbies filled with board books for toddlers. Although "library voices" are encouraged at every branch, Northside seems to draw more children than adults, making that occasional bloodcurdling scream from your toddler a bit less of a problem. The drive-up book deposit is really convenient for book returns. Any J-MRL book can be deposited in these returns, even if it wasn't checked out at this branch.

SCHLEP FACTOR: Low, thanks to the convenient shopping center location. Water fountains and spacious, clean restrooms with a changing area are available (although they ask you not to leave diapers in the trash, which can lead to some schlepping of the smelly kind). Good handicapped and stroller accessibility.

DIRECTIONS: Take 29N to the first light past the Rio Road intersection (by the Fashion Square Mall). At this light turn right into Albemarle Square Shopping Center. Northside Library is in the shopping center.

OTHER JEFFERSON-MADISON
REGIONAL LIBRARY BRANCHES

Below you will find a listing of the other local library branches and their operating hours. Each has its own unique atmosphere, so try out several and find a favorite for your family. Note that all branches below are closed Sunday.

Branch	Crozet	Scottsville	Greene County	Louisa County	Nelson Memorial
Address	Route 240 Crozet	330 Bird Street Scottsville	Stanard Street Stanardsville	103 West Street Louisa	8521 Thom Nelson Hwy Lovingston
Telephone	(804) 823-4050	(804) 286-3541	(804) 286-3541	(540) 967-1103	(804) 263-5904
Monday	1 PM–9 PM	1 PM–9 PM	1 PM–8 PM	1 PM–9 PM₄	noon–8 PM
Tuesday	1 PM–9 PM	1 PM–9 PM	10 AM–9 PM	1 PM–9 PM	noon–8 PM
Wednesday	9 AM–5 PM	9 AM–5 PM	9 AM–5 PM	9 AM–5 PM	10 AM–5 PM
Thursday	9 AM–5 PM	9 AM–5 PM	9 AM–5 PM	9 AM–5 PM	10 AM–5 PM
Friday	9 AM–5 PM	9 AM–5 PM	9 AM–5 PM	9 AM–5 PM	10 AM–5 PM
Saturday	9 AM–5 PM	9 AM–5 PM	9 AM–5 PM	2 PM–5 PM	10 AM–5 PM

BOWLING

Keglers

2000 Seminole Trail, Charlottesville   (804) 978-3999

HOURS: Daily, year-round, hours vary so call ahead. Some morning hours are available.

ADMISSION: $2.10 for youth/seniors, $2.40 for adults before 5 PM, and $3.20 for everyone after 5 PM, on weekends and on holidays.

Reservations: Permitted up to one week in advance and costs $20 per hour for up to five people.

Equipment rental: Shoes available at $2 per hour in child size 11 and up.

Supervised playroom: $3 per hour, open daily 6 PM–9 PM with extended Saturday hours.

Keglers Bowling Alley offers a lot of indoor fun for families, starting with the high-fashion footwear. Unfortunately, duckpin lanes are no longer available, but even five-year-olds can enjoy tenpin bowling if you ask for a bumper lane. The bumpers will keep the balls in the lane, keeping frustration at bay for smaller kids. Afterward, head to the back where, for a small fee, a supervised playroom with a ball pit can keep the kids entertained while you bowl or eat a quiet meal at the Breakers restaurant. The restaurant has a wide range of snacks and meals, including kids' meals with macaroni and cheese, pizza or burgers. A small arcade and billiards round out the entertainment.

Sundays are smoke-free days at Keglers (from noon to 5 PM) and smoke-free lanes are available every day. Birthday party packages are available, too.

SCHLEP FACTOR: Low before 5 PM but a bit higher evenings and weekends when guests without reservations may have to sign up on a waiting list for a lane. There are only 12 bumper lanes and they tend to go fast on weekends and evenings. The variety of entertainment and snacks makes this a great place to spend a couple of hours on a hot or rainy afternoon. Be advised that it can take over an hour to bowl a full ten frames and many kids (especially those 6 and under) will tire of the game before they are finished. On the upside, the ball pit, restaurant and arcade add enough variety to make this a really enjoyable family outing.

DIRECTIONS: Take Route 29N. Keglers is on the left, just north of the Rio Hill Shopping Center.

CLIMBING WALLS

If your kids are climbing the walls at home, bring them to one of the two local climbing walls so they can do it in style! Both locations allow kids seven and up (with a parent) to climb on their safe, indoor courses. If you have never climbed before, you should first take a class with your child to learn the basics. After that, you can pop in whenever you want for an hour or an afternoon of climbing. At both locations we recommend skipping the shoe rental for kids (they don't carry kid sizes, anyway) and bringing along a pair of flexible tennis shoes or water shoes instead.

Climbing must be done in pairs (a climber needs a spotter or belayer), making for a great opportunity to build trust along with strength. If you weigh a lot more than your child, however, don't plan on climbing; the climber can't be significantly heavier than the belayer.

Extreme Sports "The Wall"

629 Berkmar Road, Charlottesville   (804) 975-1900
http://www.xtsports.com

WEBSITE:
HOURS: Monday–Friday 10 AM–7 PM, Saturday 10 AM–6 PM, Sunday 11 AM–5 PM.

ADMISSION: $10 per day for access to the wall (only climbers pay). An introductory climb is available for $15 and requires no prior instruction.
Equipment rental: $3 apiece for shoes and harness.
Classes: Two hours for $25 (only climbers pay). The class is held Saturday mornings, and registration is required.

Kids love "The Wall" at Extreme Sports because it looks like real rocks, giving them the sensation of climbing a rock face in the Blue Ridge. The course, lit by skylights, is airy and light. Since the climbing wall is located in the back of the store, kids may find they are being cheered on by curious shoppers, too.

If you have never tried climbing before, you and your child are required to first take a two-hour course to learn the basics. The instructors here, many of whom are certified teachers, do a great job of explaining rope-tying and climbing techniques to kids. They are all very nice and easygoing with children.

SCHLEP FACTOR: Very low after you have completed the basic course. You'll find plenty of parking in the Berkmar Crossing Shopping Center. There is only one climbing wall here, so if a big group comes in you may have to wait. Call ahead to see if any groups are scheduled. Restrooms and drinking fountain are available.

DIRECTIONS: Take Route 29N to a left at the light at Rio Road. Go to the first light and take a left onto Berkmar Drive and a quick right into the Berkmar Crossing Shopping Center.

Rocky Top Climbing Club

1729 Allied Street, Charlottesville   (804) 984-1626

WEBSITE: http://www.smartsubmit.com/rockytop/index.htm

HOURS: Monday–Friday 3 PM–9 PM, weekends 11 AM–7 PM.

ADMISSION: $10 per day for use of the walls (only climbers pay).
Equipment rental: $3 apiece for harnesses and shoes.
Memberships: Available.
Classes: 1-hour introductory course for beginners is recommended and
is $35 (only climbers pay). Call for class registration.

The first climbing wall in Charlottesville, Rocky Top is still the only
dedicated climbing gym in the area. The walls here are flat, so kids don't
get quite the same sensation of actual rock climbing as they will at "The
Wall", but the variety of courses is guaranteed to keep even experienced
climbers from getting bored. If you have never climbed before, the staff
recommends a one-hour introductory course to learn the basics. The
gym also boasts racquetball courts and summer climbing camps for kids
ages 7–15.

SCHLEP FACTOR: Low, especially for those living on the east side of town. Parking is
available in front of the gym, and although it is tight and awkward, you
can usually find a space. The gym has changing rooms, restrooms, water
fountains, a drink machine and pro shop.

DIRECTIONS: Take the 250E Bypass to the light at McIntire Road. Turn right onto
McIntire and go about 1/4 mile to a right at the fork onto Harris. Take
the first right onto Allied Street and the gym will be on the right.

INDOOR PLAYGROUNDS

Planet Fun
3005 Berkmar Drive, Charlottesville   (804) 975-4386

HOURS: Daily, call ahead for operating hours, longer hours in summer.

Just one of many attractions at Planet Fun, the ball pit and sky tubes add to the fun for younger kids. The $3 ticket is good for an entire day, so kids can come and go from the playground to try out other attractions at the amusement center. Socks are required in the playground, and if you have a toddler, be prepared to follow her through the maze.

SCHLEP FACTOR: Pretty low. Planet Fun is conveniently located on Berkmar Drive with plenty of parking, a snack bar and clean restrooms with changing table. The maze is pretty high, and although a fall from ten feet up would not be possible, some younger kids get scared (meaning you will have to crawl inside and rescue them!). Kids ages 2–7 would have the most fun in this section of Planet Fun, although if you have older kids along, plenty of other amusements keep them happy, too.

DIRECTIONS: Take Route 29N to a left onto Rio Road. Turn right onto Berkmar Drive at the next light and go about a mile to Planet Fun on the right.

Playland at Pizza Hut/Taco Bell
Route 29N, Ruckersville   (804) 985-2232

HOURS: Monday–Friday 10 AM–11 PM, weekends until midnight.
Restrictions: Playland is for children under 48" tall.

Although several area fast-food restaurants have indoor playgrounds, this is by far the largest and newest. Nearly half the restaurant is taken up by the giant structure, which, best of all, is free to restaurant patrons. Kids will love the sky tubes, climbing platform, giant tic-tac-toe board and two slides that make up the play structure. Parents will love the huge variety of foods available at a reasonable price. Birthday party packages are available.

SCHLEP FACTOR: Fairly low. The restaurant is daily gaining in popularity and can get crowded on weekends or rainy, summer days. To keep the germ population at bay, the play structure is cleaned out weekly (more often if necessary) and has no ball pit. The room tends to be cool in the summer and warm in the winter, so dress accordingly. If you have kids under age 8, this is definitely worth a trip to Ruckersville.

DIRECTIONS: Take Route 29N to Ruckersville. The restaurant is on the right before the Route 33 intersection.

PJ's Arcade and Pizzeria

Mountain View Plaza, 1950 Deyerle Avenue, Harrisonburg
(540) 564-1766

HOURS: Daily, year-round, call ahead for operating hours.
ADMISSION: Ball pit/maze $2 for kids 2–12.

Located behind the Valley Mall in Harrisonburg, PJ's is a great place to take kids to unwind after shopping. The play area will keep younger children occupied with an obstacle course and ball pit, while the arcade appeals to older kids. A separate area for babies is free for kids under two. The amusement center is well-designed so parents can order pizza and keep an eye on kids in all areas of the center at the same time, making this an easy stop. Food is standard pizza/sub/soda stuff (in other words, kid heaven). Birthday party packages are available, too.

SCHLEP FACTOR: High, if you're coming to Harrisonburg just for this. Combine a trip here with shopping at Valley Mall, a visit to one of the nearby caverns, or make it a real kids' day and visit The Bull Pen which is located right down the street! Once there, PJ's is a breeze—one of those wonderful places where you can put your feet up and your kids will still have a ball.

DIRECTIONS: Take Route 29N to a left onto Route 33 at the main intersection in Ruckersville. Follow Route 33 over the mountain and into Harrisonburg. Just past the Valley Mall, turn left onto University Boulevard. Go through one traffic light to a left onto Deyerle Avenue. Follow Deyerle Avenue to the Mountain View Plaza. PJ's is inside the shopping center.

INDOOR "TAG" GAMES

Splathouse
946 Grady Avenue, Charlottesville   (804) 977-5287

WEBSITE: http://www.splathouse.com

HOURS: Daily, year-round.

ADMISSION: $30 per person for a 3-hour indoor session.

Minimum number of participants for indoor paintball is ten; families with fewer than the minimum will be grouped with others.

Reservations: Required, and should be made two weeks in advance, although short-notice players can often be accommodated. Call for availability, but no walk-ins accepted.

Minimum age: 12 years, although 11-year-olds may participate with a parent.

Splathouse, Charlottesville's "urban paintball adventure", has been entertaining area teens for five years with their suspense-filled strategy games and is now rated as one of the nation's best indoor paintball centers. Paintballs are pellets, similar to bath beads, that are filled with a brightly-colored, non-staining liquid and are fired from a gun. They sting a bit on contact, thus players must be at least 12 years old to participate. As you might have guessed, games here are much higher intensity than laser tag, with sessions lasting for three or more hours and involving ten or more games per session. Guests may choose from either an indoor playing field (the old Monticello Dairy) or one of five outdoor fields, and may also select from a wide array of strategy-based games (such as Capture The Flag). The indoor location, over 21,000 square feet, occupies an entire city block.

SCHLEP FACTOR: High, since this is not a drop-in activity. A visit to Splathouse is really more of an event than a typical family outing. The indoor facility offers restrooms, soft drinks and a pro shop.

DIRECTIONS: Take Route 29S to a left onto Barracks Road at the shopping center. Go 1 mile through 2 stoplights and at the flashing yellow light turn right onto 10th Street. Go about 20 feet to the next stoplight and turn left onto Grady Avenue. Splathouse is just ahead on the right.

Star Base Alpha Laser Tag

475 Westfield Road, Charlottesville   (804) 978-7827

WEBSITE: http://www.piedmontsports.com

HOURS: Tuesday–Thursday 4 PM–10 PM, Friday 4 PM–midnight, Saturday 10 AM–midnight, noon–9 PM Sunday, closed Mondays during school year, extended hours on school holidays (including Mondays), and in the summer. Saturdays from 10 AM–1 PM are reserved for kids 12 and under and games are 1/2-price during this time.

Family day: Sundays, where adults play free with a child's paid admission.

ADMISSION: $6.50 per game, group discounts available.

Membership: Available.

To many adults, Star Base Alpha appears to be a combination of an old-fashioned game of tag and laser surgery. To kids, this is one of the hottest attractions in Charlottesville. Players start in a briefing room where rules are explained and equipment is demonstrated. After going over a map of the play area, two teams are chosen and color-coded vests are given out. The teams are then brought to their respective bases (a star cruiser and a planet). Lights dim, fog appears and the laser battle is underway. Each participant tries to hit the opposing team's base with at least two shots without getting shot themselves. The games last about 25 minutes, and at the end, a computerized score card tells players how they fared and which team won.

SCHLEP FACTOR: Fairly low. Players should wear dark clothes to make themselves less visible to opponents (and towheads should cover up their hair!). The lasers are safe and do not cause any pain on contact. The facility can get crowded at times, but there are lots of video games to occupy kids as they wait and the staff is very friendly and helpful. There are restrooms and a snack bar, and the whole place is handicapped-accessible.

DIRECTIONS: Take Route 29S to a right on Westfield Road, one block north of the light at Greenbrier Drive. Star Base Alpha is on the left.

MOVIES

Charlottesville boasts seven indoor cinemas, assuring you that somewhere in town you will find a family flick. Although these two cinemas are among our favorites, any theater playing a G-rated movie gets high ratings! While schedules appear in *The Daily Progress*, we recommend calling the cinema for up-to-date listings.

Greenbrier Cinema
375 Greenbrier Drive, Charlottesville   (804) 980-2063

We love the Greenbrier because all seats are just $1.50 and they often have a family movie playing. If your kids can wait, most of the popular films for children (including Disney) eventually wind up at the Greenbrier.

SCHLEP FACTOR: Low. Convenient location, easy parking.

DIRECTIONS: Take Route 29N to a left on Greenbrier Drive. The cinema is on the left.

Regal Cinemas 6
The Downtown Mall, Charlottesville   (804) 979-7669

At the Regal Cinemas, kids adore the wall of candy-by-the-pound. Parents enjoy the other food selections ranging from popcorn to cappuccino and muffins. There are six theaters at the Regal; all are fairly small and offer an intimate environment for moviegoers. At least one G or PG film is typically featured. On weekends that a children's show opens, the theater often has some kind of promotional event. Staff may be dressed in costumes themed to the movie and may hand out balloons or other promotional items.

During the summer, the Regal joins forces with local corporate sponsors to provide free movies on Tuesday and Wednesdays at 10 AM. Most of the movies shown are a year or two old, but even kids who have seen the movie on video love watching it again on the big screen. Families should call each summer for current schedules and plan to arrive early, as the theater often fills to capacity.

SCHLEP FACTOR: Fairly low. The easiest parking for families is in the Omni Hotel lot; however, the theater does not validate parking for that lot. Validated parking is available in the Water Street Garage.

DIRECTIONS: Take the 250E Bypass to a right at McIntire Road. Follow McIntire through the Preston Avenue intersection to a left into the Omni Hotel parking lot. Walk to the Downtown Mall, and the theater will be straight ahead. For the Water Street Garage, continue straight past the Omni Hotel and turn left at the light onto Water Street. The parking garage will be on the left, and the theater is across the street on the Downtown Mall.

OTHER CHARLOTTESVILLE INDOOR MOVIE THEATERS:

Carmike Theater
1803 Seminole Trail (behind Pier 1 Imports)   (804) 973-4294

Jefferson Theater
110 E. Main   (804) 295-3321

Seminole Cinema
2306 India Trail (behind K-Mart)   (804) 980-3333

Terrace Theaters
1799 Hydraulic Road   (804) 977-0190

Vinegar Hill Theater
220 Market Street W.   (804) 977-4911

POTTERY

Glaze 'N' Blaze

108 Third Street NE, Charlottesville   (804) 984-5885

HOURS: Tuesday, Wednesday, Friday and Saturday 10:30 AM–8 PM, Thursday 10:30 AM–6 PM, Sunday noon–6 PM, closed Mondays.

ADMISSION: $6 per person per hour, includes use of materials, glazing and firing. Ceramic pieces sold separately.

This paint-your-own-pottery shop is a natural for children and adults alike. Kids choose an unfinished piece of pottery, select paint colors, then paint the piece in the studio. They fire the piece for you in the kiln, and you pick it up a couple of days later. Pottery pieces are sold separately and range from $2 for tiny ornaments to $30 or more for platters and such. For kids, your best bet is "Two for Tuesday" when two people paint for the price of one. Kids 6 and up love the funky, stylish decor and the snack bar. Birthday party packages are available.

SCHLEP FACTOR: Moderate. Restrooms and a snack bar with great coffee are available. There is no parking in front of the store, but there is two-hour parking along Market Street, or park in the Market Street Garage and walk the three or four blocks to the studio.

The staff at Glaze N' Blaze is wonderful with children, but some of their clientele are not as patient. Very young children (under 4) tend to fare better at The Paintin' Place.

DIRECTIONS: Take the 250E Bypass to a right at the light at McIntire Road. Follow McIntire to the light at Preston Avenue and turn left onto Market Street. Continue for several blocks then turn right into the Market Street Parking Garage. Take an elevator to the Downtown Mall level. Walk down the mall and turn left onto 3rd Street. Glaze 'n' Blaze is 1/2-block up 3rd Street.

The Paintin' Place

1709 Monticello Road, Charlottesville   (804) 295-7801

HOURS: Monday, Wednesday, Thursday and Friday 10 AM–5 PM, Tuesday 10 AM–8 PM, Saturday 10 AM–4 PM, closed Sundays.

ADMISSION: $6 per hour per person, includes use of materials, glazing and firing. Ceramic pieces sold separately. Group rates available.

Located above Lazy Daisy Ceramics, The Paintin' Place offers a paint-your-own-ceramics service in a child-friendly environment. The Paintin' Place staff is especially good with young children. Parents with more than one child will especially appreciate the loads of personal attention and hands-on help as you select and paint your pottery. They glaze and fire the pieces for you and you pick them up a few days later. Pieces range from $1 for ornaments to $25 for large pieces.

SCHLEP FACTOR: Low. The Paintin' Place offers a convenient location with plenty of parking. Although the upstairs is not handicapped-accessible, a downstairs station can be set up with advance notice.

DIRECTIONS: Take the 250E Bypass to the stoplight at Free Bridge. Turn right onto High Street. At the fork in the road, turn left onto Meade Avenue. Cross the railroad tracks, then take the third left onto Monticello Road. Lazy Daisy Ceramics/The Paintin' Place is on the right.

ICE SKATING

Charlottesville Ice Park

230 W. Main Street, Charlottesville   (804) 979-1423

WEBSITE: http://www.icepark.com

HOURS: Daily, year-round, but no public skating on Tuesdays, extended hours in the summer and on school holidays. Call for schedule.
Note: There are several hours midday between public skating sessions. Also, hockey games sometimes run over, meaning that public skating will be delayed. Call ahead to find out if games are scheduled; if so, prepare for delay.

ADMISSION: Kids 5 and under $3 for skating and rental (with a paid adult), $5.50 for skating, $1 skate rental Monday–Friday morning; Friday evenings, weekends and holidays $6.50 for skating, $2 skate rental. Seniors pay just $5 for skating and rental.
Cheap Skate Days: Wednesdays, when rentals are just 50¢

Although our hearts and minds naturally turn to ice skating in the winter, during Charlottesville's languid summer days the Ice Park is as refreshing as a box of popsicles all to yourself! Most kids ages four and up can stand up on skates, although the younger ones may need an adult hand—even if the adult hand is white-knuckling the sides of the rink! For unstable little ones, the Ice Park also offers milk crates for pushing across the ice. When the kids get tired, head into the snack bar for hot chocolate, snacks and arcade games.

Although the cost of skating can get steep for a large family, the Ice Park offers regular specials, often in conjunction with city-wide and downtown festivals and events. Special events at the Ice Park often feature a visit from the park's mascot, "I.C. Polar", too. Group and private lessons are available, and afterwards you can skate for free for the rest of the afternoon. Call for information about lessons, birthday party packages and special events.

SCHLEP FACTOR: Pretty low. Although it takes a few minutes to lace up, ice skating is a great way to wear your kids out! Wear thick socks, gloves and waterproof pants, especially for beginners, who tend to fall a lot. A supply of Band-Aids for blisters is also a good idea. Skate rentals, a snack bar, vending, lockers and restrooms are provided along with validated parking in the Omni Hotel parking lot. There is a spacious and airy lobby where non-skaters can relax and watch the action.

DIRECTIONS: Take the 250E Bypass to a right at the light at McIntire Road. At the first light, turn left onto Preston Avenue. Take an immediate right into the Omni Hotel Parking Garage. Park in the garage and walk up to the Downtown Mall. The Ice Park is immediately across from the Omni Hotel on the Mall.

ROLLER SKATING

Carver Recreation Center

4th Street NW   (804) 293-2259

HOURS: Monday, Wednesday and Friday 4:30 PM–6:30 PM September–mid June, Wednesday and Friday 5:30 PM–7 PM mid-June–August.

Admission/skate rental: Free

Minimum age/requirements: 6–18 ideally, and all children must have an adult with them.

Thanks to the Charlottesville Department of Recreation and Leisure Services, families can skate free year-round on the hardwood floor at the Carver Recreation Center, located in the heart of downtown Charlottesville. Skates are provided in sizes ranging from a child size 1 to an adult size 12. After you skate, check out some of the other fun activities available at the Center. The floor can be rented for kids' skating parties at a very reasonable fee, too.

SCHLEP FACTOR: Low. The price is definitely right for this one. Convenient location, too, with plenty of parking, restrooms and water fountains.

DIRECTIONS: Take the 250E Bypass to a right at the light onto McIntire Road. Follow McIntire to the light at Preston Avenue and turn right. Take an almost immediate left onto 4th Street NW at Wendy's. Carver is next to Wendy's.

Covenant Church Family Night Skating

1025 East Rio Road, Charlottesville   (804) 973-5536

HOURS: Thursdays year-round 7 PM–8:30 PM.

ADMISSION: Free, but skate rental is $1 per pair.

Skate size range will typically fit 5-year-olds to adults.

As a community service, Covenant Church opens their huge new gymnasium each Thursday evening for roller skating. Families are invited to lace up and spin around the wood floor to a mix of showtunes, oldies and contemporary Christian music, with a few skating games thrown in to keep the evening lively. When the kids tire of skating, they can head upstairs to a free game room with video games, billiards and air hockey overlooking the roller rink. After 8:30 PM, energetic families can stick around for an evening of basketball (see Basketball). All families are welcome; no church affiliation is necessary to participate.

SCHLEP FACTOR: Low. The church is conveniently located with plenty of parking. Occasionally, a snack stand selling chips, drinks and candy will be open during family night. Otherwise, guests will find water fountains and soda vending. The gymnasium is handicapped-accessible but the upstairs game room is not.

DIRECTIONS: Take Route 29N to a right onto Rio Road. Follow Rio Road until it becomes 2 lanes, cross a bridge and the church will be on the immediate left. The gymnasium is in the back.

Greenwood Community Center
Route 691, Greenwood

HOURS: Saturday 11 AM–2 PM October–end of April, every 2nd and 4th Friday 7 PM–10 PM year-round.

ADMISSION: $2.50 including rental, $1.50 for skating only.

Nestled amid rolling hills and luxurious estates, the tiny Greenwood Community Center offers year-round roller skating courtesy of the Albemarle County Department of Parks and Recreation. Bring your own skates or rent them at the Center, then spin around the hardwood floor to cool tunes provided by the Community Center staff. A small playground and picnic area are available, and the center can be rented for children's skating parties.

SCHLEP FACTOR: Moderate. For most families, Greenwood is not very convenient, but the drive is beautiful and the facility feels like an old-timey roller rink. The roads off Route 250 weave around, making you feel like you are lost. Don't give up!

DIRECTIONS: Take I-64W to Crozet Exit 107 (Route 250W). Turn right on Route 690, then right on Route 691. Follow Route 691 to the Community Center on the right.

Skatetown USA-Harrisonburg
100 Miller Circle, Harrisonburg   (540) 433-1834

HOURS: Tuesday and Wednesday 7 PM–9:30 PM, Friday 7 PM–11 PM, Saturday 10 AM–noon, 1 PM–4 PM, and 7 PM–midnight, Sunday 1 PM–4 PM.

ADMISSION: $2.50–$5.50, depending on the skate session; skate rental: $1 per pair. Church and school groups receive special rates and are encouraged to visit.

For more than 20 years, kids in Harrisonburg have been rocking and rolling around the skating rink on Miller's Circle. The staff here is very caring and helpful, and the facility well-maintained. The rink is huge with nice maple wood floors and lots of tunes to keep the action going.

Kids also enjoy the small arcade and Laser Tag, as well as a snack stand that sells typical kid-fare such as burgers and nachos. Saturday mornings are a great time to visit with tots. From 10 AM 'til noon, admission is only $2.50 and on Saturday afternoons skate rental is free.

SCHLEP FACTOR: High. It would take a dedicated (perhaps fanatical) skater to drive the hour to Harrisonburg for roller skating. The rink is right down the street from the JMU campus, so consider combining a trip here with the Arboretum or Life Sciences Museum on the JMU campus.

DIRECTIONS: Take I-64W to 81N to Harrisonburg. Take the first Harrisonburg exit (Exit 243). This crosses over Route 64 and turns into Route 11. Take Route 11N for about 2 miles. Turn right at Wendy's onto Miller's Circle. Skatetown USA will be directly in front of you at the end of the street.

Skatetown USA-Staunton

Barterbrook Road, Staunton   (540) 885-3798

HOURS: Wednesday 7:30 PM–10 PM, Friday 7:30 PM–11 PM, Saturday from 10 AM–noon, 1 PM–4 PM, 7:30 PM–midnight, Sunday 1 PM–3:30 PM.

ADMISSION: $3.50–$6; skate rental: $1 per pair.

Visitors to the Skatetown USA in Staunton can enjoy hours of roller skating fun set to popular music. The facility is old but is nicely maintained and is alcohol- and smoke-free. When the kids tire of skating, let them try their hands at the arcade games or fill up at a well-stocked snack bar. Kids under 12 have their own skate session on Saturday mornings from 10 AM through noon.

SCHLEP FACTOR: High. Same as for the Harrisonburg location. Skatetown is very close to the Frontier Culture Museum of Virginia. If your kids are really energetic, think about visiting after a trip to the museum.

DIRECTIONS: Take I-64W to I-81N (exit 87). Stay in the right lane on I-81 and within 1/4 mile take Exit 222. Turn right on Route 250W towards Staunton. At the 3rd traffic light turn left. Pass Wal-Mart and Lowe's, then turn right onto Barterbrook Road. Skatetown USA is ahead on the right.

SWIMMING (INDOOR POOLS)

Crow Pool at Walker Upper Elementary School

Charlottesville   (804) 977-1362

Smith Pool at Buford Middle School

Charlottesville   (804) 977-1960

HOURS: *Crow:* Monday–Thursday 2:30 PM–4 PM, Friday 2:30 PM–4 PM and 7:45 PM–9 PM, Saturday 1 PM–6 PM and Sunday noon–6 PM.
Smith: Monday–Friday 3:30 PM–4 PM, Saturday 1:30 PM–6 PM and Sunday noon–4 PM.

ADMISSION: 75¢ for children, $3 for adults (city residents); and $1.75 for children, $4.50 for adults (non-city residents). Senior and disabled rates available, as are pool passes for multiple visits.

To dispel winter blahs, throw the swimsuits in the car and head for one of the two indoor heated pools run by the Charlottesville Department of Recreation and Leisure Services. Both 25-yard pools offer daily recreational swims for families. The shallow ends of the pools are over the heads of many preschoolers, but older kids like the one-meter diving boards in the deep ends. Lifeguards are on duty and swim classes are available at both pools.

SCHLEP FACTOR: Moderate. Children 8 and under must have an adult in the water with them at all times, unless the child has passed a swim test. Arm flotation devices are discouraged for non-swimmers, and all babies must wear swim diapers. Both locations have changing rooms with lockers and showers, and both have wheelchair lifts.

DIRECTIONS: *Crow:* Take the 250E Bypass to the Rugby Avenue/McIntire Park exit. Turn right at the stop sign and go to the next light at Rose Hill Drive and turn right. When the road jogs slightly to the right, stay on Rose Hill and continue to the end of the road and into the Crow Pool parking lot.
Smith: Take the 250E Bypass to a right at the light onto McIntire Road. Follow McIntire straight through the Preston Avenue intersection and straight through the next light (at the Lewis and Clark statue) onto 5th Street. Turn right onto Cherry Avenue at the second light. Pass Tonsler Park on the left, then go through one light to a left into Buford Middle School. Inside the school property, take the road that bears to the right and park in the lower lot.

The Wintergarden at Wintergreen Resort

Wintergreen   (804) 325-2200

Hours: Sunday–Friday 10 AM–9 PM and Saturday 10 AM–10 PM year-round.

Admission: Free for children under 6, $9 children 6–12, $12 for anyone else; includes access to pool, hot tubs, steam rooms and fitness center.

Lounging beside the bright and airy indoor pool at Wintergreen on a cold winter day, you almost feel like you've been transported into August. Vaulted ceilings filled with natural light, indoor and outdoor hot tubs, plenty of lounge chairs, and the welcoming, heated pool await après skiers as well as families looking for a little cold-weather diversion. Sign up at the front desk to reserve an outdoor hot tub, then make a dash through the snow to the steaming tubs. Kids love the water basketball game and relaxed setting.

Schlep Factor: Fairly high because of the drive, although a mid-winter swim followed by dinner makes for a fun afternoon. Locker rooms provide showers (no hair dryers) and vending is available. There are quite a few steps from the parking lot up to the Wintergarden, so consider dropping off kids at the circular entrance right by the front door before parking. This may be an especially good idea in the winter when ice and snow can leave the steps slick.

Directions: Take Route 250W to a left on Route 151S. Go about 14 miles to a right on Route 664. Go 4.5 miles, then bear right at the fork into the resort. Pass the Gatehouse, then go about 3 miles up Wintergreen Drive (you will pass the Mountain Inn) until the road intersects Blue Ridge Drive. The Wintergarden is the large building on the hill. Park in the lower lot.

INDOOR MINIATURE GOLF

Natural Bridge Miniature Golf

Natural Bridge   (800) 533-1410 or (540) 291-2121 (Hotel number, they will transfer your call)

WEBSITE: http://www.naturalbridgeva.com

HOURS: Daily, year-round, opening at 8 AM, closing times vary seasonally so call ahead.

ADMISSION: Free for children 5 and under, $2 for others.

Although we wouldn't suggest driving your kids all the way to Natural Bridge for a game of miniature golf, a rainy-day visit to Natural Bridge Caverns or Wax Museum combined with a round of indoor miniature golf may be just the ticket to family harmony. Located in the downstairs of the Natural Bridge Visitor Center, this course offers windmills, bears, and other fun features (although no miniature replica of Natural Bridge). And at just $2 a game, it's a great value.

SCHLEP FACTOR: Let's put it this way, driving all the way to Natural Bridge just for the miniature golf would be like eating catsup without the hot dog. Visit one of the other attractions in the area first and let the miniature golf be your condiment. During the summer, tickets can be purchased at the course entrance, but during the rest of the year, stop by the main ticket office upstairs. Restrooms and a snack bar are located in the same building.

DIRECTIONS: Take I-64W to I-81S to exit 175. From the exit, turn left onto Route 11 and go 4 miles to the Natural Bridge Visitor Center on the left. The miniature golf course is located on the lower level of the Visitor Center.

MUSIC AND THEATER

Charlottesville is blessed with a plethora of music and theater options, from impressive community theaters and talented young classical musicians to free musical concerts and professional theatrical performances. Some of these events are ongoing, but many occur on irregular schedules or only once a year. To find out about upcoming events, check out the "Extra" section of Friday's *The Daily Progress* or the events calendar in the weekly *Observer* or the *C-ville Weekly*. Also be sure to pick up a copy of the free *Charlottesville Arts Monthly*, a small magazine published as a complimentary guide to the arts and entertainment activities in Charlottesville and Albemarle County. The magazine is available at local library branches and many arts locations.

For weekly recorded updates about cultural events in Central Virginia, call the Piedmont Council of the Arts (PCA) at (804) 980-3366. PCA also publishes a flyer in October, February and June detailing upcoming events. These flyers are available free at area libraries, McGuffy Art Center, the Virginia Discovery Museum and other locations.

MUSIC

Fridays After Five

The Downtown Mall and Amphitheater   (804) 970-3503

HOURS: Fridays 5:30 PM–8 PM from late April to late October.
Season-long and weekly schedules of performers are printed in
The Daily Progress.

This free summer concert series sponsored by the Downtown
Foundation is a showcase for local musical talent ranging from hip,
youthful music to swing orchestra. Concerts are held at the amphitheater
at the east end of the Downtown Mall and attract families as well as
students and businesspeople looking for a great start to the weekend.
Kids love to bop to the live music in front of the stage or play on the
grassy hills surrounding the amphitheater. At intermission, community
groups such as the Rope Busters jump rope team take the stage while
roving entertainers along the Downtown Mall add to the festivities.
Food, soft drinks, beer and lots of trinkets are available for sale.

SCHLEP FACTOR: Low for families with older children or for families with younger kids
that have a decent adult/child ratio. The performances can get quite
crowded, so a vigilant eye is necessary.

DIRECTIONS: Take the 250E Bypass to the light at McIntire Road. Turn right onto
McIntire and go to the light at Preston Avenue.
Water Street Garage: Continue straight to the next light and turn left
onto Water Street. Park in the parking garage on Water Street and head
east down the mall to the amphitheater.
Market Street Garage: Turn left onto Market Street. Head up Market
Street, past the Library, and turn right into the Market Street Parking
Garage.

The Prism Coffeehouse

214 Rugby Road, Charlottesville   (804) 977-7476 (97-PRISM)

WEBSITE: http://www.theprism.org

HOURS: Friday and Saturday evening (occasionally Thursdays and Sundays)
from late September–early May 8 PM for concerts.

ADMISSION: Children under 12 are 1/2 price, students over 12 receive discounted
admission, others $8–$15.
Reservations: In advance at Plan 9 Records, Spencer Gifts or Innisfree
World Artisans, or the ticket office.

Don't let the coffeehouse part of the title fool you–The Prism has been
serving up great family-friendly concerts since 1966 in an alcohol- and

tobacco-free environment. Guests are treated to a variety of professional acoustic performances; however, the majority are folk music or folk-based, featuring bluegrass, international and old time music on fiddles, banjos and guitars. Plenty of children of all ages attend the weekend performances, but kids eight and older really get into the toe-tappin', finger-snappin' tunes. The Prism also hosts a variety of free mid-week performances, although these are mostly jam sessions and are not much fun for kids.

SCHLEP FACTOR: Moderate. Although tickets are often available at the door, families should purchase them in advance to avoid disappointment. The website gives a description of upcoming events, including occasional children's concerts. There is no reserved seating, but comfortable, padded seats are available and a self-serve kitchen offers cookies, sodas, coffee and hot cocoa (donations appreciated). While the clientele at the Prism tends to be quite tolerant of families, adults should respect the fact that many guests are serious listeners of music. Disruptive children, therefore, should be removed.

DIRECTIONS: On Route 29S (Emmet Street) head towards the University and turn left onto University Avenue. Turn left onto Rugby Road at the first light and go 2 blocks. Just after you cross the Beta Bridge, the Prism is the white building on the corner on the right. Parking is available behind the building or in the adjacent Presbyterian church parking lot.

The Virginia Consort and Youth Chorale

HOURS: Performances held in February, May and December.
ADMISSION: Tickets vary but begin at $5 for students, $10 for adults.
Reservations: Tickets for up to three weeks in advance available at Thomas Ashfield Gallery, Greenberry's, Whole Foods, Blackstone's Coffee Co., Mincer's and New Dominion Bookshop.
Information: Telephone Ina Arnold at (804) 979-1565.

More than 60 children ages 10 and older make up the Virginia Consort Youth Chorale. Members, chosen by audition, perform a variety of music ranging from classical to folk. The Youth Chorale participates in all three Virginia Consort performances, but the Christmas concert, featuring a candlelight processional and brass bell choir, is the most family-friendly concert of the year.

SCHLEP FACTOR: High. We recommend these performances for concert-savvy families with children over 10. Families with antsy children will be asked to leave. This is one of the few Charlottesville attractions where dressing nicely is expected.

DIRECTIONS: Locations vary, so call ahead.

The Youth Orchestras

Youth Orchestra of Charlottesville-Albemarle (YOCA); Evans Youth Orchestra; Buford Middle School String Orchestra; Charlottesville High School String Orchestra.

Locations for performances vary so look in *The Daily Progress* for advertisements. The Performing Arts Center at CHS, Lane Auditorium and Cabell Hall are typical locations.

ADMISSION: CHS and Buford Middle School performances are usually free. YOCA and Evans performances are free for kids under 6, $3 for students, $5 for adults.

Information: Call YOCA-Evans at (804) 974-7776, Buford Middle School at (804) 296-5571, or CHS at (804) 296-5131.

The Charlottesville area has an amazing depth of musical talent evidenced by several wonderful youth orchestras. Watching these kids excelling at something they love is inspiring to children and adults alike.

YOCA and Evans are full orchestras, giving families an opportunity to see woodwinds, brass, percussion and string performers. YOCA is the older branch of the youth orchestra (performers are typically high school age) while the Evans is the younger branch, with 10–15-year-old performers. All members must either audition or have teacher recommendations to participate.

YOCA offers four performances each year: autumn, Christmas, March Concerto, and mid-May. The December performance is held in conjunction with the Evans Orchestra and offers families a chance to see both groups at the same time. Performances typically last an hour and although locations vary, are advertised in The Daily Progress. Families are welcome at all performances, although the May concert is a competition so guests must be quiet. The Evans Orchestra performs twice each year: once in December with YOCA and once on the first Sunday in May. We highly recommend the December performance for families with children 5 and up where kids will be drawn in by the familiar melodies.

The CHS and Buford Middle School Orchestras are string orchestras. CHS is an acclaimed group of 100 performers divided into beginner, concert and chamber orchestras. Three standard concerts are held each year with many more sprinkled in, including a First Night Virginia performance and the District Band and Orchestra Competition. The first two concerts, performed in conjunction with the Buford Middle School Orchestra are held the first weekend in December and the third or fourth weekend in May. A third performance held the second weekend in February is a full symphony concert. Snacks are usually sold at the hour-long performances and receptions are held for the musicians afterwards. Look for a "Meet the Musicians" night where kids can ask the musicians questions and even try out their instruments after the performance.

Buford Middle School performs several times each year: twice with the CHS Orchestra and once at the District Band and Orchestra Festival on the second Saturday in March. This festival, held at one of the area high schools, offers a chance for families to drop in and see bands and orchestras from all over the district. Snacks are sold in the lobby and the event is free.

SCHLEP FACTOR: Fairly low. The Buford Middle School performances are the most casual, with many siblings of the musicians attending, but all are family-oriented.

DIRECTIONS: Locations vary, so watch *The Daily Progress* for details.

THEATER

Ash Lawn-Highland Summer Festival

James Monroe Parkway (Route 795)   (804) 979-0122 (box office)

WEBSITE: http://www.monticello.avenue.org

HOURS: Mainstage productions held late June to mid-August at 8 PM; summer Saturday shows held July–early August at 10 AM.

ADMISSION: Saturday shows $15 for students, $22 for adults, $21 for seniors; all other days $14/$20/$19; summer Saturday Shows $5 at door, no reservations.

Reservations: Tickets may be purchased in advance or at the door. Youth days, typically three performances per season, offer reduced rates for children.

Families wishing to ease into the realm of opera and musical theater should plan a trip to Ash Lawn-Highland during the Summer Festival. Ash Lawn-Highland's Summer Opera Company has been ranked as one of the top twenty warm-weather opera companies in the world. Shows are held outside in the Boxwood Garden, so children have room to stretch, and at least one of the three shows produced each summer is family-oriented. For example, "Hansel and Gretel" played to rave reviews. All operas and musicals are fully staged and sung in English.

Family guides, available for all performances, give a child-friendly synopsis of the show and introduce opera vocabulary. To make the evening even easier and more special for families, picnic baskets and a catered buffet dinner are available, or families are welcome to bring along their own picnic.

The Summer Saturday series offers music, dancing and puppet shows for children on Saturday mornings. A different traveling theater group is featured each Saturday, so every performance is unique. Past shows have included puppet shows by Bob Brown, and Dinosaur Rock, which premiered at the Smithsonian Institution's Discovery Theater. Each year, one Summer Saturday features "Let's Make An Opera", put on by the Summer Festival Company. Families are introduced to all aspects of opera, including the elements used to make an interesting story, opera music and voices, stage sets, costumes and make-up. The audience then designs and performs their own opera. Family guides are also available for Summer Saturday performances, and suggest activities families can do at home to reinforce what they have learned.

SCHLEP FACTOR: Moderate for Mainstage performances, low for Summer Saturdays. We recommend the mainstage performances for kids 7 and older, but the Summer Saturday performances are great for children as young as 3.

Tip: Seating is not reserved so get there early, "save" your seats with sweaters or pads (folding chairs are hard!), and go picnic or play in the grounds until it's time to take your seats.

DIRECTIONS: Take I-64 to Exit 121A (Route 20S/Scottsville). Follow Route 20S through one set of lights to a left onto Thomas Jefferson Parkway. Take the Parkway past Monticello to a right onto Route 795 to Ash Lawn-Highland. If coming from downtown Charlottesville head south on 9th Street NE, which becomes Avon Street. Turn left onto Monticello Avenue which turns into Route 20S then follow directions as above.

Barboursville Four County Players

Route 33, Barboursville   (540) 832-5355 (box office)

WEBSITE: http://www.avenue.org/fourcp

HOURS: Thursday–Saturday 8 PM in August, Sundays at 5 PM. Christmas production is given each December for three weekends, Friday and Saturday at 7 PM and Sundays at 2:30 PM at the Barboursville Community Center. The Musical is held each March for three weekends, Friday and Saturday at 8 PM and Sunday at 2:30 PM at the Barboursville Community Center. Two other family-oriented shows are held for three weekends in May and October.

ADMISSION: Shakespeare and Musicals: $8 for children, $12 for adults, $10 for seniors and students; Christmas show: $6 for children, $10 for adults, $8 for seniors and students.

Season Tickets: Available at a savings.

Reservations: Tickets are available in advance by calling the box office Monday–Friday 4 PM–8 PM, or by fax at (804) 832-5424 or by e-mail at fourcp@cstone.net

Some of the best community theater for families in the area is presented by The Barboursville Four County Players. The summer stage for the group is set amid the ruins of the mansion owned by the first governor of Virginia, James Barbour. The house was designed by Thomas Jefferson, but burned to the ground on Christmas Day more than one hundred years ago. Towering old boxwoods and the four pillars of the porch form the backdrop for evening Shakespeare performances. Families can bring a picnic and eat on the grounds before the show or attend the buffet dinner (reservations required in advance). Before the show, strolling musicians and jugglers entertain children of all ages. Most children eight and up enjoy the Shakespeare performance, although plenty of pre-school children attend as well. The elaborate set and Shakespearean costumes grab kids' attention, even if the dialogue is a bit unusual for the modern child's ear.

Shows held at the Barboursville Community Center are also great for families. The Christmas program always features a family play such as "The Best Christmas Pageant Ever", and the theater is decorated for the holidays. This show is typically about two hours long with an intermission, and is fine for kids 4 and up. In March, the Players offer a major musical such as "Fiddler On The Roof" with elaborate costumes and sets. The show may be long, often 2-1/2 hours including a 20-minute intermission, so may not be suitable for very young children. May and October shows vary in content and style but are also wonderful family entertainment.

SCHLEP FACTOR: Moderate. Seating is first-come, first-served at the Ruins so families with children should arrive early and try to snag end seats. Antsy children can play quietly on the ground next to parents. Light snacks are sold at both the Ruins and the Community Center. The buffet dinner at the Ruins typically includes ham and turkey, salads, vegetables and a variety of desserts. Note that at the present time, the Community Center is not handicapped-accessible and that only porta-potty restrooms are available at the Ruins.

DIRECTIONS: *To the Barboursville Community Center:* Take Route 29N to a right on Route 33E at the main intersection in Ruckersville. Go approximately 7 miles. As soon as you enter Barboursville and see the Barboursville Fire Department on the left, look for the Community Center directly across Route 33 on the right.

To the Barboursville Ruins: Follow directions as above, but just before the Community Center, veer right onto Route 678. Follow Route 678 for about 1/2 mile. Cross over Route 20 and the Ruins are on the right.

Jefferson Children's Theater
Charlottesville   (804) 293-3570

HOURS: The 1-1/2 hour performances are currently held at Burnley-Moran Elementary School on Friday at 7 PM, Saturday and Sunday at 5 PM, two or three times per year. Each show runs for three weekends.

ADMISSION: $4 in advance, $5 at the door.

Reservations: Advance tickets are currently available at Whimsies at Barracks Road Shopping Center.

Peter Ryan, formerly an off-Broadway playwright, is enjoying a rebirth of sorts at the helm of the Jefferson Children's Theater. Performances by the Jefferson are exceptional. Ryan casts area children in the plays, and every child who auditions gets a part. The secret of the Jefferson's success is two-fold. First, since Ryan considers his venture to be community theater that just happens to use children in the casts, performances reach for a standard of excellence expected from Charlottesville community theater productions. Second, Ryan always has at least one acclaimed adult actor in his performances, which gives structure and depth to productions. Sets and costumes can be elaborate, adding to the ambiance for children. Guests can expect to see children's classics such as "Charlotte's Web" and "Charlie and the Chocolate Factory"; however, since Ryan rewrites the scripts and songs, each has an original twist. Children interested in performing in a Jefferson production should call the main number or watch *The Daily Progress* for audition information.

SCHLEP FACTOR: Low. Performances are timed and priced right for families. Since performances are broken into two segments with a ten-minute intermission, even children as young as 3 can enjoy Jefferson Children's Theater productions.

DIRECTIONS: To Burnley-Moran Elementary School where performances are currently held: Take the 250E Bypass. Burnley-Moran is on the right just before the intersection with High Street and before Free Bridge at Pantops.

Community Children's Theater

Charlottesville Performing Arts Center, Charlottesville
(804) 961-7862

HOURS: Sunday afternoons at 2 PM, four times during the school year, call for exact schedule.

ADMISSION: $8.

Season passes: $20.

Reservations: Advance tickets available at Whimsies (North Wing, Barracks Road Shopping Center) and Deck The Halls (Seminole Square). Remaining tickets are sold at the door, one hour before the performance.

For over 45 years, the Community Children's Theater (CCT) has been bringing top-quality professional theater to the children of Charlottesville. CCT sponsors four professional shows each year as well as one full-scale production featuring local children. The professional shows range from productions by Theater IV in Richmond to Chinese acrobats. All are incredible and are offered at an unbeatable price. The brochure offers descriptions of the shows for the year as well as a season ticket order form and can be obtained by calling the CCT office.

Each year, CCT brings the Missoula Children's Theater to town to conduct a week-long program with area children that culminates in a public performance. Children (grades K–12) must audition for the program (50 children can be accommodated each year) and they gain technical as well as performing experience. The show is surprisingly well-done, especially when you consider that the entire production was put together in just one week! Tickets for this show are $3 and are available at the door. For information about when the Missoula Troupe will be in town, call the CCT office.

SCHLEP FACTOR: Low. This is one of the best buys around for professional theater. Kids three and up will love the fast-moving performances.

DIRECTIONS: (To the Performing Arts Center) Take the 250E Bypass to the Dairy Road/Performing Arts Center exit. Turn left at the stop sign, go over the Bypass, bear right onto Grove Street. Turn right onto Concord and into the Charlottesville High School grounds. The school auditorium is the Performing Arts Center.

Lime Kiln Theatre

14 South Randolph Street, Lexington   (540) 463-3074

WEBSITE: http://www.cfw.com/limekiln

HOURS: Evenings at the Lime Kiln from Memorial Day–Labor Day, and on Halloween weekend. The Christmas show is held indoors at the Lenfest Center For The Performing Arts on the Washington and Lee Campus.

ADMISSION: Toddlers on laps are free, $3–$12 for children, $5–$25 for adults. For information about having the Lime Kiln Resident Company perform their current folktale for your school group, call Tracey Dickerson at the number listed above.

In historic Lexington, the ruins of an old lime kiln provide a magical setting for summer theatrical and musical productions. Unless otherwise noted on the brochure, all shows are appropriate for children, but some are specifically geared toward family audiences.

Many of the musical concerts held on Sunday evenings are family-oriented productions, as is "Stonewall Country", one of the Lime Kiln's cornerstone performances. "Stonewall Country" is the story of Lexington native General Stonewall Jackson. The play combines exciting Civil War battle scenes (complete with cannons that "fire" fireworks) and the music of Robin and Linda Williams to really engage school-age children.

The Folktale Festival, held each year for a week in May and September, is billed as "knee-slappin', toe-tappin', laugh-till-it-hurts folktales," for the whole family. Many of the folktales are based on Southern Jack Tales and can be seen at schools state-wide during the off-season.

The last outdoor shows of the year are performed on Halloween weekend. Three one-hour shows offer "frighteningly fun tales and original music for Halloween". The tales are more funny than scary; the only children shivering will be those who forget to throw a coat in the car, as the temperature dips pretty low by late evening. A Christmas performance held at the nearby Lenfest Center For The Performing Arts includes stories and Christmas carols.

SCHLEP FACTOR: Fairly high for families driving the hour from Charlottesville. Most of the performances begin around 7 PM or 8 PM, which can make for a late night. We highly recommend the family performances, however, especially for kids 8 and up. One great combination for kids studying the Civil War is to tour the Stonewall Jackson house earlier in the day, then head over to the Lime Kiln to see "Stonewall Country" in the evening. A snack stand sells popcorn, cookies, hot chocolate and the like. Strollers and wheelchairs can be accommodated (call in advance).

DIRECTIONS: Take I-64W to I-81S. Follow I-81S to exit 188B toward Lexington (Route 60W). Follow Route 60W about 4 miles through the town of historic Lexington. Go under the bridge at Washington and Lee University and continue for less than 1/2 mile to a left onto Borden Road.

Old Michie Theatre Company

221 East Water Street, Charlottesville   (804) 977-3690

HOURS: Many different performances are held throughout the year; call the theater for a recorded message about current show.

ADMISSION: $5.

Season passes: $28 for seven puppet shows.

The Old Michie Theater offers puppet shows and mainstage productions for kids by kids in a cozy theater off Water Street. Since all the productions are given by the children who are students at the Old Michie Theater, adults should have realistic expectations. Quality and length can vary, but most kids under 8 love the shows, and adults get a kick out of watching the young performers. Themes tend to be classics and fables such as Little Red Riding Hood and The Legend of Sleepy Hollow. After the show, all young fans are invited backstage to play with the puppets. The theater is an excellent place for children who wish to participate in puppet and mainstage productions, with ongoing workshops and summer camps for children as young as five. The directors have stellar reputations for their rapport with children.

SCHLEP FACTOR: Low. The theater is conveniently located, offers many productions each year and is the perfect size for young children. A snack stand sells candy and chips during intermission, and validated parking is available right across the street in the Water Street parking garage. The theater is stroller- and handicapped-accessible, although strollers should be folded for performances.

DIRECTIONS: Take the 250E Bypass to a right at the light at McIntire Road. Follow McIntire to the intersection at Preston Avenue and continue straight through the light. At the next light (by the Lewis and Clark statue) turn left onto Water Street. Follow Water Street to the parking garage on the right. The theater is directly across Water Street from the parking garage.

Soccer ball

foot ball

baseball

hockypuck

Lacrross ball

basketball

SPECTATOR SPORTS

We sent our families into the stands at a variety of local sporting events to find the most popular and easiest games to attend with kids in tow. Not surprisingly, the most popular games aren't necessarily the easiest for families to negotiate, so we have included as many tips as possible to make your outings fun. One tip that seemed to make all sporting events easier on families with young children: Bring along a pair of binoculars so kids can see the action (or the mascots) up close. And be sure to bring along change for popcorn and sno-cones!

Families willing to make the drive will find minor league hockey, baseball, and soccer in Richmond and outstanding WNBA action in D.C., all at prices that won't require you to take out a home equity loan to attend.

University of Virginia Varsity Sports

Families looking for sports action will find some kind of sporting event going on at U.Va. nearly every week during the school year. Football, basketball, soccer and lacrosse historically draw the largest family crowds, but sports enthusiasts can also see track and cross country meets, golf tournaments, baseball and field hockey games, and more. Call the U.Va. ticket office at (804) 924-8821 for information on your favorite sport or check out their website at http://www.virginiasports.com

Most of the U.Va. sports programs have Youth Days and other promotions to draw families through the gates. The best place to find out about these promotional events is the Sunday Sports Section of *The Daily Progress*, where U.Va. Sports has a weekly update.

Media guides that offer in-depth information about players are available for all U.Va. sports by telephone order only (804) 982-5500. Prices range from $4–$13, depending on the sport.

U.Va. Soccer
Klöckner Stadium

HOURS: Season runs from early September–early November, depending on the tournament schedule. Games are held on the weekends, typically at midday or early afternoon.
Information: call the U.Va. Ticket office at (804) 924-8821.

ADMISSION: $2 for kids, $4 adults, $2 seniors and are available at the gate.

The most family-friendly sport at U.Va.. is also one of the most popular sports for kids in the area. Soccer games at Klöckner Stadium always find kids running around in the grassy sidelines, hoping to get their hands on the game ball when it rolls behind the goals. The men's and women's teams each play more than a dozen home games, giving fans plenty of opportunities to enjoy top-quality NCAA Soccer. Both teams are perennial powerhouses, but the men's team is one of the strongest in the country.

Kids will especially enjoy many promotional events occurring throughout the season. Keep an eye out for the Coca-Cola Classic Tournament, Family Day, Youth Day, Adidas Day, Boo With the Hoos (a Halloween event) and more.

If you have a young soccer fan, be sure to drop by Downtown Athletic and register them for the "Cavalier of the Day" program. One name is drawn for each home game, allowing the winner to warm up with the team, follow them to the locker room and sit on the bench with them during the game, all the while outfitted in some cool new Adidas clothes.

SCHLEP FACTOR: Low (the lowest of all U.Va. athletic events). Tickets are cheap, parking is plentiful, and the timing (weekend afternoons during crisp fall days) perfect for family outings. You'll find plenty of snack stands and restrooms and, if the kids get antsy during the 2-1/2 hour games, there is plenty of room to stretch.

DIRECTIONS: Take Route 29S (Emmet Street) and go a couple of blocks past the shopping center to a right at the light at Massie Road. Park in the U-Hall parking lot one block up on the left. Klöckner Stadium is directly across the road at the corner of Alderman Road and Massie.

U.Va. Women's Basketball
University Hall
Games held throughout the week, beginning usually at 7:30 PM, mid-November–early March. Weekend games are earlier (often 2 PM).

ADMISSION: $3 for kids, $5 for adults, $3 for seniors.
Season tickets: Available, as is reserved seating with youth prices available.

HOURS: For a schedule and ticket purchases, call the U.Va.. ticket office at (804) 924-8821.

Running a close second to soccer as the most family-friendly sporting event at U.Va., the women's basketball program offers fans exciting basketball action at an unbeatable price. Sign up kids K–8th grade for the Cavalier Kid's Club so they can line up on the court pre-game and make a tunnel for the players. The players slap the kids' hands as they run through–a big thrill for little fans (see Kid's Club details below). During the game, the Cavalier mascot, cheerleaders and pep band are on hand to keep the crowd revved. Fan participation games at halftime keep the action rolling. Family-oriented promotions such as Youth Day and Mascot Day add to an already fun time for kids.

SCHLEP FACTOR: Pretty low. The main drawback for basketball games is that they normally start in the evening on school nights, making for a pretty late night once the 2-1/2 hour games are over. Look for occasional weekend games which typically start early afternoon. Parking is easy, there are plenty of snacks (orange and blue sno-cones are a favorite) and the facility is handicapped-accessible, although strollers are awkward. Unless the team is playing a noted rival, tickets are generally available at the door, making last-minute plans workable.
Note: One of the best deals in town for kids is the Cavalier Kid's Club. For $18, kids receive season tickets with seating in their own (supervised) section, a T-shirt to wear to the games, and invitations to functions such as a picnic with the players and an autograph party. Kid's Club members always get to form the human tunnel at the start of each home game, too. To date, the Kid's Club is only available for women's basketball, but in the future there may be a University Kid's Club with different perks for many U.Va. sports. To register for the Kid's Club, call U.Va. Sports Promotions at (804) 982-5600.

DIRECTIONS: See U.Va. Soccer, to University Hall.

U.Va. Men's Basketball

HOURS: 7 PM or 9 PM (earlier on weekends), mid-November–early March.

ADMISSION: $8–$10, and should be purchased in advance from the U.Va. ticket office at (804) 924-8821.
No youth discounts.
Season tickets: $275 per seat, no youth discounts. All season tickets are for reserved seats.

Although not nearly as easy (or inexpensive) as the women's games, the U.Va. men's basketball games offer lots of action and excitement for fans of all ages. The Cavalier mascot, cheerleaders and pep band add to the festivities. Family-oriented promotions such as Youth Day provide the best opportunities for kids, but make plans early. Tickets go on sale one month before each game and often sell out well in advance.

SCHLEP FACTOR: Very high, mostly because of ticket availability. Parking is more difficult than at the women's games, so arrive early for a good spot. Inside, you'll find plenty of snacks (identical to the women's games) and good handicapped-accessibility. Strollers should be left at home.

DIRECTIONS: See U.Va. Soccer.

U.Va. Lacrosse

Men's games: Klöckner Stadium; Women's games: the artificial turf field behind University Hall.

HOURS: Mid-February–early May.

ADMISSION: $2 for children, $4 for adults, $2 for seniors, available at the Gate.

U.Va. Lacrosse games are a great way for families to spend a spring afternoon. Lacrosse is a big sport in Charlottesville, and both the men's and women's games see many families through the gates. Although there is no Youth Day for lacrosse, kids can sign up at Downtown Athletic for the "Cavalier of the Day" program. Each lucky winner (one for each home game) gets some spiffy new duds courtesy of Reebok, and warms up and sits with the team during the game.

SCHLEP FACTOR: Low. Tickets are readily available and parking is easy. Fans will find snacks and restrooms for both the men's and women's games.

DIRECTIONS: See U.Va. Soccer.

U.Va. Football

Scott Stadium

HOURS: Early September–end November.

ADMISSION: $22–$26 per seat purchased in advance from the U.Va. ticket office at (804)-924-8821.

Season tickets: $118 for five home games.

"Hoos On The Hill" season tickets for kids under 18: $25.

All prices and categories will change after the stadium renovation is complete.

Although U.Va. football tickets aren't inexpensive, an afternoon of tailgating and football makes a great outing for families with kids 7 and older. To snag a parking spot, arrive three hours before game time. Pack along a picnic and discover why tailgating before the game has become almost as much fun as the game itself.

There is plenty of action in the stadium to keep older kids interested through the three to four hour games. Try to arrive at least 15 minutes before game time so the kids can see the U.Va. Cavalier ride horseback into the stadium and hear the fireworks go off. The U.Va. Cheerleaders often hand out complimentary pompoms before the game at the lower level, too. Halftime festivities include music and various entertainment.

For kids, the best game of the year is Youth Day, when free hot dogs and drinks are served at the stadium, and The Cage at University Hall is filled with games, moonwalks and other kid-pleasing activities.

SCHLEP FACTOR: Fairly high. Tickets should be bought in advance (up to one month) from the U.Va. ticket office. University Hall and the Fontaine Avenue area are the best bets for parking, but arrive very early as the lots swell to capacity hours before the game. Parking at University Hall is free with shuttle service to Scott Stadium, or drive down streets around the stadium where many homes and businesses open up their parking lots to fans. Although you will pay about $10 per car for a parking space in this area, you will be only a short walk from Scott Stadium. For families with kids, we highly recommend purchasing tickets for the Hill, where you can spread out a blanket and have a bit more elbow room. If you have a stadium seat, there is very little wiggle room. Note that umbrellas are not allowed in the stadium.

DIRECTIONS: *To U-Hall:* See U.Va. Soccer.

GYMNASTICS

Classics Gymnastics

2327 Seminole Trail, Charlottesville   (804) 978-4720

HOURS: Three meets held December, early and late spring (call for exact dates).

ADMISSION: Free.

At Classics Gymnastics' three meets, fans can see girls as young as 9 compete in bars, beam, floor and vault. These gymnasts are all seasoned athletes who have had many years of training before they reach the competitive level, assuring fans of an impressive display of strength, grace and agility.

The best meet of the year for fans is the Classics Invitational, held the second week in December. During this two-day event, families can watch teams from all over the state compete. Large meets like this one are a bit like a three-ring circus: routines are being performed on all the apparatus at the same time, so even fans who drop in for a short time can see a little bit of everything.

For this and all meets, be sure to call and ask when the optional routines will be performed. Optional routines are the individualized routines the gymnasts perform (in contrast to the compulsory routines which are the same for all the gymnasts). This part of the competition is much more exciting to watch, and kids get more of a feel for each athlete's strengths and personality. Fans can watch the action from the sidelines or, for a bird's eye view of the events, from the upstairs viewing area.

SCHLEP FACTOR: Low. Thanks to Classics' recently expanded gym, there is more room for fans to stretch. Meets typically last all day or longer, making it easy to drop in and out of the event. There are restrooms with a changing table, toys to occupy little ones, and usually a snack stand. In case your kids catch the gymnastics bug while they are there, the gym also offers classes for boys and girls 2 and up.

DIRECTIONS: Take Route 29N to a right at the light at Wal-Mart. Follow the access road to the Antiquer's Mall shopping center. Classics is on the corner across from the Antiquer's Mall.

ICE HOCKEY

U.Va. Hockey

Charlottesville Ice Park, Charlottesville   (804) 980-3357

WEBSITE: http://www.cvilleproperties.com/hockey.htm

HOURS: Select Saturdays 9:45 PM, select Sundays 12:00 PM, late September—early March.

ADMISSION: $3 for children/students, $5 for adults.

Charlottesville families can enjoy great hockey right in their own backyard when the U.Va. Hockey team takes the ice at the Charlottesville Ice Park. Although the U.Va. team is technically a club at the University, they have won the Atlantic Coast Collegiate Hockey League title for three years in a row. The team plays a 16-home game schedule to a lively crowd. Collegiate hockey is great for families, in part because no fighting on the ice is tolerated. Occasionally the U.Va. Cavalier mascot or the Ice Park mascot, I.C.Polar, drops by, adding to the festivities. Games typically last two hours with two intermissions, and the Ice Park DJ keeps things lively by playing pop music during down times. A free program gives fun facts and pictures of the players. Families new to the sport can usually get tips from the fans on rules of play. After the game, players will sign autographs and talk to the kids if there is enough interest from the fans.

Kids who fall in love with the game won't need to go far for instruction; the Ice Park offers hockey lessons and leagues for boys and girls.

SCHLEP FACTOR: Low, especially for the Sunday games. The Ice Park has many amenities including bleacher seats, snacks and spacious restrooms to make your visit easy. Validated parking is available next door in the Omni Hotel parking lot, too.

DIRECTIONS: Take the 250E Bypass to a right at the light at McIntire Road. Go to the first light and turn left onto Preston Avenue. Take an immediate right into the Omni Hotel Parking Garage. Park in the garage and walk up to the Downtown Mall. The Ice Park is immediately across from the Omni Hotel on the Downtown Mall.

POLO

Virginia Polo Center

Old Lynchburg Road, Charlottesville
(804) 977-POLO or (804) 979-0293

HOURS: Friday evenings and Saturday afternoons June–August, Friday and Saturday evenings in October–November. Call the Polo Center at (804) 977-7656 for exact game times.

ADMISSION: Children always free, adults may be asked to pay a nominal entry.

Polo games at the Virginia Polo Center are great events for children of all ages. Several polo clubs use the center, but in general, kids are invited to stroll around the barn or to the visiting club's trailers to pet the horses and talk to the players. The friendly and enthusiastic players take the time to explain the elaborate equipment as well as provide interesting details about the horses. During the game, the announcer gives running commentary about what is happening so that even novices can easily follow the action. Pack a picnic and any refreshments your family might need as no food is available. In late October, the Center hosts a big tournament. Many people tailgate at the event, and barbecue is usually sold.

In the winter, indoor polo is played at the arena. These games are still family-oriented, but not as much fun for kids as the outdoor games.

SCHLEP FACTOR: Low. These games make a great drop-in evening activity for families. Restrooms are available in the arena Parking is sometimes free, otherwise $2 depending on which club is using the field.

DIRECTIONS: Take I-64 to Exit 120 (5th Street Exit). Go south on 5th Street (headed away from Charlottesville) for 3-1/2 miles to a left on Forest Lodge Lane and follow signs to the Virginia Polo Center.

HOW DO THEY DO THAT?

Unique Tours for Kids.

One wonderful thing about kids is their endless curiosity about the world around them. Just about anything can capture the imagination of a child. These tours are meant to indulge and foster this natural curiosity. Some of the tours require groups or advance reservations, but others are designed for individual families to drop in and learn. Find one that suits your family or group and dig in!

Many of the tours in this section welcome families. Sites that encourage drop-in guests have directions listed. Sites that require advance reservation for tours have no directions. Ask for directions to the site when you make reservations.

ANIMALS

Carolton Farm and Fiber

5401 Carolton Lane, Barboursville   (540) 672-2935

WEBSITE: No website, but e-mail: carolton@dragnet.net

HOURS: Tuesday–Saturday, April and May.

ADMISSION: 50¢ per person

Tours: Guided 2-hour tours by reservation only (call as far in advance as possible for tour reservations—some groups make arrangements in the fall for the following spring). 10–25 children for tours; all ages are welcome. Drop-ins are welcome during April and May for self-guided tours.

When you arrive at Carolton Farm and Fiber you'll instantly know you're in sheep country. Emma, the farm's sheepdog, is likely to guide (or herd) you into the farm where Barbara and Gorden Tinder have raised sheep since 1956. The Tinders offer tours during lambing season so visitors can see exactly what goes into the labor-intensive process of producing top-quality wool. Children first walk through the barn and are shown how to care for the lambs and sheep. Participation is a big part of the learning experience as kids hold and bottle-feed lambs, guide sheep through chutes, help dispense medications, etc.... Next is a trip to the shop to learn about spinning and weaving. Older kids get a chance to card the wool while younger children listen to a story. Bring a blanket and lunch to picnic on the grounds after your visit, and be sure to bring your camera! If you have an animal-loving group of any age, this is an experience you don't want to miss.

Iron Rod Farm

2955 Earlysville Road, Earlysville

ADMISSION: Free.

Contact Larry or Leslie Sidwell at (804) 973-8407 up to two weeks in advance to schedule tours.

Tours: Daily, except Sundays, year-round, although there are no tours on Saturdays in the summer. Spring tours are best for younger children when there are lots of babies on the farm.

Tour Minimum: None, although maximum is 25 children, preschool age and older.

Over the years, Iron Rod Farm has been practically swallowed up by the Charlottesville suburbs, but continues to produce top-quality French Alpine goats for a national market as well as goat cheese for local inns and restaurants. The Sidwells are farmers of the old school, warm and friendly and willing to proudly show families or groups around their property. The farm tour is hands-on and perfect for antsy pre-schoolers. Kids get to feed the goats by tossing hay from the loft, and watch (or sometimes help) as the goats are machine- or hand-milked. Families who visit in the spring can also bottle-feed the baby goats and may even get to see a goat being born! Older kids or 4-H groups will get a more in-depth tour that offers more specific information about goat farming, including information on showing and raising the animals. Pamphlets about raising dairy goats are also available.

Lower Sherwood Llama Farm

Route 795, Charlottesville

ADMISSION: Free.

Call Paige McGrath at (804) 286-2288, one day to one week in advance for tours.

Tours: Available year-round, but late fall and spring are best when there are babies on the farm.

Tour Minimum: None, but a maximum of 60 preschool–early-elementary children.

Lower Sherwood Farm near Carter's Bridge is gaining a reputation among area preschools for offering one of the best animal tours in the area. Guests are first led inside the llama pen where more than 50 of the gentle and curious creatures live. If children remain still and quiet, the llamas will surround the group, and many of the older animals will allow guests to pet them. Kids who visit during the spring or late fall will also get to visit the pen where female llamas and their babies are kept. Tours are tailored to each group's age and interest, but children can learn a little llama history, find out why llamas are kept on modern farms, and find out what makes a good llama.

   After a one-hour tour, guests can explore two ponds, see the horses and bunnies, and picnic in the grassy areas that surround the beautiful farm.

Meadow Sweet Farms

Lovingston

ADMISSION: Free, but donations are appreciated.

Overnight stays for in-depth study are available on a limited basis for $75 per person.

Call Jean or Sherry Blanchette in the evening (7:30 PM–10:30 PM) at (804) 263-6652, one week or more in advance to arrange tours.

Tours: By reservation.

Tour Minimum: None, but a maximum of 100 children ages 7 and older. Small groups and families are preferred.

Families and groups willing to make the 45-minute drive to Lovingston will find one of the most extraordinary learning opportunities in the area. Here, guests can visit Meadow Sweet Farms, where Jean and Sherry Blanchette have dedicated their lives to the preservation and conservation of displaced captive wildlife. Although a variety of animals can be found on the farm, the Blanchettes' passion and focus is the conservation of wildcats, as evidenced by the cougars, bobcat, lynx, African Jungle cat and South American Geoffrys cat that make their home on the farm. The Blanchettes have rescued the animals from laboratories, fur farms and under-trained private owners and now use the animals to teach the public. Guests can expect to learn details about each species, including their behavior and habitats, as well as identification and conservation efforts. Rather than simply listen to a lecture about animal behavior, the Blanchettes encourage groups to observe the animals firsthand. Tours, therefore, are better suited to small groups which will be less disruptive to the animals. Guests wishing to have a more in-depth experience may choose to stay overnight in an apartment on the farm.

ART

McGuffy Art Center

2nd Street NW, Charlottesville
Call Joan Cabell at (804) 973-2988 (residence) to arrange formal tours.
Tours: Formal tours by reservation, one month in advance.
Tour Minimum: Ten or more children from first grade–high school.
Families are welcome to drop in and observe any artist.

The McGuffy Art Center, once a school named for William McGuffy of McGuffy Reader fame, is today a wonderful co-operative studio where families and groups can watch a variety of artists at work. During formal tours, kids will get in-depth presentations from two or more artists. Glassblowing, sculpture, drawing, painting, photography and dance are but a few of the disciplines offered. There's always something new and different on the tour.

In addition, families are invited to drop in any time and observe any of the artists as they work. Guests should visit quietly and not interrupt the artists at work, although artists will often offer information to visitors. McGuffy has four large galleries (including the renowned Second Street Gallery) where families can drop in and see an impressive array of art. Guests can also purchase art supplies at the McGuffy Art Store located on the second floor of the center.

After your visit, stop by McGuffy Park, adjacent to the Art Center. This small park has a playground and is a great spot for a picnic.

Note: Many of the artists at McGuffy offer classes for children and adults in drawing, printing, pottery, modern dance, etc.... To receive information about classes, call the McGuffy and ask to be placed on the mailing list.

DIRECTIONS: Take the 250E Bypass to McIntire Road; turn right. At the light, turn left and then immediately get into the left lane and make a sharp left turn onto High Street. Take the 1st right onto 2nd Street NW. McGuffy is on the right.

FOOD

Albemarle Baking Company

York Place, Downtown Mall, Charlottesville
Call Gerry Newman at (804) 293-6456, one week in advance to arrange tours.
Tours: May be unavailable during high demand times, such as graduation weekend or Thanksgiving.
Tour Minimum: None, but a maximum of 20 per tour, preschool–elementary.

Gerry Newman will bring small groups through his bakery to see all kinds of goodies in the works. Kids will love seeing oversized versions of appliances they all have at home (mixers, ovens, etc.). If you ask in advance, Gerry may even arrange for kids to bring home a sample of his baked goods. The bakery has a huge glass window where you can see baking going on even without a pre-arranged tour, so if you are on the Downtown Mall, drop by York Place for a look and a whiff!
Hint: If your group is on the Downtown Mall for this tour, be sure to read the listing for Chaps Ice Cream Parlor in our Dining section for a great deal on group meals for kids.

Auntie Ann's Pretzels

Fashion Square Mall, Charlottesville
ADMISSION: $5 per person covers project, samples and drink.
Call Mary Harrington at (804) 974-7532, at least one week in advance.
Recommended group size: 10–30.

Auntie Ann's has their 1-1/2 hour tours down to a science. Groups first view a "History of the Pretzel" video and enjoy pretzel and drinks. Kids then tour the kitchen and try their hand at rolling out their own pretzel (a lot like making playdough snakes!). These pretzels are then baked into edible treats or cooked longer and made into magnets or pencils. (Choose which you would like in advance for the entire group.) If your group can't come to Auntie Ann's, make arrangements for them to come to you. This tour makes a great birthday party for younger children.

Krispy Kreme Donuts

1805 Emmet Street (Route 29N), Charlottesville
Call any Assistant Manager at (804) 923-4007 two days in advance for a free group tour that includes a complimentary donut and lemonade for each child.
Best tour time: 10 AM–11 AM, when the donuts are being made, or in the afternoon when cake donuts are made.
Minimum number: None, but a maximum of 15 children, ages 4 and older.

At Krispy Kreme Donuts, kids can watch donuts as they bake and travel along a conveyor belt, over a vat of hot oil and through an icing waterfall. Families who visit at not-too-crowded times can also ask a manager to come out and explain the process in greater detail. Groups that call in advance are also given the chance to dip and add sprinkles to a donut that they are then allowed to eat. The friendly staff even throws in a glass of lemonade for each child, too.

DIRECTIONS: Krispy Kreme is located on Route 29, just south of the Hydraulic Road intersection.

Pepsi Cola Bottling Company

1150 Pepsi Place Charlottesville   (804) 978-2140
Call Mr. Flint three weeks in advance to arrange a one-hour tour.
Tour Minimum: 15–50, preschoolers–teens.

The Pepsi Bottling Company welcomes more than 1,200 area kids each year into their processing plant. Tours begin with a short video, then move to the plant where more than 1,000 bottles of soda are filled and capped every minute. Next, kids find out how the product is packaged and loaded for shipping. After a few games, including a recycling exercise, each child leaves with a free can of soda.

VIRGINIA PRODUCTS

Blue Ridge Pottery

Stanardsville   (540) 985-6080

HOURS: Daily, 10:30 AM–4 PM, longer hours in summer.
Drop-in tours are welcome, although large groups should call ahead since space inside the studio is limited.
Potters are generally working during business hours, but call ahead if you want to make sure.
Occasionally, the studio offers a two-hour workshop. Call for details.

Drop by the tiny studio at Blue Ridge Pottery to see potters working at the wheels, busy creating the pottery they sell in the on-site store and at craft shows throughout the area. From the stacked blocks of clay to the two giant outdoor kilns, your kids will see pottery in every stage of development.

After touring the studio, walk next door to a shop where the finished pottery, souvenirs, and ice cream cones can be purchased. The store was once the Golden Horseshoe Inn and served as Stonewall Jackson's headquarters during the war. Inside the store, kids can try their hand at a variety of folk instruments and marvel over the indoor water gardens found at every turn, including one which pours from the underside of the stairwell. In warm weather, pack a picnic lunch and enjoy the beautiful outdoor water gardens and landscape.

Occasionally the studio offers a two-hour workshop giving participants a chance to try their hand at the potter's wheel. Although kids generally don't have the muscular development necessary to operate the wheel, they are welcome to participate with an adult.

DIRECTIONS: Take Route 29N to a left on Route 33W in Ruckersville. Pass through the village of Stanardsville. Blue Ridge Pottery is on the left, about 8 miles from downtown Stanardsville.

Route 11 Potato Chip Factory

Middletown   (800) 294-7783

HOURS: Informal drop-in tours Fridays 10 AM–6 PM, Saturdays 9 AM–5 PM.
ADMISSION: Free.

Tours: In-depth tours are available for school (including homeschool) groups of any size on Friday mornings by reservation only. Call Sarah at the above number for reservations.

Although tiny Middletown is more than two hours from Charlottesville, we had to include the Route 11 Potato Chip Factory in our tours. Here, kids won't see huge machinery doing all the work, but an old-fashioned factory where potatoes are still peeled and sliced by hand into a vat of oil. The entire process from peeling and slicing to cooking, salting and hand-packing can be viewed from behind huge glass windows on Fridays and Saturdays. Although this drop-in viewing is available all day, arrive early in the day to see the most action.

On Friday mornings by appointment, school groups can get an in-depth tour of the factory where they will learn "more than they ever wanted to know about making potato chips."

And of course, after both the formal and informal tours, samples of the many different varieties of chips produced here are available.

DIRECTIONS: Take Route 29N to a left onto Route 231 in Madison. In Sperryville, take Route 211 to Route 522 toward Front Royal. In Front Royal, get on I-66W until it dead ends into I-81. Go 1 mile on I-81 to the Middletown exit. Follow signs to the center of town. The factory is just south of the only stoplight in Middletown.

Virginia Metalcrafters

1010 E. Main Street, Waynesboro   (540) 949-9432
Self-guided tour hours: Monday–Thursday 9 AM–4 PM year-round.

Visitors can watch molten brass as it is poured into hand-formed sand molds in the Virginia Metalcrafters foundry in Waynesboro. Since the viewing is from behind an observation window, no reservations are required. The shop also sells items similar to the ones made in the foundry.

DIRECTIONS: Take I-64W to exit 99 (Afton/Waynesboro). Turn left onto Route 250 and go 1-1/2 to 2 miles to the store (a colonial house with white columns) on the left.

WINERIES

For information about tours, contact the Jeffersonian Wine Grape Growers Society at (804) 296-4188 or call the vineyard directly.
Tours: Generally year-round, although many require appointments during the winter.

Charlottesville wineries are blossoming into well-respected businesses with award-winning products. Most of the local vineyards offer drop-in tours, which combine a bit of gardening, chemistry, biology and history to give visitors an understanding of how wine is made and the history of growing grapes in Virginia. Each winery is different but most tours are informal and fine for children over 10 (sans tastings at the end). The following is just a partial list of local vineyards that offer tours. Call ahead for directions and hours of operation.

Jefferson Vineyards
1399 Thomas Jefferson Parkway, Charlottesville   (804) 977-3042

Near Monticello, this vineyard is producing wine on the same land Jefferson's friend and associate Filippo Mazzai cultivated for grapes in the late 1700s.

Oakencroft Vineyard and Winery
1486 Oakencroft Lane, Charlottesville   (804) 296-4188

The closest winery to Charlottesville, Oakencroft is just 5 minutes from Barracks Road Shopping Center.

Rose River Vineyards and Trout Farm
Route 648, Syria   (540) 923-4050

This vineyard offers a trout farm adjacent to the winery.

Prince Michel Vineyards
Route 29N, Madison   (540) 547-3707

The largest winery in the area, Prince Michel offers a museum and a fancy French restaurant well as tours.

White Hall Vineyards
5190 Sugar Ridge Road, White Hall   (804) 823-8615

This relatively new winery at the base of the Blue Ridge Mountains offers a smaller, more intimate experience for guests. The staff is exceptionally nice and the beautiful property is great for an informal picnic after your tour.

THEATRICAL PROPS

Enchanted Castle Studio
Natural Bridge   (540) 291-2353

HOURS: Daily 10 AM–6 PM July and August, weekends only in June, September and October, Memorial Day weekend, closed rest of year.

ADMISSION: Children 3 and under for free, $4 for children, $5 for adults, senior and group discounts available. Drop-ins welcome.

The Enchanted Castle is one of those places that you pass on the highway, then jerk your head around for a second look. Out front, a winged rhinoceros stands guard over the castle-shaped compound. Peeking out over the top, a pig stands ready to bungee-jump from a 40-foot tower. Go ahead. Turn around, and just for fun, tour Mark Cline's studio where fiberglass props of all sizes are made for restaurants and amusement parks. During this zany, Willy Wonka-style tour, kids can see how simple wood and metal frames are wrapped in chicken wire, cotton and fiberglass, then finished with carved Styrofoam details and paint. Sometimes visitors will see how figures are animated with motors and joints. Since Mark likes to try out his latest creations on tour groups, kids get a sneak preview of attractions that will soon be bound for Putt-Putt golf centers, Six Flags and other high-profile locations. Aptly described as the "Universal Studios of Appalachia", the Enchanted Castle is a fun diversion from the serious historical stuff so prevalent in our area.

DIRECTIONS: Take I-64W to I-81S (near Staunton) to exit 180A (Route 11S). Follow Route 11S for 1/2 a mile to the Enchanted Castle on the right. (You can't miss it; it's the only joint with a winged rhino on the front lawn).

Natural Bridge Wax Museum Factory

Lexington   (540) 291-2426

WEBSITE: http://www.naturalbridgeva.com

HOURS: Daily, year-round, but call ahead for current operating schedule. Factory tours close 1/2 hour before the museum.

ADMISSION: (Good for both the Museum and the Factory tour): Children 6 and under for free, $3.50 for children, $7 for adults.

After touring the Natural Bridge Wax Museum, bring the kids downstairs to see how these amazingly realistic figures were made. Two videos detail the history of wax figures and describe the steps in making them. In between the shows, kids will see firsthand the various stages a figure goes through before its completion. If you visit from 10 AM–2:30 PM, you can observe the artisans at work, although since it takes up to six months to complete a figure, only a small part of the process can be seen on any given day. For more information on the Wax Museum, see the listing under Museums.

DIRECTIONS: Take I-64W to I-81S to exit 175. Turn left onto Route 11 and go 4 miles to the Wax Museum and Visitor Center on the left.

BALLOONING

Balloons Over Virginia

Ashland   (804) 798-0080

Call Henry Rosenblum to arrange a date, at least one month ahead.

ADMISSION: The presentation is free.

Minimum age: 1st grade and older.

Requirements: A large field or auditorium is needed to set up the balloon, as well as a slide projector if your group wants the slide show.

Okay, confess. Have you ever raced through the countryside, your head hanging out the window, kids cheering you on from the back seat in pursuit of a hot air balloon you spotted on the way to the grocery store? Spotting a hot air balloon floating over the Virginia countryside brings out the kid in all of us, so this is one tour that will please young and old alike. Henry Rosenblum and his crew are the official balloon company for the state of Virginia. (They fly the Virginia Is For Lovers Balloon seen in the Department of Tourism ads.) Although your group can't really go to them, they will bring their balloon to your school or other large group. Henry brings geography, math, and science to life in a fabulous age-appropriate talk on how balloons work and what is involved in the manufacture and piloting of a balloon. If you have a slide projector, he also has a great slide show of the balloon competitions in which they have participated. Afterwards, the guys inflate the balloon (yep, the real one) and show the kids the scientific principles at work, along with plenty of "oohs" and "ahhs". If you have a large auditorium, they can even bring an old balloon so kids can walk around inside it once it is inflated. These guys are hard to schedule—this is a hobby, they are firefighters by trade!—but really worth the effort.

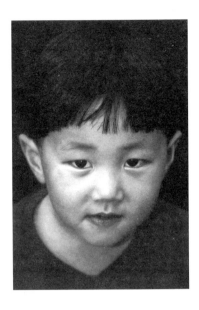

RICHMOND AND BEYOND

Load up the kids, head for I-64, and in just one hour you can be in a major metropolitan city filled with fun family activities. Although we have hit many of Richmond's highlights in this chapter, there is much more to this city than we can do justice to here. For more comprehensive information, we recommend two publications. First, the Sabot School publishes *Richmond Is For Children*, a book now in its 4th edition that reviews hundreds of family-oriented attractions in Richmond. The book is available for $15 and can be purchased directly from the Sabot School at (804) 288-4122. Second, *Richmond Parents* is a wonderful monthly publication that will keep you abreast of the special events and exhibits for families in the Richmond area. The coverage of the Richmond Children's Festival alone is worth the $15 annual subscription. *Richmond Parents* subscriptions can be purchased by calling the publisher at (804) 673-5203.

AMUSEMENT PARKS

Paramount's Kings Dominion

Doswell   (804) 876-5000

WEBSITE: http://www.pkd4fun.com

HOURS: Daily late March–early October; daily June–August, mostly weekends otherwise. Hours vary so call ahead for up-to-date schedule.
Hurricane Reef (the adjacent water park) hours: Weekends in May, then daily June–early-September from 11 AM until either 6 PM or 8 PM, depending on the closing time of the rest of the park.

ADMISSION: *For both the amusement park and the water park:* Free for children 2 and under, $22.99 for children 3–6 years or under 48" tall, $31.99 for anyone 7 years or older or over 48" tall, group and senior rates available.
Coupons that provide discounted admission are available each year. Call or check out the website for current sponsors.

The 400-acre Kings Dominion, the most visited attraction in the Richmond area, is a must-see for families who love amusement parks. Upon entering the park kids are measured and given color-coded armbands that determine what they will be permitted to ride. Once banded, kids can choose from seven different themed areas with more than 40 rides varying from tot-sized to world-class, lose-your-lunch rollercoasters. For younger children, Kidzville boasts the Kidz Construction Company, a hands-on play area, and lots of rides sized just for tots. Most little ones also enjoy the Hanna-Barbera cartoon characters that roam the park, and middle-grade kids especially like the Nickelodeon area, Splat City. Shows are available all day throughout the park and offer visitors a chance to take a break from the rides.

In the summer, have the whole family wear swimsuits underneath their clothes to cool off in Hurricane Reef, the adjacent 6-acre water park. Here you'll find a splash pool and little slides for toddlers, a variety of flumes for older kids and a Lazy River for the entire family. The water park makes a great stop when pounding the pavement becomes unbearable, but it can get crowded on hot days.

SCHLEP FACTOR: Let's just say you and your kids will sleep really well after a visit here. Actually, as theme parks go, this isn't so bad. The 45-minute drive from Charlottesville is easy, and once inside amenities are plentiful. Food inside the park is plentiful, too, but pricey. Some families choose to pack a picnic and eat outside the gates. Swimsuits must be worn on the attractions at Hurricane Reef, but clothes must be worn in the rest of the park. Lockers and changing rooms are available right inside the water park. Strollers are a must for kids under 5.

Tip: Before you hop right into the out-to-the-street line to purchase tickets only to find out a 1/2-hour later you are in the wrong line (a mistake many first-timers make), check out the signs over the ticket windows. There's usually a minimal wait in the correct line.

DIRECTIONS: Take I-64 E to I-295N just outside of Richmond. Follow I-295N to I-95N. Take Exit 98 (King's Dominion Exit) and bear right. Go through one stoplight and bear right into the park entrance.

INDOOR PLAY CENTERS

Discovery Zone

1530 N. Parham Road, Richmond   (804) 270-3376

HOURS: Daily, year-round, Monday–Thursday 1 PM–7:30 PM, Friday and Saturday 10 AM–9 PM, Sunday 11 AM–7 PM.

ADMISSION: $4.99 for kids under 38" tall, $6.99 for kids over 38" tall. Parents play free, as do children under one year who are accompanied by a paying child.
Laser tag, skill games and rides are extra.

This huge indoor play center offers ball pits, sky tubes, obstacle courses and slides in two play areas, one for kids over 38" tall and one for kids under 38" tall. When the kids are pooped from climbing through the tunnels, head over to The Art Factory for art activities or to the arcade for rides and skill games. Older kids will get a kick out of the laser tag ($6.99) and the karaoke station. A snack area sells Pizza Hut pizza, popcorn, pretzels and other goodies.

SCHLEP FACTOR: Low–High (a.k.a. depends on what kind of mood you're in). This Discovery Zone is on the east side of Richmond and there are plenty of activities to keep kids 12 and under busy for an afternoon. Although parents are encouraged to join the kids in the play area, many choose to watch the action from the sidelines. Be advised that socks are required for play and that weekends and rainy days can be extremely busy. Discovery Zone is right down the street from the Regency Mall.

DIRECTIONS: Take I-64E to the Parham Road South Exit (exit 181). Head south (right) on Parham Road to the Parham Plaza (look for K-Mart, which is also inside the plaza). Discovery Zone is inside the Parham Plaza Shopping Center.

JAMES RIVER EXCURSIONS

Riverboat Cruises on the Annabel Lee

3011 Dock Street, Richmond   (804) 644-5700

HOURS: *Lunch Cruise hours:* Wednesday–Friday noon–2 PM, Saturday 11 AM–1 PM, Sundays 1 PM–3 PM April–mid-October.

ADMISSION: $14.95 for children under 13, $21.95 for adults, slightly higher for Sunday Brunch.
Kiddie Cruise hours: Thursdays 11 AM–1 PM July–August.
$13 for children, $17.50 for adults, group rates available.
Reservations: Required, and should be made a week or more in advance.

The Annabel Lee, a Mississippi River paddleboat replica, offers family-friendly cruises down the James River. During the ten-mile journey, guests fill up on Southern dishes at the buffet and enjoy live entertainment and ongoing narration about sites along the James. Evening cruises are available, but for children we recommend the more casual two-hour lunch cruise or Sunday Brunch cruise. Families can move between the outside Starlight Deck and the two indoor, climate-controlled decks. Older kids will enjoy the bingo games for which Annabel Lee souvenirs are given as prizes.

During the summer, special two-hour kiddie cruises run every Thursday and feature clowns, storytellers, magic and the like. Kid-pleasing food such as pizza and baked chicken is served on the buffet, and every child receives a balloon creature and has their hand painted. Special birthday party packages are available for the kiddie cruises, too.

In December, the Annabel Lee hosts a Lunch With Santa cruise complete with Christmas decorations, caroling and other live entertainment. (Although kids who are deathly afraid of the Jolly Old Elf will be none too happy to be stranded aboard a ship with him for two hours!)

SCHLEP FACTOR: Low. Getting to the pier is pretty easy and visitors will find plenty of parking available at the dock. We find that kids ages 5 and up really enjoy the regular lunch cruises, although younger ones may get antsy by the end. Even 3-year-olds will enjoy the Kiddie and Santa cruises. Be sure to bring your camera! Call for handicapped accessibility.

DIRECTIONS: Take I-64E to I-95S to the Franklin Street Exit (exit 74B). Turn left onto Franklin Street then right onto 15th Street. Go to the first stoplight and turn left onto Main Street. Go about 6 blocks to 21st Street and turn right. Go 2 blocks to a left on Dock Street. Annabel Lee will be on the right.

Richmond Raft Company

4400 E. Main Street, Richmond   (804) 222-7238

HOURS: March–November, weather and water depending.

ADMISSION: $35 per person for Upper Section and Lower Section trips, $48 for Falls of the James trip.

Trips last from three to six hours.

Minimum age/requirements: Children must be at least 12 years old to participate in the Lower Section and Falls of the James trips, and 3 feet tall for the Upper Section trip.

Reservations: Required, and should be made in advance.

Groups with fewer than six members may be combined with other groups to fill the raft, or may choose to buy out the extra seats on the raft to have the raft to themselves.

Make plans with the Richmond Raft Company to experience what may be the only urban whitewater rafting experience in America. Families need not have any rafting experience to get in on the thrill of paddling through the Class IV rapids that slice through the heart of downtown Richmond–just a hankering for adventure and a sincere desire to get soaked. All equipment and instruction is provided, some of it baptism-by-fire as your guide helps your group navigate the river.

Families with kids over 12 can choose from either the Lower Section trip, a fast-paced adventure over the wildest rapids in the area, or the Falls of the James trip, a day-long excursion over both the smaller rapids in the Upper Section and the heavy duty stuff on the Lower Section. The Falls of the James trip includes lunch on the river. Families with younger children can get in on the fun on the Upper Section trips, with milder Class I and II rapids and more opportunities for swimming.

SCHLEP FACTOR: Fairly high considering you are combining an hour plus drive, cooler-packing and lots of water into one afternoon. Wear a swimsuit and bring sunscreen and a change of clothes. Wetsuits are provided at no extra charge during chilly or rainy weather.

DIRECTIONS: Take I-64E to I-95S in Richmond. Take Exit 74B (Franklin Street). Turn left onto Franklin Street, then right on 15th Street and left onto E. Main Street. Follow E. Main Street through 4 traffic lights, past Poe's Tavern to the Richmond Raft Company on the right.

MUSEUMS

Children's Museum of Richmond

740 Navy Hill Drive, Richmond   (804) 788-4949

HOURS: Daily, year-round Monday 9 AM–5 PM, Tuesday–Friday 9 AM–1 PM, Saturday 10 AM–5 PM, Sunday 1 PM–5 PM. Open extended hours in the summer and for some school holidays.

ADMISSION: Children under 2 for free, $3 for children 2–12, $4 for adults.

Make-believe is the order of the day at the Richmond Children's Museum. Kids can dress up in costumes and perform on stage, be part of a television news studio crew and see themselves on camera, or go on a shopping spree in the grocery store. The most popular exhibit here is the 40-foot replica of a Virginia limestone cave, complete with stalactites, stalagmites and cool, clammy air. Kids don imaginary headlamps (flashlights to imagination-deficient grown-ups) for a realistic, knee-crawling exploration of the cave. Aboveground, kids will find lots to do in the art studio and computer center. Changing exhibits are offered as well, and include themes such as primary colors and neighborhoods. The museum makes an effort to complement other activities and exhibits occurring around town. When the Museum of Fine Arts hosts an Egypt exhibit in the summer of 1999, for example, the Children's Museum will have a child-oriented Egypt exhibit.

In the summer, the Children's Museum sponsors the Peanut Butter and Jam children's concert series, and in late May, the Soap Box Derby and Family Festival.

In early 2000, the Children's Museum will move to a new 42,000-square-foot facility next door to the Science Museum on Broad Street. This five-fold expansion will catapult the museum into the big leagues, potentially making it one of the top ten children's museums in the country. Seven different learning environments, a children's performance pavilion and a 6,000-square-foot outdoor learning garden are but a few of the features the new location will offer.

SCHLEP FACTOR: Moderate because of the drive from Charlottesville and the downtown location. Try to avoid arriving or departing during morning and afternoon rush hour, as the museum is right downtown.

DIRECTIONS: Take I-64E to I-95S to Exit 75 (Downtown/Coliseum/3rd Street) and bear right off the ramp. Turn left at the first light onto Jackson Street. Go 3 blocks to a left on Navy Hill Drive. The museum is on the left. Parking is available in front of the museum or in the pay lot across the street. *Note:* After the move in 2000, follow directions to the Science Museum of Virginia.

Science Museum of Virginia

2500 W. Broad Street, Richmond   (804) 367-6552 or (800) 659-1727

WEBSITE: http://www.smv.mus.va.us

HOURS: Monday–Saturday 9:30 AM–5 PM, Sunday 11:30 AM–5 PM; Memorial Day–Labor Day the museum is open Friday and Saturday until 7 PM.

ADMISSION: Children under 4 for free, $4 for kids 4–12, $5 for those over 12 years, $4.50 for seniors. Free for ASTC members.
IMAX tickets are $4 or $3 if purchased in combination with the Science Museum ticket.

The Science Museum of Virginia, located in the historic Broad Street Train Station, is one of the most popular attractions in Richmond. More than 250 exhibits covering topics such as computers, electricity, aeronautics and chemistry do a super job of explaining some very complex ideas, but you have to be able to read the directions on each exhibit to know how to use them. This museum, therefore, is better suited to grade- schoolers and older, although younger children enjoy climbing into the Piper Cub and the Friendship 7 spaceship replica, and everyone will love the huge Foucault pendulum in the rotunda. If you visit with a non-reader, be prepared to examine the exhibits together. The aeronautics exhibits, including a flight simulator and a paper airplane test station, are especially well-done. Also, don't miss the IMAX theater shows. Science-oriented films are shown on a five-story domed screen that makes you feel as if you are part of the action.

Special events are offered throughout the year, but two of our favorites are the Model Railroad Show, held the first two weekends in November, and the Scooper Bowl, held on a Saturday in late June. At the Model Railroad Show, guests view a huge assortment of miniature trains on a variety of layouts. At the Scooper Bowl, kids can eat their fill of Breyer's ice cream and participate in other summer-related festivities.

If you are a member of the Virginia Discovery Museum, or of any ASTC-affiliated museum, your admission is free and you receive discounts on the IMAX films.

SCHLEP FACTOR: Moderate, but much higher if your child can't read! The museum is a 1-1/4 hour drive from Charlottesville and has good handicapped and stroller accessibility. Free parking is offered, and restrooms and water fountains are plentiful, but note that there is no longer a restaurant in the museum (although there are several vending machines in the basement). As you exit the Museum parking lot, a right onto Broad Street will lead you past every imaginable fast-food eatery and, beyond, to a variety of casual dining chains and an enclosed mall.

Note: In early 2000, the Richmond Children's Museum will be moving next door to the Science Museum, doubling the fun on this section of Broad Street!

DIRECTIONS: Take I-64E to Exit 78 (Boulevard). Take a right off the exit ramp and go through several lights to a left on Broad Street (1st major intersection). The museum will be at the 3rd stop light on the left.

Virginia Museum of Fine Arts

2800 Grove Avenue, Richmond   (804) 367-0844

WEBSITE: http://www.state.va.us/vmfa/index.html

HOURS: Tuesday–Sunday 11 AM–5 PM, Thursday 11 AM–8 PM. Closed Mondays and major holidays.

ADMISSION: Free, but a $4 donation is suggested. Separate fee for special exhibits. Strollers are available at no charge.
Children's Art Resource Center workshops are $6 per person, $5 for members. Reservations are required in advance and can be made by calling (804) 367-8148.

This world-renowned museum is filled to its 350,000 square-foot brim with art from ancient times to modern. It is surprisingly accessible to families thanks to the accommodating staff and the Children's Art Resource Center. Although the Art Resource Center is no longer available for drop-ins, Saturday workshops for children are offered for two different age groups, two or three times a month. These workshops offer an art explorative activity based on some aspect of the main gallery. One recent theme, for example, was Behind The Art, where children learned about behind-the-scenes careers in art, such as museum curator and exhibition designer. Kids then became artists and created a mini-museum to display their works. School groups are invited to use the Art Resource Center by reservation during the week for the Art In Action program.

In the main gallery, pick up a Family Guide which will lead you to areas most interesting to children. One favorite is the new Discover Silver Gallery, a permanent exhibit where kids learn about the history and properties of silver through lots of hands-on activities. Kids make rubbings patterned after silver designs, handle pieces of silver, silver plate and pewter, and learn how to tell which is which, and other related activities. After leaving the silver exhibit, be sure to check out the collection of Russian Faberge eggs, the Egyptian and African displays, and the fun and colorful art nouveau displays in the West Wing.

After your visit, browse the gift shop and have lunch or a snack in the Arts Cafe, where kids can eat outside by the fountain or inside in inclement weather.

SCHLEP FACTOR: Pretty low (especially for an art museum). The museum is stroller- and handicapped-accessible (with strollers available to borrow) and the Arts Cafe provides a perfect rest stop. Afterwards, consider a trip to Maymont or Byrd Park just a few blocks away.

DIRECTIONS: Take I-64E to exit 78 (Boulevard). Follow Boulevard (Route 161S) for 1-1/2 miles through 9 stoplights. After the ninth light, turn right onto Grove Avenue and right into the parking lot.

★ Money Museum at the Federal Reserve Bank and Belle Isle

701 E. Byrd Street, Richmond   (804) 697-8108

HOURS: Monday–Friday 9:30 AM–3:30 PM. Closed bank holidays.

ADMISSION: Free.

The Money Museum, on the ground floor of the Federal Reserve Bank, details the history of money from ancient times to modern. Coins from around the world, primitive and colonial coins, and gold and silver bars are on display, as are items once used for barter such as tobacco and animal skins. Other displays explain the minting of coins and the safekeeping of money.

Although the Money Museum is fascinating, it is a quick (half hour or less) visit, so afterwards stroll down the canal to Belle Isle for one of the most scenic walks in the city. At the back of the Federal Reserve Building, walk down 7th Street, which runs alongside the James River, until it turns into Tredegar Street. From Tredegar Street, walk across the suspension bridge to Belle Isle. On the bridge, kids love the traffic noises from the Lee Bridge, which runs right overhead. Belle Isle is a small island that at different times was home to a prison, a quarry and an iron mill. On the island, you can see the ruins from these past industries plus whitewater rapids on the James, the Richmond skyline, fishermen, and wildlife such as river otters and great blue herons. Walk all the way around the island (about a mile) and enjoy the rocky shoreline, a pond with a dock at the old quarry site and the scenery. Walk back across the suspension bridge to complete this 1-1/2 mile walk. The entire walk is stroller- and handicapped-accessible and is quite safe, although children shouldn't climb on the ruins.

Walk back towards the Federal Reserve and enjoy the new Riverwalk, featuring electric barge rides on the Haxall Canal, a re-creation of the Kanawha Canal. The first section of the Kanawha was completed in 1795 and was surveyed by George Washington. Although the lock on the Haxall Canal is not operational for boats, there will be demonstrations showing how the original locks worked. The Riverwalk area will also have interpretive signs detailing the history of the canal and industry along the river as well as shops and cafes.

PARKS AND NATURE

Byrd Park

Boulevard Avenue, Richmond

HOURS: Richmond Children's Festival is held in the park the second weekend in October from noon–5 PM both days. For a brochure, call the Arts Council at (804) 355-7000.

ADMISSION: Paddleboats are available on Fountain Lake for $5 per hour.

Byrd Park is adjacent to Maymont Park and offers three lakes, one with paddle-boat rentals in the summer, stroller-friendly asphalt trails and a playground. In the summer, the Festival of the Arts is held at the amphitheater. This series of free performing arts shows includes concerts, dances and drama.

Each October, Byrd Park hosts the Richmond Children's Festival, which attracts more than 60,000 visitors in just two days and is the largest free children's festival in the country. Each year the festival celebrates a different culture with food and exhibits. In 1997, for example, India was the focus. Performers demonstrated Indian dances and sports, and there was a replica of an Indian village where kids could try on saris and turbans, taste authentic Indian cooking or try native dance steps. Other exhibits feature activities not related to the cultural theme. International Stage hosts dancers from countries around the world. Puppet shows, ballet performances, pony rides and much, much more can be found at the Festival.

SCHLEP FACTOR: Pretty high, although a visit during the Children's Festival is a must. During the Festival, don't try to park at or near Byrd Park. Instead, take the free shuttle from the parking lots at the University of Richmond Stadium. Pets, coolers, and glass are prohibited, but a stroller for pooped toddlers is highly recommended.

DIRECTIONS: Take I-64E to Exit 78 (Boulevard). Follow Boulevard until it dead-ends at the Columbus statue. Turn left into the park.

Lewis Ginter Botanical Garden at Bloomendaal

7000 Lakeside Avenue, Richmond   (804) 262-9887

WEBSITE: http://www.lewisginter.org

HOURS: Daily year-round, 9 AM–5 PM, with extended weekend hours from April–October.

ADMISSION: Free for children under 2, $3 for children 2–12, $5 for adults, $4 for seniors. Group rates available.

Bloomendaal, a Victorian home that has served as a bicycle club, a children's hospital and a private residence, is now enjoying its most fragrant renaissance as Lewis Ginter Botanical Gardens. On this 80-acre estate, visitors can stroll through 18 acres of spectacular gardens. A visit in the spring is a must, when the bulbs, rhododendrons and azaleas are in bloom, although a visit any time of year is an indulgence of the senses.

For kids, Lewis Ginter offers a Children's Garden planted with flowers, fruits and vegetables from around the world. A butterfly garden, with information on how kids can attract butterflies to their own yard is popular, as is a hands-and-nose-on herb garden with tips on identifying herbs. Two other treats in the Children's Garden are the digging areas, complete with shovels, where kids dig in the sand and mulch, and a huge sundial where kids stand in the middle and let their shadows "tell" the time. Over the next three years, the Children's Garden will undergo an expansion to include a maze and other fun features.

Outside the Children's Garden (if you can drag them out), be sure to visit the Henry Flagler Perennial Garden, which boasts three acres of perennials in room-like settings. In front of the Tea House, kids will enjoy an Oriental garden complete with waterfall and lake with koi and other fish. A bridge leads to an island garden planted with bug-eating venus flytraps and pitcher plants.

After your visit, stop by the new Visitor Center where you will find a large gift shop and a restaurant serving upscale, self-serve (and child-friendly) lunches and snacks. Bring your food outside to the patio and eat lunch overlooking the gardens.

Special events are geared toward families, and one, the World Gardenfest for Children, was designed especially for kids. This festival, held in July, features food and plants from around the world. During the Gardenfest of Lights in December, visitors are treated to cider, cookies and carolers, and the gardens are dressed in thousands of lights bearing botanical themes. The roses, for example, have lights arranged to look like roses climbing up the branches, and the willows are draped in green lights. Gardenfest of Lights begins in mid-December and runs through the rest of the month from 5:30 PM through 10 PM (closed Christmas Eve, Christmas Day and New Year's Day). A special Mother's Day celebration features a light jazz concert, food and the gardens in full bloom.

SCHLEP FACTOR: Low, especially for garden lovers. If your kids aren't nature enthusiasts, make your first visit during one of the special events when there are other activities going on. The new Visitor Center and expanded Children's Garden will make this an even better outing for families.

DIRECTIONS: Take I-64E to I-95N. Keep to the right and take Exit 80 (one of the first exits). Turn right onto Hermitage Road which turns into Lakeside Avenue. The gardens will be on the left, just past Hilliard Road.

★ Maymont Park

1700 Hampton Street, Richmond   (804)358-7166

HOURS: Daily year-round, 10 AM–7 PM April–October, 10 AM–5 PM November–March.
Indoor exhibits have more limited hours and are closed on Mondays.
Snack bar hours: Tuesday–Sunday 10 AM–5 PM, April–October.

ADMISSION: Free, although donations requested at the mansion, the Children's Farm and the Nature Center.
Tram rides: $1 for children, $2 for adults, available Wednesday–Sunday noon–4 PM, May–September, and on weekend afternoons April and October.
Carriage rides: $2 for children, $3 for adults, offered weekends April–November noon–4 PM.
Call the park for a free schedule of upcoming events or to join the Maymont Foundation.

A trip to Maymont Park is much more than a quick playground stop; this 100-acre Victorian-era estate has enough activities to occupy the most energetic kids for an entire day. Several special events at Maymont are well worth a visit, although arrive early before the parking lot fills to capacity. On Easter Sunday, the park hosts an egg hunt, visits from the Easter Bunny, bonnet-making stations, food and entertainment. Victorian Day in mid-October brings everything Victorian to the Maymont House, including a carriage parade, old-timey bicycles, a fortune teller, a Victorian tea and Victorian games. Our favorite event is the Victorian Christmas celebration, held on the first weekend in December. The home is decorated; the aroma of hot apple cider, ginger cookies and roasted chestnuts fills the air; and Father Christmas is on hand to visit with children. A special kids-only holiday store, located near the gift shop, allows children to shop (with help from attendants) for inexpensive gifts for their parents. Maymont also sponsors the Flower and Garden Show in February, although it is not held at the park. Because of its size, Maymont offers two separate entrances (three when the new Nature and Visitor Center open).

Spottswood Entrance: At the Spottswood entrance to the park, visitors will find a Children's Petting Farm, the wildlife exhibit, an aviary and, in

1999, the new Nature and Visitor Center. Restrooms and a snackbar are also at this entrance.

The Children's Farm is home to a variety of domesticated animals. Bring your quarters for the animal food dispenser so the kids can feed the goats, sheep, llamas, donkeys, cows, peacocks and chickens. The barn is open from noon–5 PM year-round (closed Mondays). As you continue past the barn, a steep paved hill leads the way to the wildlife exhibit. Bears, elk, bison, deer, a bobcat and other wildlife make their homes here.

At the bottom of the hill, visitors turn left to view the aviary and bison, and the new Nature and Visitor Center. This multi-million-dollar structure will have its own parking lot and will house a 126-foot river aquarium detailing the falls of the James River, a river otter exhibit, and six other educational galleries with themes ranging from Virginia geology to nocturnal animals. Two discovery rooms will be available, one with hands-on exhibits for toddlers and one with ongoing experiments for older children. Several large classrooms will accommodate school groups (reservations required). The Nature Center alone will be enough to occupy children for an afternoon and will make a great rainy day stop. A cafe will offer sandwiches and patio seating.

After visiting the bison and/or the Nature Center, cross the bridge and turn right to see the Birds of Prey exhibit and the black bears. You may continue along this path to the Japanese Garden and then on to the other side of the park, or return to the barn and take a tram ride to the Maymont House. Day-use tickets for the trams are available at the tram stop. The tram, which makes three stops in the park, is a good idea for families with small children. Another option would be to get back in your car and drive to the other entrance. Whichever you choose, be advised that families who continue on foot will have a lot of walking ahead of them, as well as a long set of steps in the Japanese garden to get up to the house.

Hampton Street Entrance: At the Hampton Street entrance, families will find the Maymont House, the carriage house, a gift shop, a snack bar and the Italian and Japanese gardens. Families may wish to take a half-hour tour of the Maymont House, the Victorian home built in the late 1800s by the Dooley family. The home is a Timetravelers site and has details kids enjoy such as a swan-shaped bed and rocker, among other animal-motif items, and stained-glass windows.

Nearby, families will find a gift shop, carriage rides and the carriage house where the horse-drawn carriages are stored. Tickets for the 15-minute carriage rides are available at the carriage stop near the house. Afterwards, head down the hill behind the carriage house to see the beautiful and fragrant Italian gardens, built in 1910. Some families will be ready to call it a day after the Italian gardens; if you do, you will miss one of the best features of the park. Take the steps from the Italian garden down to the Japanese garden. Here, a 45-foot waterfall cascades into a pool, ponds with arched bridges and stepping stones beckon, and

Japanese plantings abound. Kids will love the bamboo maze located near the waterfall, the huge koi in the ponds, and the stepping stones.

SCHLEP FACTOR: Moderate. Families with young children may wish to make several trips to Maymont rather than try to see it all in one day. Do bring a stroller, even for independent preschoolers. Snack bars at the Spottswood entrance and at the gift shop sell hot dogs, hamburgers, sandwiches, ice cream, sno-cones and the like. Be advised that Maymont is strictly a pedestrian park (except for strollers or wheelchairs) and that no pets, kites or flower-picking is allowed. Not all areas of the park are handicapped-accessible.

DIRECTIONS: Take I-64E to Exit 78 (Boulevard). Go south on Boulevard to the end (the Columbus statue will be right in front of you).
For the Spottswood Entrance: Turn right at the statue then follow the brown signs to the parking lot off Shirley Street.
For the Hampton Entrance: Turn left at the statue and follow the brown signs to Hampton Street.
For the Nature Center Entrance (opening mid-1999): turn left at the statue then right into Byrd Park and follow the signs.

THEATER

Theatre IV Family Playhouse
114 W. Broad Street, Richmond   (804) 344-8050

HOURS: Four shows each year, all during the school year, Friday–Sunday, with several matinees available. Call for a schedule.

ADMISSION: $14–$18 per seat, and should be bought in advance by calling the box office.
Season subscriptions: A variety is offered for discounted tickets and other perks.

Folks in Charlottesville may be familiar with Theatre IV from their performances through the Community Children's Theater. Home for this award-winning group is the Empire Theater, which was built in 1911 and is the oldest theater in the state. Four full-scale productions are performed each year at the Empire, each running for 2-1/2 weeks. These theatrical presentations combine live music, dramatic scenery and elaborate costumes with professional performances by the Theatre IV troupe. Past performances have included "The Adventures of Pinocchio" and "Treasure Island", among other fairy tales and fables. All are magnificently staged and well worth the drive to Richmond.

SCHLEP
FACTOR: Fairly low, thanks to the exceptional quality of Theater IV productions. Performances are 1–1-1/2 hours long, some with intermissions. The best way to ensure seats for these popular performances is by subscribing. A variety of subscriptions is available and offers great flexibility. If you don't have a subscription, reserve tickets up to one month prior to the opening of the show.

Inside the theater, guests will find restrooms with changing tables, and (usually) a snack stand that sells sodas, crackers and candy. The theater is stroller- and handicapped-accessible. Strollers are parked in the lobby during performances.

DIRECTIONS: Take I-64E to I-95S toward Norfolk/Petersburg. Exit I-95S at Belvedere Street (Exit 76B). At the end of the ramp, turn left at the stop sign onto Lee Street. Go to the 2nd light and turn right onto Adams Street. At the Broad Street/ Adams Street intersection, the theater will be on the corner, but continue through the light to the Theatre IV parking lot on Adams Street then walk back to the theater. Signs will assist you.

SPECTATOR SPORTS

Richmond Braves (Baseball)
3001 N. Boulevard, Richmond   (804) 359-4444 or (800) 849-4627
WEBSITE: http://www.rbraves.com
HOURS: April–mid-September, Monday–Saturday, usually beginning at 7 PM, Sunday games at 2 PM.
Call the ticket office for a complete schedule or for a pre-recorded message about upcoming games.
ADMISSION: Lap kids under 2 are free for all levels, $8 for box seats (first tier seats), $6 for press box (lower ten rows of the upper tier), rows 11 and up are $3 for kids 12 and under, $5 for adults, $3 for seniors.
Season tickets and group discounts: Available, call for details.

The Richmond Braves, the top AAA-farm team for the Atlanta Braves, play a whopping 72 home game schedule at their 12,000 seat stadium, The Diamond. Many big-leaguers put their time in at The Diamond, one of the finest minor league ballparks in the country. Kids will love the Diamond Room Restaurant right behind first base where they can get an almost-dugout view of the game along with dinner. Diamond Duck, the team's mascot, is always on hand, as is a roving four-man band and a clown who makes balloon sculptures for the kids. The Diamond also boasts a scoreboard just like in the big leagues that shows instant replays and close-ups of the fans during the 2-1/2 hour game.

After two games near the Fourth of July, the Braves host Richmond's premier fireworks show, and in August, Boy and Girl Scouts are invited to camp in the outfield with their parents after the game. Movies are shown on the Diamondvision scoreboard and McDonald's provides breakfast the next morning. Birthday party packages are available, and include tickets to the game, a personalized cake, hot dogs, drinks, Richmond Braves goodies for the birthday child and more.

SCHLEP FACTOR: Low. The Diamond is right off I-64 with plenty of parking available in the adjacent lot ($3). Tickets are available at the gate. Inside, fans will find subs, hot dogs, popcorn, beer, ice cream and other ballpark fare. No reservations are necessary for The Diamond Room Restaurant, which offers both buffet and menu items. The entire facility is handicapped-accessible, although strollers should be left at home.

DIRECTIONS: Take I-64E to Exit 78 (Boulevard). Turn left onto Boulevard and the Diamond will be on the left.

Richmond Kickers (Soccer)

Office: 2320 W. Main Street, Richmond   (804) 644-5425

WEBSITE: http://www.richmondkickers.com

HOURS: May–Labor Day weekend on select Fridays and Saturdays at 7 PM. There are a few mid-week games as well. Call the office for a complete schedule or for a pre-recorded message about upcoming games.

ADMISSION: Children 3 and under for free, $6 for children, $8 for adults; purchase tickets at any Richmond area Arby's for a $2 discount.
Season tickets and group discounts: Available.

Families can now watch professional soccer in Richmond thanks to the Richmond Kickers, part of the professional soccer A-League. The Kickers play a 14 home game schedule at the University of Richmond City Stadium. The team is the top farm team for the D.C. United and one of the most successful franchises in professional soccer. At every game, fans are not just treated to exceptional soccer but also to a carnival-like atmosphere in the stadium. Interactive games such as moonwalks and rock climbing walls are available, and Shasta the Clown is on hand for balloon sculptures and face painting. On the field, kids will enjoy the antics of the team mascot, a yet-to-be-named kangaroo. Pre-game, all kids under 18 are invited onto the field to create a human tunnel for the players, and post-game, the team remains on the field to sign autographs.

The Kickers have one of the hottest birthday party packages in town, too. For approximately $10 per person, party-goers are treated to a game, pizza and cupcakes, a visit from the mascot and clown and an appearance from the birthday child's favorite Kickers player. For an additional fee, autographed T-shirts and balls can be arranged.

In the summer, the Kickers host week-long soccer camps for boys and girls, both half- and full-day, featuring Kickers players as coaches.

SCHLEP FACTOR: Low. The University of Richmond Stadium is easy to find (it's the same stadium that hosts the NCAA Men's Soccer Final Four) and there is plenty of free parking in the adjacent lot. Tickets are always available at the gate. In the stadium, fans will find snacks such as hot dogs, pretzels, soft drinks and candy. Be sure to bring along some extra cash for the kids' activities sprinkled throughout the stadium. Although some are free, some have an extra fee. The stadium is handicapped-accessible, but strollers should be left at home.

DIRECTIONS: Take I-64E to I-95S (the Downtown Expressway). Take the Rosewood Avenue exit. At the end of the ramp, turn left onto McCloy Street. The University of Richmond stadium is immediately on the right.

Richmond Renegades (Ice Hockey)

3 Richmond Coliseum, Richmond   (804) 643-7825

WEBSITE: http://www.renegades.com

HOURS: Mid-October–early April, usually Friday and Saturday 7:35 PM, some Sunday games at 4 PM. Call the office for a complete schedule or for a recorded message about upcoming games.

ADMISSION: Lap kids 2 and under for free, kids 3–12 half price, $15 for arena level, $9 for lower corner, $7 for upper level. Season tickets and group discounts: available.
Tickets may be purchased by calling Ticketmaster at (804) 262-8100.

Hockey fans can watch the Renegades, a farm team for the San Jose Sharks, battle for the puck at The Freezer in the Richmond Coliseum. Most of the 35 home games are fairly tame, although parents should be aware that fights occasionally break out on the ice. Two intermissions during the 2-1/2 hour games give fans plenty of time to stretch their legs, but the action really never stops. Music is provided by Richmond-area radio stations; there are on-the-ice activities; and The Gade, the alligator mascot, is on hand to toss Frisbees, T-shirts and other souvenirs into the crowd. For $1, fans can purchase a foam hockey puck and during intermission throw them to a designated area on the ice. The puck that lands closest to the target wins a prize ranging from a signed jersey to a mountain bike.

After all games, players sign autographs in the autograph booth, and after most Sunday games, fans can bring their skates and join the players on the ice for autographs, conversation, and a bit of ice skating fun. Birthday party packages are available; they include tickets to the game, pizza, cupcakes and giveaway items for each child and a visit from The Gade. Call the office for information on all special events and parties.

SCHLEP FACTOR: Moderate. Although tickets are usually available at the gate, your best bet is to call Ticketmaster in advance. We highly recommend attending the Sunday afternoon games, which tend to be more family-friendly.

There are two parking lots adjacent to the Coliseum (about $3) but you'll have to arrive early to snag a spot. Otherwise, park in one of the many parking lots along Leigh Street. Inside the park, snacks include hot dogs, pizza, ice cream and candy. The Coliseum is handicapped-accessible, but strollers should be left at home. Because of the length of the game and the (possible) walk to the Coliseum, Renegades' games are best for families with kids over 7.

DIRECTIONS: Take I-64E to Exit 75 in Richmond. Turn left onto Leigh Street and the Richmond Coliseum will be on the right.

AND BEYOND...

Although Williamsburg is a bit farther than the other attractions found in this book, we simply couldn't help ourselves. Many of our families visit Williamsburg every year, for the amusement and water parks, the history or a combination. Just 1-3/4 hours from Charlottesville, a visit to any one attraction still makes a feasible day trip.

If you choose to spend a weekend or more in Williamsburg to see all of the attractions, we highly recommend visiting Colonial Williamsburg first and then moving on to the amusement parks. Kids appreciate the experience of the historic area more if they haven't had a taste of the high thrills first.

★ ## Colonial Williamsburg
Williamsburg

WEBSITE: http://www.history.org
Call the Visitor Center at 1-(800) HISTORY for brochures, reservations and tickets.

ADMISSION: Tickets are offered at three levels:
Patriot's Pass: Admission to all exhibits and museums for one calendar year; $19 for children 6–12, $34 for adults.
The Colonist's Pass: Admission to most exhibits and museums for two days; $17 for children 6–12, $30 for adults.
The Basic Pass: Admission to many exhibits and museums for one day; $15 for children, $26 for adults.
Look for summer packages that include lodging and admission to Colonial Williamsburg, Busch Gardens and Water Country.

Colonial Williamsburg, the site of one of America's earliest colonies, is now one of the nation's largest living history museums. Visitors can see the Governor's Palace, the Capital, the Courthouse, and the powder magazine as well as a number of trade sites that realistically portray colonists' lives just before the Revolutionary War. In all, more than 500 buildings over 173 acres are on display—enough to keep even the most energetic families hopping for days. We can't hope to cover everything Colonial Williamsburg has to offer, but instead encourage families to visit the website and call for free brochures. Area libraries also carry the picture book, *A Colonial Town: Williamsburg*, by Bobbie Kalman. This book offers a great overview of buildings kids can visit today, as well as age-appropriate history that will help make a visit meaningful to children.

Upon arrival in Williamsburg, families should first drop by the Visitor Center for tickets, tours, dinner reservations and the *Visitor's Companion*, a free publication that lists special events. The Visitor Center has several gift shops and restaurants, videos about the area and shuttle buses to the historic sites.

The Duke of Gloucester Street is the main street through Colonial Williamsburg, with houses, shops and taverns lining each side. The apothecary, milliner, shoemaker and saddlemaker, and the Greenhow store (general store) are easy sites to visit with kids and offer reproduction souvenirs. Since many of the colonists were illiterate, all of the signs have pictures that give a clue about what each store offers for sale which kids enjoy deciphering. Our families enjoy eating lunch in one of the taverns, where servers in period attire offer 18th-century food. Chowning's Tavern is especially good for kids, but plan to arrive early for lunch to avoid a long wait for a table. Also, on the Duke of Gloucester Street, children's colonial costumes are available to rent for the day.

The famed Governor's Palace has guided tours which are fine for kids over 7 and next door is the public gaol (jail) where Blackbeard and his band of pirates were held after their capture.

Two museums are also included in all passes; one, the Abby Aldrich Rockefeller Folk Art Center, is fun for children 5 and up. Don't miss the reconstructed slave quarters at Carter's Grove Plantation. While the mansion tour at Carter's Grove should be skipped if you are touring with kids, the interpretors at the slave quarters do an excellent job of describing slave life at Williamsburg. Carter's Grove is a short drive from the historic area.

Several child-oriented tours are offered at Colonial Williamsburg, including the Young Recruit Program for boys and the Colonial Girls Program. Children dress in period costumes and try their hand at tasks boys and girls would have done in the 1770s. A third program, Felicity in Williamsburg, is based on the American Girls series of books about a young girl growing up in Williamsburg in the late 1700s. All three tours require participants to have Patriot's Passes as well as pay an additional fee. Call for reservations and details.

SCHLEP FACTOR: High, if you are going for the day, but lower if you plan to spend a weekend or more. Our families rate Colonial Williamsburg as a must-see attraction for kids 7 and older, but is very difficult with toddlers. The area has every imaginable hotel, from budget to luxurious, many of which offer packages that include lodging and tickets. The website has many of the packages listed, or call for information. No matter how long you visit, your family will do plenty of walking, so bring along a stroller for children under 5.

DIRECTIONS: Take I-64E to Exit 238 in Williamsburg. Follow the green and white Colonial Williamsburg signs to the Visitor Center.

Busch Gardens

Williamsburg   (757) 253-3350

WEBSITE: http://www.buschgardens.com

HOURS: Daily, opens 10 AM, closing times vary (call ahead) mid-May–August, limited days March–early May and September–October.

ADMISSION: Children under 3 for free, $28 for children 3–6, $35 for children 7 and up–adult, $30 for seniors; Twilight $22.45 for children 3–6, $29.50 for children 7 and up–adult.
Multi-park tickets allowing admission to Busch Gardens and Water Country USA are $54.50 adult or child.

Offering top-notch amusement rides in a beautiful setting, Busch Gardens will please both children and adults. Nine villages from four different Old World countries provide the backdrop for gut-wrenching roller coasters such as Alpengeist, the world's tallest and fastest hanging roller coaster, and The Big Bad Wolf, a hair-raising suspension roller coaster. Little kids love the Land Of The Dragons with scaled-down rides and lots of interactive play features. The Royal Preserve Petting Zoo featuring the Anheuser-Busch Clydesdales pleases kids of all ages. Each village has shows and food. We recommend the German Festhaus for German food and dancing amid ornate decorations. Typical American fare is available throughout the park as well.

SCHLEP FACTOR: High, because of the drive, but surprisingly low once you are in the park. The beautiful landscaping and European ambiance make this park easier on adults than other amusement parks. Try to arrive at the park opening and eat meals at off-times to avoid crowds. Strollers are recommended for all kids under 5 (even indignant ones will want it by the end of the day).

DIRECTIONS: Take I-64E to exit 242A/B. Follow Route 199 2 miles to Route 60. Take Route 60E 1-1/2 miles to the entrance. Highway signs for the park are clearly marked along the way.

Water Country USA

Williamsburg   (757) 253-3372 or (757) 253-3350

WEBSITE: http://www.watercountryusa.com

HOURS: Daily, opens 10 AM, closing times vary (call ahead) mid-June–August, limited days in May and September.

ADMISSION: Children under 3 for free, $19.50 for children 3–6, $27 for adults; Twilight (after 3 PM) $16.40 for adult or child. Senior, group and military discounts available.

Multi-park tickets allowing unlimited use of Water Country and Busch Gardens for any three days in a two-week period is $54.50 adult or child.

With more than 30 rides and attractions spread over 40 acres, Water Country is the mid-Atlantic's largest water park. Older kids love the thrilling water slides such as Aquazoid, where riders plunge down semi-darkened tunnels amid flashing laser lights. Cow-A-Bunga and H2O UFO are two children's play areas with shallow water and lots of interactive and climbing features. Families will also enjoy the group ride down Big Daddy Falls (not appropriate for tots), an enormous wave pool, and a theater with dive shows. There are lots of dining choices available throughout the park.

SCHLEP FACTOR: High. Water Country is great fun when the weather heats up, but as the temperature climbs, so do the crowds. The water is heated, making early-season or cloudy-day visits a good option to avoid crowds, although bring along a cover-up to keep kids warm between rides. Plan on arriving early and have your kids go straight for the big water slides, which tend to develop long lines by late morning. In the afternoon, when everyone else is sizzling in line, your family can relax by the wave pool. Each family member should bring a towel and a pair of water shoes. Extra clothes can be stored in rental lockers.

DIRECTIONS: Take I-64E to Exit 242A/B. Follow Route 199 to the entrance. Highway signs for the park are clearly marked.

NORTHERN VIRGINIA AND VICINITY

Northern Virginia and Washington, D.C. offer far more family attractions than we can review in this book. If you are interested in digging deeper into District attractions, we highly recommend another school guide, *Going Places With Children in Washington, D.C.*, published by the Green Acres School in Rockville, Maryland. Here we have included our favorite Northern Virginia destinations for your family to explore.

Noted (★) attractions are Timetravelers sites. Kids have their free Timetravelers passports stamped at participating attractions. After they collect six stamps in one season (April–October) they send in the passports for a free T-shirt, a certificate signed by the Governor of Virginia and a chance at other neat prizes. For more information see the section in the Getting Started chapter.

ANIMALS

Reston Animal Park
1228 Hunter Mill Road, Vienna   (703) 759-3636

HOURS: Monday–Friday 10 AM–3 PM Spring–Fall; weekends 10 AM–5 PM; Summer Monday–Friday 10 AM–5 PM weekends 10 AM–6 PM.

ADMISSION: Kids under 2 for free, $8.95 for children 2–12 and seniors, $9.95 for adults.

VIP Package: $11.95, includes elephant and pony rides, as well as a portion of animal food. Reduced rate in cooler months.

This animal park, located just ten minutes from Tyson's Corner, has both common and exotic animals, many that kids can pet and feed. The main barn houses most of the petting zoo animals such as ponies, goats, pigs, llamas and sheep, as well as a few animals kids can see up close but can't touch, such as a zebra and camels. Elephant and pony rides are offered here, too. Nearby, a variety of monkeys, bears, giant tortoises and reptiles can be viewed and exotic birds are scattered throughout the park. A hayride, included in the admission fee, takes guests through fields filled with fallow deer, bison, elk, emus and a Watusi steer with eight-foot horns. Kids won't be able to touch the animals, but since there are no barriers the animals can come right up to the wagon. A pond with an observation deck, picnic area, snack stand and gift shop round out the offerings.

In the summer, the park hosts special events such as puppet and reptile shows. Call ahead for information and hours.

SCHLEP FACTOR: High. Although kids love to see the animals at the park, families driving all the way from Charlottesville just for this will likely be disappointed. Instead, combine a trip here with a trip to The Water Mine Family Swimmin' Hole, to Colvin Run Mill Historic Site, or to Tyson's Corner for shopping and lunch at the Rainforest Cafe. All are within minutes of the animal park. The park is stroller- and handicapped-accessible, and the snack stand sells soft drinks, snacks, ice cream and candy.

DIRECTIONS: Take Route 29N to Route 28N in Centerville. Follow Route 28 to Route 7 (Leesburg Pike). Go east (right) on Route 7 for about 8 miles to a right on Baron Cameron Avenue. At the first traffic light turn left onto Hunter Mill Road. The Animal Park is immediately on the right.

HISTORIC

★ ## Colvin Run Mill Historic Site
10017 Colvin Run Road, Great Falls   (703) 759-2771

WEBSITE: No website, but send e-mail to colvinrunmill@hotmail.com

HOURS: March–December Wednesday–Monday 11 AM–5 PM; January–February Wednesday–Monday 11 AM–4 PM. Closed Tuesdays.

Tours: On the hour; the last tour begins an hour before closing time.

ADMISSION: Free, and tours of the mill and house are free for children under 5, but $2 for children 5–15, $3 for students 16 and over, $4 for adults, $2 for seniors.

Puppet show tours: $3 per child, held every Thursday at 1 PM.

Grinding: Can be seen on the first and third Sundays of the month, April–October, noon–2 PM, weather permitting.

Colvin Run Mill, a gristmill built in the early 1800s on land once owned by George Washington, today offers visitors a chance to see how grain was processed nearly 200 years ago. Visitors can see the beam scale, a grain elevator and the large grinding stones powered by a 20-foot oak water wheel and wooden gears. Grinding still takes place at the gristmill on the 1st and 3rd Sundays of the month, but a video that shows the grinding is available for viewing anytime. Also don't miss the 19th-century miller's house that offers a museum about the families who lived at the mill and a grain elevator that kids can operate. An interpretive barn and blacksmith's shop also are on site, as is the General Store which served the community in the early 1900s. Today the General Store sells products ground at the mill as well as penny candy, souvenirs and hand-crafted items. The pot-bellied stove, wooden floors and bins with old-fashioned toys like jacks, tops and cornhusk dolls makes kids feel as though they have just stepped back in time.

Families with preschoolers will want to visit on a Thursday for a special tour of the mill. Kids stroll from one site to the next, along the way encountering Marvin the Miller and several other puppet friends that tell them in an age-appropriate way about the mill and the process of grinding grain.

Several special events make a visit to Colvin Run Mill especially fun for kids. "Autumn Traditions", held on a weekend in October, offers lots of hands-on exhibits, woodworking, cider-pressing, and apple butter-making. The "Country Christmas" event, held on a December weekend, showcases Victorian Christmas decorations, music, visits with Father Christmas and crafts. Colvin Run Mill also hosts an Easter Egg hunt, a Halloween program and a great Father's Day celebration featuring free or inexpensive ways for kids to "treat" their dads. Admission is charged for some special events. Call ahead for dates.

Schlep Factor: Moderate. This is a great stop for 1–2 hours, but should be combined with either a trip to the Water Mine at Lake Fairfax Park, Reston Animal Park or to Tyson's Corner for shopping and dinner. All are within minutes of Colvin Run Mill, as is Wolf Trap Farm Park.

Directions: Take Route 29N to Route 28N in Centerville. Follow Route 28N to Route 7 (Leesburg Pike). Go east (right) on Route 7 for about 8–10 miles to a left on Colvin Run Road.

★ George Washington's Mount Vernon and Pioneer Farm

Mount Vernon   (703) 780-2000

Website: http://www.mountvernon.org

Hours: Daily, April–August 8 AM–5 PM, March, September, October 9 AM–5 PM, November–February 9 AM–4 PM.

Admission: Children 5 and under for free, $4 for children 6–11, $8 for adults, $7.50 for seniors; fee includes admission to the house and farm and use of the mini-bus.

Tours and Events: Call to request a brochure.

Although George Washington's home near Alexandria has been open to the public for years, the recent addition of the Pioneer Farm now makes the plantation one of the most family-friendly attractions in Northern Virginia. There are enough activities to fill an entire day, but it is reasonably priced enough to visit for a couple of hours as well.

As visitors enter, they first approach the mansion and a number of outbuildings. Since mansion tours are self-guided with docents available to answer questions, we recommend that even families with very young children try to take a peek inside. Visitors will see furnishings that graced the house when Washington lived here, including the bed in which he died. The house has been restored to look as it did in the last year of Washington's life, right down to furniture placement. The 18 outbuildings are also self-guided (although audio tours are available for $2) and have signs explaining their use in Washington's day. After strolling around the outbuildings, guests can either hop on a free shuttle or take a five-minute downhill walk to the Pioneer Farm.

Washington's 16-sided barn has been carefully re-created on the four-acre Pioneer Farm. Families can see horses thresh wheat in the barn and, from March-November, can participate in a variety of farm activities. Staff in period attire demonstrate the farming techniques Washington used when he farmed the same land. The sheep, chickens and horses will delight even the youngest visitors.

After visiting the farm, head down to the wharf for a 45-minute sightseeing boat tour of the Potomac. At $5 for adults, $4 for seniors and $3 for children, the tour is very reasonable compared to others along the Potomac.

For weary visitors, a mini-bus runs every 1/2-hour, providing free transportation from the farm and wharf back to the main entrance.

Many special tours and events run throughout the year at the plantation. Call ahead or pick up a brochure at the entrance. Schlep factor: Low, unless you are touring in May or June when Mount Vernon is very crowded. We recommend avoiding these months, if possible. The drive through Old Town Alexandria (via the George Washington Parkway) is very scenic, winding beside the Potomac with many good picnicking spots along the way. In addition, Mount Vernon offers a full-service restaurant and a more casual snack bar. Three shops, several restrooms (with baby-changing stations) and a post office round out the facilities. Mount Vernon offers excellent stroller and handicapped accessibility.

DIRECTIONS: Take Route 29N to I-66E to I-495S. Follow I-495S to Alexandria and exit at the Route 1N exit. Take the 1st right at Franklin Street, then turn right at Washington Street, which is the George Washington Parkway. Follow the Parkway all the way to the end to Mount Vernon (about 8 miles).

OLD TOWN ALEXANDRIA

Alexandria

The Alexandria Convention and Visitors Association
(800) 388-9119

HOURS: Daily, year-round, 9 AM–5 PM.

Tours: One-hour walking tours leave from the Ramsey House daily at noon April–November; $3 for children, $5 for adults.

In her heyday, Alexandria was a busy seaport with a vital link for the colonists to Europe. Today, visitors can still see many homes and businesses that were built in the 1700s. We recommend that families visiting Old Town first stop by the Alexandria Convention and Visitors Association, located in the historic Ramsey House at 211 King Street. Here guests can get information about the many historic sites in town and pick up a free visitor's parking pass which will allow you to park free at any metered space. Families participating in the Timetravelers program (see the chapter on Getting Started) should note that several Alexandria attractions are also Timetravelers sites. One of our favorite historic sites in Old Town is Gadsby's Tavern Museum on North Royal Street where guides in period costume lead guests through the restored tavern, bedrooms and the ballroom once frequented by George Washington. The tavern still serves lunch, dinner and Sunday brunch by reservation (703) 548-1288. Families with children will do well to choose one historic site to visit, then, after your tour, park near the end of King Street where the road meets Union Street and the Potomac River. Within a block of the intersection of King and Union, you will find:

>*Ben and Jerry's Ice Cream Parlor*
>*Olsson's Books and Music* has a good selection of children's books and music.
>*The Torpedo Factory Art Center* (a converted WW II factory) where over 150 artists and craftspeople work. Kids can talk to the artists and watch them at work.
>★*The Alexandria Archaelogy Museum.* In this working laboratory, archeologists continue to piece together Alexandria's rich history.
>*The Torpedo Factory Food Pavilion* and *Potomac Riverfront* are located on the water side of the Torpedo Factory. There are lots of dining choices in the food court, and the waterfront has walkways, benches and parks for running off steam. Street performers and musicians add to the ambience.
>*The Why Not Shop*, located up King Street away from the water, is a much-loved children's store that sells quality clothing and toys.

Two other especially noteworthy stops on King Street in Alexandria are within walking distance of the King/Union Street intersection, but a real stretch for tired toddlers. One is the Masonic Temple, which has an observation deck and a fascinating pair of elevators which are far apart on the ground floor but almost touch each other at the observation deck level. Take a ride up for a great view of the city. A Likely Story, one of the best children's bookstores we have ever visited, is also located on the opposite end of King Street.

On the first Saturday in December at 10 AM, the Scottish Christmas Walk is held in Old Town. Scottish clans march down the streets dressed in full regalia. Bagpipes and bodhrans and a contingency of Scottish dogs please children of all ages.

SCHLEP FACTOR: Fairly high. Old Town Alexandria is spread over sixty acres. Try to focus your visit on a small historic tour, then head to the riverfront to relax. Parking in Old Town is not easy, so be sure to pick up a free parking pass at the Ramsey House. Even parking at the Ramsey House is difficult, with only street parking and pay lots available. Families visiting from summer to mid-fall or during special events should arrive early to secure parking. Cameron Run Water Park and Mount Vernon are just a hop, skip and a jump away from Old Town.

DIRECTIONS: Take Route 29N to I-66E to I-495S (toward Alexandria). Take the Route 1 exit (exit 1). Follow Route 1 (Patrick Street) several blocks until it intersects King Street. For the Ramsey House and the King/Union Street tour described above, turn right onto King Street. For the Masonic Temple and A Likely Story, turn left onto King Street.

MUSEUMS

Newseum and Freedom Park

1101 Wilson Boulevard, Arlington
(703) 284-3544 or (888) NEWSEUM
WEBSITE: http://www.newseum.org
HOURS: Year-round 10 AM–5 PM Wednesday–Sunday; closed Mondays, Tuesdays, Thanksgiving, Christmas and New Year's Day.
Timed entry passes are given out beginning at 9:45 AM each day.
ADMISSION: Free.

The Newseum, opened in 1997, is the world's first interactive museum dedicated to exploring how and why news is made. Kids can visit the Ethics Center to learn about the tough choices journalists must make in reporting the news, see the greatest news stories of all time in the News History Gallery, and go behind the scenes to see how news programs are produced in the Newseum Broadcast Studio. Best of all, kids are offered a chance to go on-camera and create their own television broadcast, which then is played back for the museum visitors. The tape can be purchased for $10 and makes a great souvenir. Kids will also enjoy the 126-foot long video news wall which plays news stories as they happen. The Newseum is great for kids 10 and up and/or those with a high interest in journalism. Younger kids who don't have a good understanding of the news, however, will be bored to tears.

Before you leave the museum, be sure to visit Freedom Park. This rooftop park, adjacent to the museum, has exhibits celebrating the pursuit of freedom around the world. *A Walk With Freedom*, an interactive guide for kids available at the museum information desk, will help kids understand the Freedom Park exhibits. A toppled statue of Lenin, large segments from the Berlin Wall and a monument commemorating slain journalists are but a few of the exhibits they will find here (along with a great bird's-eye view of the Washington and Jefferson Monuments).

SCHLEP FACTOR: Pretty high, especially if you have younger kids in tow. Although admission to the museum is free, the adjacent parking garage is $5. Wheelchairs, strollers and backpacks are available for loan at the coat check room; although since the Newseum targets older kids, we suggest leaving little ones at home for this attraction.
Note: To control crowds, timed-entry cards are handed out at the entrance. To avoid a long wait to enter the museum, plan to arrive before opening time to secure a card. Inside, the Newseum store sells lots of great news-related items, and the News Byte Cafe offers drinks and light snacks. Arlington National Cemetery and Iwo Jima are a short drive away.

DIRECTIONS: Take Route 29N to I-66E to the Key Bridge Exit. Get into the right lane and bear right onto Fort Myer Drive. Get into the left lane and go up the ramp on the left side of Fort Myer Drive. Turn left onto Wilson Boulevard and go through one stoplight at North Lynn Street. The Newseum is on the left just after the intersection, and a parking garage is adjacent. Allow about 2 hours to drive from Charlottesville.

MUSIC AND THEATER

Wolf Trap Farm Park

1624 Trap Road, Vienna   (703) 255-1868 (to be added to the mailing list), (703) 255-1827 (information on children's performances)

HOURS: Late May–mid-September.

ADMISSION: $10 and up (everyone, including babies, pays). Call Pro-Tix at (703) 218-6500 for tickets.

Wolf Trap, America's National Park for the Performing Arts, provides outdoor and covered seating for its summer concert series. Held almost nightly in the Filene Theater, performances range from opera to blues to rock, and some are suitable for or intended for families. In addition, special children's events, hosted by the National Park Service, are held throughout the summer at the Theater In The Woods.

At the end of the summer, Wolf Trap hosts the International Children's Festival. This not-to-be-missed two-day event features songs, dances and costumes from around the world. For information on this event, call the Fairfax County Arts Council at (703) 642-0862.

SCHLEP FACTOR: Fairly high, since Wolf Trap is 1-1/2 hours from Charlottesville. The family performances, thankfully, are typically held early in the day.

DIRECTIONS: Take Route 29N to Route 28N in Centerville. Follow Route 28 to Route 7 (Leesburg Pike). Go east (right) on Route 7 for about 10 miles to a right on Trap Road.

SPECTATOR SPORTS

Washington Mystics (WNBA)

Washington, D.C.

WEBSITE: http://www.wnba.com/mystics

HOURS: June–August at 7 PM. (Half of the home games are on weekends.)

ADMISSION: Lap kids under 3 for free, otherwise $8–$25 per seat; can be purchased up to one month in advance through Ticketmaster at (202) 432-SEAT.

To get on the Mystics mailing list, write them at: 601 F Street, Washington, D.C. 20004

We admit it. The MCI Center is not in Northern Virginia. The MCI Center is smack-dab in the middle of Washington, D.C. But we couldn't help ourselves. Even families who don't normally enjoy sporting events will be totally blown away by the Washington Mystics, Washington's franchise in the women's NBA. During their inaugural season the team had the league's highest attendance record, attracting more than 16,000 fans to each game. At least 15 home games are held at the MCI Center each summer, all of them wonderful family events featuring great basketball, shows, giveaways and games. Halftime performances range from contortionists to indoor fireworks and always include the Mystics Mayhem, a pep squad of kids ages 7–19 who cheer and dance on the court. After each game, 200 lucky fans are invited onto the court for an autograph session. The Mystics host many special events throughout the season to add even more to the festivities. Check out their website for upcoming events.

SCHLEP FACTOR: High, but really worth it. The MCI Center, where the games are played, is an attraction in itself, featuring the MCI National Sports Gallery, a two-level interactive sports museum that is incredible for kids, and The Discovery Channel Store: Destination D.C., a four-story interactive store. Other shops and dining are located here, and Chinatown, the National Archives and several museums are an easy walk from the center. Games last about two hours, but plan to arrive several hours early to experience the MCI Center and surrounding areas. Parking is available in an adjacent garage and in other lots close by. Expect to pay $15–$20 for game parking. Traffic and parking are typically not a problem for weekend games and security is exceptional.

DIRECTIONS: Take Route 29N to I-66E. Stay on I-66E into Washington, where it becomes Constitution Avenue. Turn left onto 7th Street and go a couple of blocks to the MCI Center on the right.

WATER PARKS

All the water parks in Northern Virginia are public regional parks. While the admission fees are reasonable, the size of the crowds may not be. Consider arriving right after the park opens or after 5 PM to avoid the crush of people inevitable at these favorite hot-weather hangouts. One nice feature about these parks is that since they are all relatively small (compared to Water Country) you are less likely to lose a child. Parents who hate the stress of the big water parks will be able to relax and give older children a bit more freedom. Be sure to bring along towels and water shoes for each member of the family. Each park has rental lockers and plenty of food options.

Each of these water parks will please different age groups. Cameron Run is best for kids 7 and up who are good swimmers. Splash Down is a lot of fun for kids under 13 or for those who are not adept swimmers. The Water Mine is great for kids 6 and under or children who still delight in lots of imaginative play.

Cameron Run Regional Park

4001 Eisenhower Avenue, Alexandria   (703) 960-0767 (pool)

HOURS: *Pool:* Daily 10 AM–7 PM Memorial Day weekend–Labor Day (hours vary so call ahead).

ADMISSION: $8 for those under 48," $10 for those over 48"; everyone, including babies, pays.
Twilight Admission (after 5 PM): $4.50 for those under 48", $5.50 for those over 48".
Tube rentals for the wave pool: $3 plus a $2 refundable deposit.
Batting cages and miniature golf: mid-March–October, an additional fee charged. Hours vary.

The granddaddy of the Northern Virginia water parks, Cameron Run has the only wave pool in Northern Virginia and boasts several high-thrill water slides as well. An extensive kiddie section offers calf-deep water, small slides, and a mushroom waterfall with climb-on water creatures. Little ones have their own baby pool with water bubblers and a gentle waterfall. The pool is especially popular with kids 7 and older thanks to the 40-foot high, three-flume water slide and, of course, the 500,000-gallon wave pool that simulates a day at the beach. A snack bar sells pizza, burgers, hot dogs, ice cream and sodas. Outside the water park, Cameron Run also has an 18-hole miniature golf course, batting cages, and a fishing pond. Coolers, private rafts and arm flotation devices are not allowed, and swim diapers are required for babies.

SCHLEP FACTOR: Moderate to high, mostly because of the nearly 2-hour drive from Charlottesville. Spacious bathhouses with lockers and showers makes the trip easier. We recommend Cameron Run for families with children 7 and older who know how to swim. The park is reasonably close to Mount Vernon.

DIRECTIONS: Take Route 29N to Route 66E to I-495S. Follow I-495S to Exit 3A (Eisenhower Avenue) Go to the stoplight at the end of the exit ramp and turn left onto the connector. Go to the 2nd light and turn right on Eisenhower Avenue. Follow the signs to the park.

Splash Down Water Park at Ben Lomond Park

7500 Ben Lomond Park Drive, Manassas   (703) 361-4451

WEBSITE: http://www.pwcweb/splashdown

HOURS: Late May–early September, weather permitting.

ADMISSION: Children 1 and under for free, $7.95 for those under 48" tall, $10.95 for those over 48" tall, $5.95 for spectators.
Group pricing, season passes and twilight discounts are available.

Hop in your car and in less than 1-1/2 hours you and your kids can be zooming down one of two 70-foot waterslides or floating down the Lazy River on an innertube. Splash Down, a relatively new Northern Virginia water park, has 11 acres of fun for kids of all ages. Two tots' areas with smaller waterslides, climbing structures and plenty of interactive water features keep the little ones happy, while a pool with a log walk and a lily pad walk, waterslides and several other water areas entertain older kids. When the kids get hungry, favorites like ice cream and pizza are available, as well as sandwiches, fries and lots of candy. No coolers are permitted inside the park, but picnic areas are provided outside the gates.

Although teens could get bored at Splash Down in a couple of hours, this is our favorite water park for families with kids under 13 or for kids who are not adept swimmers. One more perk: Splash Down uses salt water in most of their pools. Little ones don't like the taste and are therefore less likely to swallow the water.

SCHLEP FACTOR: Surprisingly low for so much fun! You will find a free parking lot right next to the park, but arrive early for a good spot.

DIRECTIONS: Take 29N to I-66E. Follow I-66 a short distance to the Manassas (Route 234S) exit. Take Route 234S for 1.1 miles to a left on Sudley Manor Drive. Take Sudley Manor Drive for 3 miles to a left onto Ben Lomond Drive into the park. (Watch for brown park signs to help guide you from I-66.)

The Water Mine Family Swimmin' Hole at Lake Fairfax Park

Reston   (703) 471-5414

WEBSITE: http://www.co.fairfax.va.us/parks

HOURS: Daily, 10 AM–8 PM Memorial Day–Labor Day, although hours vary when school is in session, so call ahead.

ADMISSION: $7.95 for those under 48", $9.95 for those over 48", and everyone, including babies, pays.
Group pricing, season passes and twilight discounts are available.

The Water Mine, run by the Fairfax County Park Authority, exercises young imaginations as much as young bodies. Legend has it that Prospect Pete was mining for gold at Lake Fairfax and instead found water. The theme of this tiny water park is around Prospect Pete and the Old West, with a craggy old mountain as the centerpiece with two slides that empty into the water below. In addition, the park boasts four more water slides shaped like a covered wagon, a log, a barrel, and a frog with a slide for a tongue. The shallow water also has climb-on critters, obstacle courses, and The Lost Mine, an interactive climbing feature with waterfalls, tunnels and a slide. A separate baby area has lots of bubblers, sprays and other tot-friendly features. When the kids get hungry, a snack bar sells candy, ice cream, sodas, chips and hot dogs. In addition, the park always contracts a concessionaire to sell other items, such as pizza.

The Water Mine is just one small part of Lake Fairfax Park. Other features include a large lake with paddleboat rentals and a tour boat, a carousel, a miniature train, hiking trails and camping. One nice perk: guests of the water park also receive unlimited rides on the carousel and miniature train.

SCHLEP FACTOR: Low for the amount of fun your (younger) kids will have. Because of the park's imaginative play areas, size, and proximity to Charlottesville, this is our favorite water park for kids under six. All of the water slides are under 14', so the park does not attract many teens. In 1998, the park had to close early several times when capacity was reached, so arrive early or after 5 PM. Reston Animal Park, Colvin Run Mill, Wolf Trap Farm Park, and Tyson's Corner are within minutes of the park.

DIRECTIONS: Take Route 29N to Route 28N in Centerville. Follow Route 28 to Route 7 (Leesburg Pike). Take a right on Route 7E for about 8 miles to a right on Baron Cameron Avenue. At the 2nd traffic light turn left into Lake Fairfax Park.

DINING AND SHOPPING

Since you've had kids, have your dining and shopping experiences have become limited to any place with a drive-through window or a toll-free number? If so, this chapter may be just the ticket to rediscovering the variety of shopping and dining that Charlottesville has to offer. For more information on local shopping, dining and attractions, pick up a copy of *The Charlottesville Guide,* published three times a year by Carden Jennings Publishing, the same folks who bring us the wonderful *Albemarle Magazine*. This free publication can be found at local hotels, the Visitor Center, and other tourist venues, or can be seen on-line at http://www.cjp.com/guide.

DINING

When we asked our families which restaurants were kid-friendly in Charlottesville, one response was, "Aren't they all?" True, Charlottesville is such a family town that kids are welcome in almost every restaurant. The following were considered exceptional by our families. Chains such as Chili's, Pargo's and Ragazzi's aren't included here, but many are great for kids, too, offering children's menus, coloring books and other perks.

Although we have heard of toddlers who will sit still through a restaurant meal, we have never actually met one. If you have kids under 5, pack a small diaper bag with miniature containers of playdough, a ziplock bag with markers and crayons, a pad of paper and a few other small, quiet toys or books. Keep this "restaurant bag" in the car to make meals out more enjoyable for everyone.

Casual dining

If you are looking for a casual, everyday kind of place to take the family, nothing too pretentious, too expensive, or too rattled by patrons under 4 feet tall, look no further.

Anna's Pizza No. 5
115 Maury Avenue, Charlottesville   (804) 977-6228

We aren't sure if there are Anna's numbers 1–4, but Anna's #5 is in the Fry's Spring neighborhood and serves a mix of students, families, and local teams, post-game. The kids love the pizza and the juke box. Parents love the can't-do-too-much-damage ambience and the fact that there are enough tables so wiggly children are not a problem. They also serve pasta, subs, salads...an old-style pizza joint.

Baja Bean
1327 W. Main Street, Charlottesville   (804) 293-4507

Choose indoor seating at booths or tables, or sit outside in the courtyard cafe and munch on Tex-Mex fare at this Corner restaurant. The restaurant is noisy enough that even a loud toddler won't get a second look.

The Brick Oven

Rio Hill Shopping Center, Charlottesville   (804) 978-7898

The Brick Oven serves creative Italian fare in a casual, friendly atmosphere. Everyone gets their way with "half-and-half" pizzas; children can order kid-pleasing toppings on one side, while Mom and Dad can pile on the artichoke hearts, basil, pesto and garlic on the other. The high-chair set gets a free "fistful" of spaghetti or ziti, and a children's menu is also available.

The Chiang House

1240 Seminole Trail (Route 29N), Charlottesville   (804) 973-0881

The Chiang House offers both Chinese and Japanese cuisine in a very festive environment. Kids love the teppan-yaki tables where the chef cooks at the table, all the while entertaining guests with a mix of humor and cooking wizardry. The indoor and outdoor goldfish ponds are also a hit and often mesmerize babies.

The College Inn

1511 University Avenue (The Corner), Charlottesville   (804) 977-2710

One of our favorite spots for family meals on the Corner, the College Inn is locally owned and offers excellent Greek salads and pizza. The restaurant is family-friendly and usually not too crowded, even when U.Va. is in full swing. Our families' favorite spot to sit is the section right at the entrance, a few steps up with three tables. This area helps confine the clamor, allow for a kids' and a grown-ups' table and keeps down the "disturbing others" factor. This is especially great when two families combine for a dinner out.

Crozet Pizza

5794 Three Notch'd Road, Crozet   (804) 823-2132

Imagine a pizza place so popular that you need reservations for dinner. Crozet Pizza is said to have the best pizza in the state, but dropping in with hungry kids can be a big mistake. Call ahead for reservations or for take-out. Kids will enjoy the wall completely covered with business cards and the wall of photographs of world travelers wearing Crozet Pizza T-shirts. A schlep from Charlottesville, but worth the trip. Too crowded for wandering toddlers.

The Dogwood Restaurant
10 Center Court, Palmyra   (804) 589-1155

Here's a novel idea: how about a restaurant that combines exceptional quality food with an atmosphere that welcomes children? The owners of the Dogwood Restaurant in Palmyra have three children of their own and know the challenges of dining with kids. They have designed their restaurant to support the family dining experience. Adults can enjoy entrees such as cornmeal-crusted bluefish in spicy peanut sauce or shrimp and andouille sausage jambalaya, while the kids have their own (really inexpensive) less exotic meal. Coloring books help keep kids entertained while they wait for their meal. All entrees are reasonably priced, and, best of all, kids 5 and under eat free!

Guadalajara
Two Charlottesville locations:
395 Greenbrier Drive   (804) 978-4313
801 E. Market Street   (804) 977-2676.

Offering some of the most authentic Mexican food in town, Guadalajara has waitstaff who are excellent with children and will even teach them a Spanish phrase or two if prompted. The service is fast, the food tasty, and the decorations and free tortilla chips keep the kids busy. At the Greenbrier Drive location, kids like the counter covered in pennies, and two televisions that play Spanish stations. Try to arrive early for easy seating.

Hard Times Cafe
1309 W. Main Street, Charlottesville   (804) 979-3991

If your family has a hankering for chili, there is no place in town like Hard Times Cafe. Three kinds of chili—Texas, Cincinnati and vegetarian—are made from scratch from turn-of-the-century recipes. The non-veggie chilis are heavy on the meat; some of our families prefer the vegetarian version with peanuts and lots of veggies. Burgers (veggie and not), hot dogs and a few other items are available as well. Wash down dinner with draft root beer, or for the grown-ups, ales and beer. Tenderfoot portions are available for small appetites, and fun "chili parlor" music adds to the ambience. Be advised that the place is literally crawling with television sets, which some parents love but some loathe. The best part is that since the place is cavernous, it rarely gets too crowded.

The Hardware Store

316 E. Main Street (on Downtown Mall), Charlottesville
(804) 977-1518

Located in a renovated hardware store on the Downtown Mall, the Hardware Store Restaurant is a big hit with kids. Creating a perfect hardware store atmosphere right down to the toolbox of condiments that accompanies your sandwich, the restaurant is a great stop for burgers (both veggie and not) and other fare on the huge menu. Kids will also enjoy browsing through the adjoining chocolate shop where an imaginative array of chocolate novelty items are sold. The service here is typically slow, so don't stop by if you are pressed for time.

The Ming Dynasty

1417 Emmet Street, Charlottesville   (804) 979-0909

Vegetarians, calorie-watchers and harried parents will all have a great meal at the Ming Dynasty. While typical Chinese fare is offered at this family-owned restaurant, the Ming specializes in a huge assortment of vegetarian and low-fat entrees. Parents will especially appreciate the exceptional waitstaff and large menu. A lunch buffet and Sunday brunch are good family choices, but the restaurant is never really crowded, making any meal here quick and easy.

The Nook

415 E. Main Street (on Downtown Mall), Charlottesville
(804) 295-6665

This restaurant is a great spot for leisurely weekend breakfasts with the kids. While many eateries around town are swamped during the morning, the Nook typically has easy seating. Breakfast is served until 11 AM, then sandwiches and the like are served early afternoon until closing in this child-friendly diner. In the warm weather, the lovely outdoor seating is very relaxing and cool, especially for breakfast.

Northern Exposure

1202 W. Main Street, Charlottesville   (804) 977-6002

This downtown restaurant, owned, as you may have guessed, by a couple of uprooted Yankees, is a good choice for family dining. Two outdoor patios (one on the roof and one covered and heated at street level) are a good choice for noisy little ones, or opt for indoor seating next to the huge mural where you will find paper-covered tables and crayons where kids can design their own masterpieces. The menu has a number of vegetarian and heart-healthy selections, inventive pasta dishes, and signature ice cream flavors (made locally by Tony at Chaps). A kids' menu and warm bread keep little tummies happy, too.

Oregano Joe's
1252 Emmet Street, Charlottesville   (804) 971-9308

Serving creative Italian food, Oregano Joe's is one of the most child-friendly restaurants in town. Coloring books help keep little ones occupied, and if that doesn't work, the staff has been known to entertain while the grown-ups finish their meal. A children's menu assures kids can find something they like, but, hey, this is Italian food. Even the pickiest eater won't have a problem here. Really convenient Route 29N location with plenty of parking, too.

Sloan's
1035 Millmont Street, Charlottesville   (804) 979-2879

Sloan's patio seating and huge menu, including a children's menu with items named after the owner's kids, makes this a good family dining spot. Coloring books with crayons and lots of fun appetizers help, too. Try a "Beta Bridge" for dessert—two donuts with ice cream, whipped cream and toppings. Yummm...big enough to share.

Southern Culture
633 W. Main Street, Charlottesville   (804) 979-1990

What makes Southern Culture special are those three little words every mother loves to hear—cooks-to-order. The owner loves children, and his chefs will whip up pretty much anything your child wants to eat, yet adults can get a great Southern meal, too. A children's menu is available, to boot. Bonus: The kids are given crayons to decorate the paper-covered tables. Go early for best seating. Nice Sunday brunch, too.

Tiny Mac

Albemarle Square Shopping Center, Charlottesville   (804) 974-6542

Tiny Mac, begun by the Sloan family of Sloan's Restaurant fame, changed hands in 1998 but continues to offer good family dining north of town. Homey food such as meatloaf, macaroni and cheese and burgers are served in a casual, not-too-crowded environment. Young children will find plenty of room to squirm, and cups with tops. A children's menu and the convenient location makes this a good choice for families with young kids.

Vinny's New York Pizza and Pasta

Two locations: Intersection of Routes 29N and 33, Ruckersville (804) 985-4731, and 2800 Hydraulic Road, Charlottesville (804) 964-1040

Vinny's offers good pizza, salad and subs in two kid-friendly environments. The staff is very accommodating to families, even offering free eats to area kids who bring in good report cards. Both locations offer take-out and dining rooms. Arrive early for easy seating.

A Quick Bite

If you are trying to squeeze in dinner or a snack between soccer practice and the 6 PM show, or just need to minimize dining time and the thought of processed fried chicken cut into cute little shapes makes you want to...well, you know: try one of these instead.

Bellair Market

Route 250W just west of the intersection with 250 Bypass, Charlottesville   (804) 971-6608

Not typical gas station fare, Bellair Market has some of the best sandwiches around, and picky eaters can also choose from a wide assortment of convenience items. Eat at the tables or get carryout for a picnic in the park.

Bodo's Bagels

Locations in Charlottesville:
1418 N. Emmet Street   (804) 977-9598
505 Preston Avenue   (804) 293-5224
1609 University Avenue (on The Corner)   (804) 293-6021.

No secret here: Bodo's is the favorite among families, couples, singles, students and locals alike. One family summed it up: "Good food, good music, fast service." We'll add "good price" to that. Even when the line is out the door, you're only minutes away from a hot fresh bagel. And if the music is too loud or too hard for kids, just ask: they'll change it.

Casella's Pizza

Barracks Road Shopping Center, Charlottesville   (804) 979-7011

If you are at Barracks Road at lunchtime, stop at Casella's for pizza for the kids, soup and salad for you. The staff is great about cutting pizza into bite-size pieces for toddlers and bringing your tray to the table if your hands are full. Dinnertime turns Cassella's into a table-service restaurant, and although it is still casual and friendly, the service is slower.

Revolutionary Soup

108 SW Second Street (off the Downtown Mall), Charlottesville
(804) 296-7687

Six varieties of soup are offered each day at Revolutionary Soup. Grab
a seat inside and enjoy the funky atmosphere, or ask for your soup to go
and find a sunny spot along the Downtown Mall. At least one soup
offered each day appeals to kids, but be advised that the restaurant is not
stroller- or handicapped-accessible.

Simeon Market

1330 Thomas Jefferson Parkway (halfway between Monticello and Ash
Lawn-Highland), Charlottesville   (804) 977-8200

If you are visiting Monticello or Ash Lawn-Highland or are just in the
vicinity of the TJ Parkway during lunch, stop in at Simeon Market for a
gourmet sandwich or excellent pizza. They also do custom picnic
baskets.

Sylvia's Pizza

310 E. Main Street (on Downtown Mall), Charlottesville
(804) 977-0162

Not the place for those who have trouble making decisions, Sylvia's has
more than a dozen pizza selections lined up to tempt your tastebuds.
Tempura pizza, fresh basil and mozzarella pizza, eggplant parmesan
pizza...the list goes on and on. But for the picky eaters, you can also get
plain cheese. The pizza is served cafeteria-style on paper plates. Sylvia
does a big lunchtime crowd, so we recommend visiting by 11:30 AM or
after 1 PM.

Two Moons Cafe

Two locations in Charlottesville:
109 NW 14th Street (on The Corner)   (804) 923-3494
110 NW Second Street (on Downtown Mall)   (804) 293-5709

Two Moons offers dirt-cheap Tex-Mex food made-to-order from high
quality ingredients. The atmosphere is casual, the servers friendly and
fast. The Corner location offers a full-service restaurant that features
free-range meats, produce grown in their own garden, and lots of
vegetarian options. The downtown location is a walk-up "burrito hut."
Order lunch, then find a spot on the Downtown Mall or in Lee Park to
munch.

THE "EXOTICS"

If your kids turn up their noses at anything more adventurous than peanut butter, skip this section. These restaurants don't offer typical kids' fare; however, they all offer a glimpse into another culture without leaving Charlottesville. All welcome children and go out of their way to help tailor meals to young tastebuds. For less adventurous souls who nonetheless need an occasional change of pace, consider Guadalajara Mexican Restaurant (above) or one of the several Chinese restaurants in our Casual Dining listings.

The Flaming Wok
1305 Seminole Trail (Route 29N), Charlottesville   (804) 974-6555

Families will find a variety of Asian cuisine at the Flaming Wok, including Korean, Japanese and Chinese. Their specialty is Stone Korean Barbecue which guests cook for themselves at the table. Sushi and sashimi, as well as familiar Chinese food is offered, too. The Oriental decorations are appealing and the waitstaff is exceptionally good with kids. An inexpensive lunch buffet and a karaoke room are also offered.

Golden Kris Malaysian
Rio Hill Shopping Center, Charlottesville   (804) 964-1700

The cafeteria setting belies the exotic food served up at the Golden Kris. The owner/host is very helpful in giving dining tips to picky eaters. Service is fast, and a television plays cultural shows from Malaysia (you can ask for the videos to be turned on if one isn't playing). Convenient location and reasonably priced, too.

Maharaja Indian
139 Zan Road (Seminole Square Shopping Center), Charlottesville
(804) 973-1110

Kids like the authentic Indian decor and waitstaff at Maharaja. Colorful, airy curtains adorn the windows, and, in warmer months, outdoor seating is available. Since the food is prepared while you wait, you can request almost any dish to be toned down for a milder introduction to what is typically quite spicy cuisine. A lunchtime buffet offers a variety of not-too-spicy Indian dishes, including a rice pudding and tandoori chicken, both of which often appeal to kids. They also have great baked-to-order Indian breads, which spice-avoiding kids adore.

Thai!

1773 Seminole Trail (Gardens Shopping Center), Charlottesville
(804) 964-1212

Charlottesville's only Thai restaurant is very accommodating to
children. An exotic interior with a shallow river and trickling waterfall
are intriguing, and the waitstaff bends over backwards to make kids feel
at home. Ask for suggestions for young palates, but we recommend
steering clear of anything with lemongrass, which is too strong for most
kids' taste buds.

Tokyo Rose

2171 Ivy Road (Ivy Square Shopping Center), Charlottesville
(804) 296-3366

This is one of the few places where people clamor for a seat on the floor!
Arrive early to snare these high-demand traditional Japanese tables.
Kids love the opportunity to take off their shoes and sit on the floor for
dinner. Add chopsticks and let the fun begin. Tempura, teriyaki, and even
some sushi appeal to kids (try cooked egg or shrimp, California rolls or
vegetarian sushi) and the dessert tray is worth behaving well for! Several
other Japanese restaurants have opened in recent years and all are fine
for adventurous eaters of all ages.

THE "FANCIES"

Imagine that Aunt Julia is visiting from the city. She wants to take you out for dinner. Somewhere nice. With the kids. Uh-oh. These restaurants are not for every day, but if your children are old enough to sit through a meal and not yodel "The Star Spangled Banner" into their water glasses, these restaurants can work!

The Lafayette Hotel

Main Street, Stanardsville   (804) 985-6345
Reservations: Required for lunch or dinner.

Imagine eating fresh mountain trout almandine with crab stuffing in downtown Stanardsville with your children. Stop laughing! Former Boar's Head chefs Whitt Ledford and Nick Spenser are now making culinary magic in Greene County at this restored 1840s inn. A flexible children's menu is offered, or bring the family for the extensive Sunday brunch buffet ($8.95 for adults, $7.95 for children). Kids will enjoy the two fireplaces that warm the dining room and the candlelit tables. Dress is casual and parents will love the great food at very reasonable prices. This is one fancy restaurant where even toddlers are accommodated, although we find that younger children tend to fare better at lunch.

The Old Mill Room at The Boar's Head Inn

Route 250W, Charlottesville   (804) 972-2230

Head over to the Old Mill Room before 6 PM or so, and you will typically find the place nearly empty. Kids enjoy finding the Boar's Head theme scattered throughout the lodge (don't let them miss the vat of chocolate coins bearing the emblem at the restaurant exit) and an after-dinner stroll to see the ducks on the lake. The huge Sunday brunch buffet is a good option for families with young kids who don't like to wait for their food. The restaurant is very quiet, so this is probably not the place for a fussy baby or rambunctious toddler.

Duner's Restaurant

Route 250W at Owensville Road, Ivy   (804) 293-8352

The casual atmosphere in Duner's belies the upscale food served here. Well-known for their wizardry with seafood, Duner's also offers a range of entrees, one of which is always vegetarian. Our families like this off-the-beaten-track restaurant, noting especially the appetizers, hot sourdough bread, and desserts (what else do you need?). Although the restaurant is too crowded for small children, kids don't have to get too spiffied up for a dinner here and most kids won't have too much trouble selecting an entree from the unpretentious menu.

Clifton-The Country Inn

1296 Clifton Inn Drive, Charlottesville   (804) 971-1800
Reservations: should be made at least 24 hours in advance, much sooner for weekends in the fall.

Dining at Clifton Inn is more of an event than a meal. The two-hour dinners, served in a 200-year-old inn, have only one seating each evening. Guests begin the night with cocktails, which can be enjoyed over a game of croquet, by the lake, pool, or gardens, or at the game table. Before dinner the chef gathers the guests and explains how the evening's entrees are prepared. Guests are then brought into the dining room for either a four- or five-course meal. The food is upscale yet simple, featuring local, seasonal ingredients (in kid-speak, nothing too weird). A beef and a seafood entree are typical, but special requests can often be accommodated with advance notice. Since the dinners are long, they are appropriate only for children over 12. The prix-fixe dinners are $48 Sunday through Thursday and $58 Friday and Saturday.

The "Joints"

These are the dining spots that have been around forever. Don't expect a gleaming, modern environment (or coloring books, for that matter) in these local hangouts. What you will find in each is true atmosphere that portrays old Charlottesville in a way that chain restaurants can't.

Riverside Lunch
1339 Long Street, Charlottesville   (804) 971-3546

Locals used to call Riverside Lunch the "Boar's Head East" because of the great food. You'll find truckers, old-timers and business people in this little joint, feasting on what many call "the best burgers in town."

Spudnuts
309 Avon Street, Charlottesville   (804) 296-0590

Potato flour may be the secret behind the spudnut, but a glass of ice-cold milk drawn from one of those huge old metal dispensers is a required accompaniment. You can overhear some interesting conversations at Spudnuts, but you won't hear anything at all if you don't go early. Spudnuts closes at 2 PM on weekdays and at noon on Saturdays (closed Sundays).

Taiwan Garden
9 University Shopping Center, Charlottesville   (804) 295-0081

Probably not the Chinese restaurant you would choose to impress your boss, but for just a little more time and money than fast food, you can have a delicious hot meal at one of the oldest (possibly the oldest) Chinese restaurants in Charlottesville. Many entrees are under $8 and are big enough to feed two hungry kids, but order a sampling and bring home the leftovers. The waitstaff is very accommodating to families, and, in all the years we have been visiting Taiwan Garden, we have never had to wait for a table. Great, fast take-out, too!

The Tavern

Emmet Street just south of Barracks Road, Charlottesville
(804) 295-0404

The chocolate chip pancakes and waffles are worth the wait at the tavern, where breakfast is served until closing. Long lines are typical at the Tavern on weekends, so don't bring the kids when they are really hungry.

Timberlake's Drug Store and Soda Fountain

322 E. Main Street (on Downtown Mall), Charlottesville
(804) 296-1191

Mr. Timberlake moved his drugstore to Main Street in 1917 and it has been there ever since. The soda fountain has moved from the front of the store to the back, but from the spinning bar stools customers can still order fresh lemon or limeade, sandwiches, root beer floats and milkshakes (regular to drink with a straw, or extra thick that needs a spoon). Afterwards, view the photos of Timberlake's through the years that are scattered about the store, and take a stroll down the Downtown Mall.

The Virginian

1521 W. Main Street (on The Corner), Charlottesville   (804) 984-4667

This tiny restaurant, wedged into The Corner like a long splinter, has served Charlottesville for 75 years. The food (which includes a children's menu) is very good and includes a wide variety of American fare. The charm of the Virginian, its size, is a problem if you have a large family. Booths are only large enough to seat families of four or fewer (comfortably, anyway).

The Best Part...Dessert

Blackstone's Coffee

Albemarle Square Shopping Center, Charlottesville   (804) 973-1332

You'll be hard-pressed to find a coffee shop as child-friendly as Blackstone's. On a recent visit, our waiter bypassed the adults, dropped to eye-level and asked the children if everything was to their liking. There is a fireplace with comfy chairs and games in the back, and a case full of tempting desserts (although the entrees were not spectacular). On weekend evenings, Blackstone's has free music and the kids are invited. This is a great after-the-movies dessert and conversation spot for the entire family.

Chaps

223 E. Main Street (on the Downtown Mall), Charlottesville
(804) 977-4139

Chaps is a perennial favorite in Charlottesville, thanks in part to the excellent homemade ice cream and in part because of owner Tony La Bua, who jokes with the kids and remembers regulars. The Fifties decor with records on the wall and seafoam green booths is fun, too. Tony offers children's groups (school, parties, scouts, etc...) who call in advance a hot dog, soda, chips and an ice cream cone for a pittance.

Espresso Corner

100 14th Street (on the Corner), Charlottesville   (804) 293-6641

If you're running errands on the Corner with the kids, pop into this hip spot for great smoothies, cookies, muffins and coffee. Couches and games makes this an easy stop with kids.

Kohr Brothers Frozen Custard

1881 Seminole Trail (Route 29N), Charlottesville   (804) 975-4651

Kohr Brothers recreates an old-fashioned Atlantic City-style shop in its Route 29N location, complete with a working carousel. Customers are treated to creamy, delicious frozen custard (like soft-serve ice cream, only better) and kids can ride the carousel for free with a purchase. Kohr's also has a store in Fashion Square Mall, but if you want the atmosphere and the carousel, you'll have to come here.

Krispy Kreme
1805 Emmet Street (Route 29N), Charlottesville   (804) 923-4007

If a creme-filled donut is your idea of dining, then this is the place for you. Although we excluded chains in our listings, Krispy Kreme was worth a mention because a free tour comes with every purchase. From their place in line, children can watch the donuts as they are being made. The frosting waterfall draws "ahhhs" from kids of all ages. There is also a drive-through if you prefer to eat on the run.

THE "OUT-OF-TOWNERS"

These are the restaurants that, although not right down the street, are worth a stop. If you're visiting an out-of-town attraction, check to see if one of these is nearby.

Generous George's Positive Pizza and Pasta Place
3000 Duke Street, Alexandria   (703) 370-4803

Generous George's is a quirky family restaurant with carousel animals for decor as well as lions, giraffes and tigers for climbing. Pizza, with any topping you can imagine as well as a few you can't, is the mainstay, but the "positive pizza pie," a pizza crust topped with entrees like fettuccini alfredo or lasagna, is the star. A free Generous George T-shirt comes with every child's meal. As you might expect, this place is crawling with families.

Graves Mountain Lodge
Syria   (540) 923-4231
Reservations: Required

Folks come from miles around and even make the drive from Washington, D.C., for dinner at the Lodge. Meals are served family-style at long pine tables and feature a different entree each night. If you are visiting during warm weather, bring along a change of clothes for the kids so they can wade in the stream in front of the lodge, and plan to take a hike or a horseback ride along the lodge's trails. There is just one seating for dinner. If you're late, you'll have to wait 'til breakfast. Reservations are required.

Rainforest Cafe
Lower level, Tyson's Corner Mall, Tyson's Corner   (703) 821-1900

Imagine eating lunch with trumpeting elephants, a volcano erupting nearby, a thunderstorm brewing overhead. Overstimulating? Maybe, but definitely entertaining for kids. The Rainforest Cafe, boasting enough live animals to have a curator on staff, combines Disneyesque animation and sound effects with a huge menu. Guests first queue up for a "passport" (basically a souped-up reservation with names such as "Toucans" or "Rhinos"). When the reservation is called, guests follow a guide on safari into the restaurant.

A large shop is adjacent to the restaurant and continues the rainforest theme. This is a great stop after visiting the rainforest exhibit at the National Zoo or any of the Tyson's Corner/Reston attractions, but be prepared for a wait (especially on weekends); the restaurant is very popular.

To reach Tyson's Corner Mall from many of the Northern Virginia attractions listed in this book, continue east on Route 7 for about 6 miles past Colvin Run Mill to the mall on the left.

Rowe's Family Restaurant
Rowe Road (right off the I-64/I-81 interchange), Staunton
(540) 886-1833

Rowe's Family Restaurant, featured in a recent "Gourmet Magazine" article, is the place for homey comfort food. Parker House rolls, macaroni and cheese, and unbelievable pies top the menu, but guests can eat breakfast, lunch or dinner here. A children's menu, crayons and high chairs are available, and the staff is wonderful with kids. Families leave feeling as stuffed and pampered as they would after a visit to Grandma's. Come early during the dinner hour to avoid a wait. (Hint: Rowe's is an easy drive from the Frontier Culture Museum of Virginia.)

Sweet Things Ice Cream Shoppe
106 W. Washington Street, Lexington   (540) 463-6055

Sweet Things offers fantastic homemade ice cream in an old-fashioned ice cream parlor setting. Located in historic Lexington, Sweet Things is close to the Lime Kiln and just a hop away from Natural Bridge. Or stroll over after visiting the Stonewall Jackson house.

Tea at The Jefferson
W. Jefferson and Franklin Streets, Richmond   (804) 788-8000

Hours: Thursday–Sunday 3 PM–4:30 PM
Admission: $12.50 per person; Teddy Bear and Santa Teas priced higher.
Reservations: Required for all teas, and should be made well in advance for the Santa and Teddy Bear Teas.

The Palm Court in the opulently-restored Jefferson Hotel is the icing on the tea-cake for tea party aficionados. Dressed in their Sunday best, children love the teeny sandwiches and cookies, and the tea and cocoa served in real porcelain tea cups. Each Friday a harpist plays at the tea, and the third Saturday of each month is a Chocolate Lover's Tea featuring a buffet of chocolate items. Ask about special children's events such as the Teddy Bear Tea, held the first Sunday of each month, which features a clown (teddy bear guests are welcome at no extra charge), and the Santa Tea in December where Santa and Mrs. Claus are featured guests. After tea, walk through the Hotel and admire the luxurious touches such as the grand staircase and old paintings. Although the Jefferson is not the place for rowdy kids, it makes practicing manners fun!

Wright's Dairy Rite
346 Greenville Avenue (Route 11), Staunton   (540) 886-0435

Since 1952, customers have come to Wright's Dairy Rite for burgers and malts served at their car, ordered from a "Servusfone" at their parking place. It may be hard to explain to kids born in the 90s how this is different from a drive-thru window, but it is one of those great little hidden spots you won't find in most tourist brochures. Supposedly the Statler Brothers used to hang out at the Dairy Rite before their rise to stardom.

SHOPPING

We have to admit a weakness here. Free Union Country School families tend to be an outdoorsy lot. We have families who have rafted raging rivers, rappelled sheer rock faces, backpacked to places most people will only read about in National Geographic, but the thought of entering a mall with children in tow leaves many of us white as milk, quivering in our mud-caked boots. Our weakness works to your advantage. We have cut to the chase here; although many stores have toys or children's departments, we have only included the best family shopping in our area. Now if only there were guided trips to the mall....

CHILDREN'S BOUTIQUES

Sherry's Children's Collection
The Millmont Shops, Millmont Road, Charlottesville
(804) 979-5300

Sherry's specializes in up-scale clothing, shoes and accessories for infants through teens. Sherry's is also the only place in town shoppers will find premium Peg Perego highchairs and strollers, and Britax car seats, as well as other high-quality baby products and furniture. Convenient parking, exceptional service and a children's play area make this boutique an easy stop.

Whimsies
North Wing, Barracks Road Shopping Center, Charlottesville
(804) 977-8767

Whimsies offers a huge selection of top-quality children's clothing, shoes and accessories. Parents and grandparents alike will appreciate the knowledgeable and helpful sales associates and children's play area.

BOOKS

Although no longer served by a large contingency of independent booksellers, Charlottesville continues to boast a wide variety of bookshops. Listed here are a few of the larger shops in town that offer children's books. In addition, Charlottesville is blessed with over a dozen used book stores, many of which offer children's titles.

Barnes and Noble

Barracks Road Shopping Center, Charlottesville   (804) 984-0461
HOURS: 9 AM–11 PM Monday—Saturday, 9 AM–9 PM Sunday.

In the back of Barnes and Noble you will find the largest selection of children's books in the area. The staff encourages hands-on browsers, making this a great place to curl up with a child and a book. Two storytimes are offered each week for preschoolers. Stories are read in the small theater, and refreshments (usually cookies) are served. Children 7 and older have their own book club where the classics in children's literature are read and discussed. During your visit, check out the Barnes and Noble Jr. flyer for upcoming special events, which occur pretty often and can include author visits, parties and visits from popular children's book characters. The cafe at the front of the store is great for a snack, and, best of all, when everything else in town is closed, Barnes and Noble is usually open!

Green Valley Book Fair

Mt. Crawford   (800) 385-0099; (540) 434-0309
WEBSITE: http://www.gvbookfair.com

The Green Valley Book Fair began 25 years ago in the barn of an old family farm near Staunton. Today, the book fair occupies over 20,000 square feet and offers new books in over forty categories, all discounted 60%–90% off retail. An extensive children's selection offers titles from all of the major publishers, as well as plush toys from Gund. Throngs of customers from all over the mid-Atlantic flock to the six annual fairs, so come early for the best selection. Fair schedules vary each year but are typically held for 1-1/2–2-1/2 weeks in March, May, July, August, October and late November through mid-December. You can also purchase items through their website, but we recommend visiting in person for the unique ambience. The Book Fair can get very crowded, so be sure to bring adequate supervision for young children.

DIRECTIONS: Take I-64W to I-81N near Staunton. Take Exit 240 at Mt. Crawford. Take Route 682E for 1-1/2 miles, then turn left onto Route 681 at the Green Valley sign. (Approximately 1 hour from Charlottesville).

New Dominion Bookshop

404 E. Main Street (on the Downtown Mall), Charlottesville
(804) 295-2552

This relatively small bookstore on the Downtown Mall is chock-full of carefully selected books, including high quality children's books. The old polished-wood bookshop ambience, a staff of true readers and a willingness to special order make this a haven for book lovers. Stop over during your next stroll down the Downtown Mall.

SECOND TIME AROUND SHOPS

One of the nicest things we can do for our environment (and pocketbooks) is to purchase used clothing, books, equipment and furniture. While the following stores are the largest local vendors of used children's items, there are many other second-time-around shops, including several used book stores and clothing consignment shops. Craft-loving kids should stop by the Creative Re-Use trailer at the McIntire Recycling Center for free craft supplies ranging from fabric scraps and wallpaper samples to pompoms and packing peanuts. In addition, many locals eagerly await two huge annual flea markets that benefit Focus—A Women's Service Organization and the SPCA. Here savvy shoppers will find toys and games, children's clothing and equipment. A third bargain hunter's dream is the annual Friends Of The Library Book Sale. Held each March to benefit the Jefferson-Madison Regional Library, this sale offers thousands of titles in a variety of categories and always features an outstanding selection of children's books.

Kids Kaboodle

Rio Hill Shopping Center, Charlottesville   (804) 974-7063

The owner of Kids Kaboodle has a brutally selective eye for merchandise brought to her shop for consignment. Only like-new items are selected for her shelves, which can make life difficult for consignors but assures shoppers they will find top-quality clothes at very reasonable prices. The store also sells women's and maternity clothes, children's shoes and baby equipment.

Play It Again Sports
Rio Hill Shopping Center, Charlottesville   (804) 973-2638

Both old and new sports equipment can be found at Play It Again Sports. We especially like this shop for used ski equipment, ice skates and already-broken-in baseball gloves, but shoppers will find an assortment of reasonably-priced equipment for many different sports.

TOY STORES

Also note that the Virginia Discovery Museum on the Downtown Mall has a small gift shop with many selections under $5 and Teacher's Edition on the lower side of the Village Green Shopping Center on Commonwealth Drive has educational books, games and posters for teachers and parents alike.

Copernicus
100 E. Main Street (on the Downtown Mall), Charlottesville
(804) 296-6800

This toy store offers a nice selection of "thinking" and science toys and is a favorite stop for kids. Puzzles, games, experiments, books and the like line the shelves, with plenty of allowance-priced items, too.

Shenanigans
North Wing, Barracks Road Shopping Center, Charlottesville
(804) 295-4797

This colorful, friendly store encourages hands-on browsers and offers a great selection of high-quality toys. The selection ranges from pricey imported dolls to inexpensive grab bags of stickers. Playmobile and Brio are featured, as is a big, yet choice, selection of children's books, lots of dress-up, games and art projects. Knowledgeable and helpful sales associates and free gift-wrapping make Shenanigans an easy stop.

OTHER CHILDREN'S SPECIALTY STORES

Hush Little Baby

1905 Commonwealth Drive (Village Green Shopping Center),
Charlottesville   (804) 295-8388

This tiny store debuted in 1998 and carries a small but thoughtful selection of innovative products for babies up to one year old as well as maternity clothes and accessories. Many items found in the store can't be found anywhere else in the area. The store also has several rental programs, including breast-pump rentals.

O' Baby

113 4th Street NE (off the Downtown Mall), Charlottesville
(804) 245-8484

A studio of Art Effects Inc., O' Baby offers very cute handpainted furniture and accessories for children's rooms as well as personalized gifts, fabrics and crib linens. The owners will also handpaint murals for children's rooms, playrooms, etc... The store is only open Tuesday through Saturday, or other days by appointment, so be sure to call ahead before stopping over.

THE MALLS

Families looking for more shopping in the area will find enclosed malls in Staunton and Harrisonburg in addition to the malls listed below. Energetic shoppers who crave more selection can venture to Northern Virginia to Tyson's II Mall (on Route 7 in Tyson's Corner) or Fair Oaks Mall (on I-66 just past Manassas). Both are family-oriented, mega-malls filled with restaurants and shops that suit a wide variety of styles and tastes. Tyson's II also offers a Rainforest Cafe (see our Dining chapter). Take care not to confuse Tyson's II with the Galleria Mall, located right across the street.

Downtown Pedestrian Mall

Main Street, Charlottesville

The Downtown Pedestrian Mall, an outdoor mall in the heart of downtown Charlottesville, is a wonderful place to stroll with children.

Brick-lined streets, historic buildings, fountains and fun sculptures are the backdrop for many family-friendly stores and eateries. The Virginia Discovery Museum and the outdoor amphitheater where Fridays After Five concerts are held anchor one end of the mall, and the Charlottesville Ice Park and Regal 6 Theaters, the other. In between are the historic Paramount Theater (currently under renovation) and The Jefferson, a theater that offers discounted movies. More family entertainment just off the mall can be found at Glaze 'n' Blaze, a paint-your-own-pottery studio.

Many small, locally-owned shops with children's selections can be found on the Downtown Mall, including Copernicus Toy Store (see Toy Stores), O'Baby (see Other Children's Specialty Shops) and April's Corner, which offers women's and girls' clothing as well as a few toys and books. Art Needlework sells yarn and needlework supplies, including kits appropriate for children, and Innisfree World Artisans sells wares from around the world, including unusual toys, all at reasonable prices. No fewer than five used bookshops make their homes on the Downtown Mall, as does New Dominion Bookshop (see Books, above). Cha Cha's and O'Suzannah sell fun, funky gifts, although both have enough fragile items to exclude visits from the stroller set.

Food choices abound (see Dining) including Chaps Ice Cream, Baskin-Robbins and lots of outdoor cafes and street vendors. Albemarle Bakery, located inside York Place, offers lots of great bakery items and a large plate glass window where kids can watch as the cookies and breads are made.

Parking can be found at the Market Street and Water Street Parking Garages as well as at other smaller lots surrounding the mall. Many Downtown Mall merchants validate parking for two hours in the parking garages. Street parking is limited.

Fashion Square Mall
Route 29N and Rio Road, Charlottesville

The only enclosed mall in Charlottesville, Fashion Square Mall has undergone something of a renaissance in the last five years. It has become much more family-friendly, adding stroller rentals and a number of shops designed especially for kids. There are now quality children's clothing stores such as Gap Kids and Gymboree. Two bookstores, Waldenbooks and B. Dalton Books, offer children's departments with both classics, and new titles. Both are very tolerant of young, hands-on browsers. Stride Rite Shoes, KB Toys, The Disney Store and World of Science all cater to families, as well, and many other shops have children's selections. Baseball card enthusiasts frequent Cavalier Sports Cards and many girls enjoy the inexpensive jewelry and accessories at Claire's. The mall lacks a food court, but offers Blimpie, Sbarros Italian Eatery, and Chick-Fil-A for meals.

SEASONAL CALENDAR

Special events for families happen throughout the year in Central Virginia. The following are annual events that offer children's activities or otherwise enrich the experience of the attraction that hosts them. For more information on these and more seasonal events, check out the "Extra" section of the Friday *The Daily Progress*, and listings in the weekly *Observer* and *C-Ville Weekly* (both free at newsstands around town). For downtown Charlottesville events, check out the Downtown Foundation's website at http://avenue.org/downtown.

JANUARY

New Year's Day Family 5K Fun Run
Free Union
New Year's Day   (804) 293-3367

Sponsored by the Charlottesville Track Club amid beautiful scenery in Free Union.

Stonewall Jackson Birthday Celebration
Lexington
January 21   (540) 463-2552

City-wide celebration of Lexington's favorite son includes free tours and birthday cake at his home.

FEBRUARY

Valentine's Day at Wintergreen
Wintergreen
Valentine's Day   (804) 325-2200

Cupid on the slopes, parties, and lots of fun kid activities and family-oriented events.

Maymont Flower and Garden Show
Richmond
Late February   (804) 358-7166

Inside the Richmond Coliseum, gardens in full bloom, including trees, shrubs and flowers, ponds, waterfalls and fountains help shrug off winter blahs. Lots of gardening information, too. Admission fee.

MARCH

Friends of the Library Book Sale
Charlottesville
mid-March   (804) 977-8467

Huge used book sale with proceeds benefitting the J-MR Library. Held
in two segments, the first offering children's books.

Virginia Festival of the Book
Charlottesville
mid-March   (804) 924-3296

A four-day celebration features interviews, readings, panel discussions,
book signings and more. Lots of children's activities.

Pepsi Snowblast
Wintergreen
March   (804) 325-8171

Kids' games, music, campfire and snowboard demonstrations on the
mountain at Wintergreen Resort.

APRIL

Fishin' at Onesty Pool
Charlottesville
Early April   (804) 970-3260

During Spring Break (for city schools), the city Department of
Recreation and Leisure Services fills Meade Park with more than 300
trout and invites families to spend a day fishing. Trophies are given for
the first catch each day. Small fee for each fish caught.

Easter at Wintergreen

Wintergreen

April   (804) 325-2200

Easter egg dyeing workshops, Easter egg hunt at stables and on the mountain at Wintergreen Resort.

Easter Egg Hunts

Charlottesville

Easter

Various groups sponsor community-wide egg hunts at the Downtown Mall and Charlottesville High School. Check *The Daily Progress* for details.

Graves Mountain Lodge Spring Fling

Syria

April   (540) 923-4231

Popular event with fly-fishing demonstrations, horseback rides, bluegrass music and arts and crafts sale. Fee for admission, and some activities have fees.

Spring Court Days Craft Festival

Charlottesville

Mid-April   (804) 296-8548

Craft show, sale, demonstrations, entertainment, and food in Lee Park off the Downtown Mall. Lots of children's crafts, face painting, etc. Free admission but fees for face painting, etc.

Annual Dogwood Festival

Charlottesville

Mid–late April   (804) 961-8924

Almost two-week event that features a carnival with rides in McIntire Park, fireworks, barbecue and parade. Admission fee for some events.

Fridays after Five begins

Charlottesville

Late April–early October   (804) 970-3503

Popular outdoor concert series showcases local musical talent in the amphitheater on the Downtown Mall. Food, drink, and roving entertainers. Free.

Foxfield Races

Charlottesville

Late April   (804) 293-9501

Afternoon of steeplechase horse races and tailgate parties at the Foxfield Race Course on Garth Road. Admission fee.

MAY

Crozet Arts and Crafts Festival Spring Show

Crozet

Early–mid-May   (804) 977-0406

Juried fine arts and crafts show at Claudius Crozet Park in Crozet featuring 125 of the nation's best artists and craftspeople, music, dancing, and food. Some kid's crafts and activities such as face painting. Admission fee.

Ash Lawn-Highland Kite Day

Charlottesville

Mother's Day   (804) 293-9539

Kite flying and prizes for the entire family in the fields at Ash Lawn-Highland. Admission fee for spectators, free for participants.

Wintergreen Country Fair

Wintergreen

Memorial Day   (804) 325-2200

Petting zoo, frog jumping event, homemade ice cream and more at Wintergreen Resort.

Graves Mountain Lodge Festival of Music

Syria

Weekend after Memorial Day   (540) 923-4231

Popular three-day bluegrass music festival with food, fishing and horseback rides. Many people camp for the duration of the event. Admission fee.

Discovery Dash

Charlottesville

Late May   (804) 977-1025

Footrace for children at the U.Va. Track to benefit the Virginia Discovery Museum. Pre-registration with fee.

JUNE

Free Kids' Movies at the Regal Cinema

Charlottesville

Tuesdays and Wednesdays all summer   (804) 979-7669

Beginning in June, families can see favorite children's movies free at 10 AM, Tuesday and Wednesdays, at the Regal Cinema 6 on the Downtown Mall. Arrive early for seating.

Batteau Night in Scottsville

Scottsville

Mid-June   (804) 286-9267

A batteau encampment, entertainment, crafts, demonstrations and music at the public boat ramp on the James River in Scottsville. Free.

Ash Lawn-Highland Summer Festival

Charlottesville

Late June—mid-August   (804) 293-4500

Professional productions of opera and musicals performed on the lawn at Ash Lawn-Highland throughout the summer. Admission fee.

JULY

Plantation Days at Ash Lawn-Highland

Charlottesville

Weekend closest to July 4th   (804) 293-9539

Independence Day celebration including 18th century crafts, living history interpreters, demonstrations, music, dancing, food and more at historic Ash Lawn-Highland. Admission fee.

Crozet Fireman's Festival

Charlottesville

Early July   (804) 296-5850

Rides, games, music, dancing, fireworks, parade, and food at the Claudius Crozet Park in Crozet for two weekend evenings. Admission fee.

Free Union Fourth of July Parade

Free Union

Sunday closest to July 4th   (804) 978-1351

A participatory parade where children and parents can ride their bikes, pull wagons and otherwise parade through Free Union with lots of spectators to cheer them on. The parade begins at 4 PM at the Free Union Baptist Church and ends at Free Union Country School. Free.

Independence Day Celebration

Charlottesville

July 4th   (804) 980-3861

Fireworks, band concerts, games, and some rides at McIntire Park, sponsored by the Charlottesville/Albemarle Jaycees. Admission fee for some events.

Scottsville Celebrates Independence Day
Scottsville
July 4th   (804) 286-2623

Old-fashioned Fireman's Parade and fireworks to celebrate the 4th in Scottsville. Free.

Fourth of July Jubilee
Wintergreen
July 4th   (804) 325-2200

Arts and crafts show, hayrides, kids' Olympics, and a petting zoo (at the stable) at Wintergreen Resort. Admission fee for some events.

Madison County Fair
Madison
Early July   (540) 948-4661

Carnival, fireworks, agricultural displays at the Young Farmers Fairgrounds. Admission fee.

Summer Saturdays at Ash Lawn-Highland
Charlottesville
Mid-July–early August   (804) 293-4500

Beginning in July, a series of family programs including music, dance, drama and puppetry introduces children to outdoor theater, including opera on the lawn at historic Ash Lawn-Highland. Admission fee.

AUGUST

Greene County Fair
Greene County
August   (804) 985-8282

Carnival rides, music, agricultural exhibits and food. Admission fee.

Meet the Team Day
Charlottesville
Early August   (804) 982-5600

Come out to the artificial field behind U-Hall to meet the U.Va. football team, get autographs and take pictures. Free.

SEPTEMBER

Albemarle County Fair
North Garden
Early September   (804) 293-6396

Carnival rides, entertainment, games and contests as well as agricultural shows and displays for a week in North Garden off Route 29S. Lots of children's entertainment and participatory events. Gorgeous mountain views. Admission fee.

Jazz Festival
Charlottesville
Early September   (804) 296-8548

Great local jazz performers and food at the Downtown Amphitheater.

State Fair of Virginia
Richmond
Mid-September   (804) 228-3200

For two weeks the fairgrounds at Strawberry Hill in Richmond come alive with carnival rides, big-name entertainment, games, exhibits and food. Similar to county fairs, only much bigger and with paved walkways but no mountain views. Admission fee.

Taste of the Mountains Main Street Festival
Madison
September   (540) 948-4455

Appalachian crafts such as spinning, weaving, basket-making, quilting, wood carving are demonstrated to the strains of Appalachian music. Petting zoo and food. Free admission, and free bus transportation from parking at Madison County High School.

Scottsville James River Fishing Jamboree

Scottsville
Early September   (804) 286-4800

All-day fishing and family fun event with bluegrass music, giveaways
and prizes in child and adult categories at the public boat ramp in
Scottsville. Entry fee for participants.

Barracks Road Charity Fair

Charlottesville
Mid-September   (804) 977-4583

Local non-profit groups host crafts, baked goods and children's activities
such as sand art and face painting at the Barracks Road Shopping
Center. Free.

Annual Hawk Migration

Afton Mountain
Mid-September–late October

Bring binoculars and watch the hawks migrate for the winter. The Inn at
Afton often has researchers camped out in the parking lot. Observe from
atop Little Calf Mountain, Turk Mountain on Skyline Drive, or Duncan
Knob on Massanutten Mountain. Tip: Hawks follow the spine of a
mountain, on the west side with an updraft. Free.

International Children's Festival of Wolf Trap

Vienna
Late September   (703) 642-0862

Huge two-day event with music, dance, puppetry and other performing
arts events for children. Hands-on arts and crafts activities and food.
Admission fee.

Foxfield Races
Charlottesville
Late September   (804) 293-9501

Full day of steeplechase horse races and tailgate parties at the Foxfield Race Course on Garth Road. Admission fee.

OCTOBER

Fall Court Days Craft Festival
Charlottesville
Early October   (804) 296-8548

Craft show and sale, demonstrations, entertainment, and food at Lee Park near the Downtown Mall. Some children's crafts and activities such as face painting. Free admission, but fee for activities.

Fall Festival and Sheep Dog Trials
Orange
Early October   (540) 672-2935

Shearing, spinning, and weaving demonstrations as well as sheep dog trials at historic Montpelier. Two-day event held the first weekend in October. Lots of hands-on kids' activities. Admission fee for those over 16 years.

Apple Harvest Festivals
Charlottesville
October

Various apple growers host weekend apple harvest events that typically include music, apple butter making, crafts and apple picking (at orchards). A few popular events at Graves Mountain Lodge (two weekends), Carter Mountain Orchard (two weekends) and several Nelson County apple growers. Watch *The Daily Progress* for details.

Richmond Children's Festival
Richmond
Second weekend in October   (804) 355-7200

Largest free children's festival in the country, themed around a different culture each year and held in Richmond's Byrd Park. Dancing, music, drama, professional performances, hands-on activities, and food. Not to be missed. Admission fee.

Madison Harvest Festival
Madison
Second Saturday in October   (540) 948-4455

Old fashioned sorghum-making festival including soap-making, quilting and antique farming demonstrations and a pancake breakfast behind Madison County High School on Route 29. Nominal admission fee.

Festival 1893 (Victorian Day)
Richmond
Mid-October   (804) 358-7166

Everything Victorian comes to Maymont Park, including a carriage parade, old-timey bicycles, a fortune teller, a Victorian tea, games, shopping and much more. Many kids' activities. Held near the Maymont House. Free admission, but fee for some activities.

International Food Fest
Charlottesville
Mid-October   (804) 296-8548

A one-day celebration of Charlottesville's cultural diversity held on the Downtown Mall. Food and entertainment from nearly a dozen countries around the world are featured. Free.

Crozet Arts and Crafts Festival Fall Show
Crozet
Mid-October   (804) 977-0406

Juried fine arts and crafts show, music, entertainment and food at the Claudius Crozet Park in Crozet. Some children's crafts and activities such as face painting. Admission fee.

Mountain Heritage Weekend
Wintergreen
First weekend in October

Apple butter making, music, horse-drawn carriage rides and more at Wintergreen Resort.

Spirit Walk
Charlottesville
Late October   (804) 296-1492

Evening walking tours of downtown Charlottesville featuring living history interpreters who play the roles of famous Charlottesville residents from the past. Sponsored by the Albemarle Historical Society. Admission fee and reservations.

Halloween Celebration at Wintergreen
Wintergreen
Halloween   (804) 325-2200

Chairlift "Ghost Express" rides, haunted house, jack-o'-lantern carving, and trick-or-treating at Wintergreen Resort.

Community Halloween Trick-or-Treating
Charlottesville
Halloween
Trick-or-treating for the kids is held at 4 PM sharp on the Lawn at U.Va., in the evening at Fashion Square Mall, on the Downtown Mall and at other shopping centers around town. Free.

Discovery Museum Halloween Party
Charlottesville
Halloween   (804) 977-1025

Special Halloween party for kids under 5 with decorations, activities, and food at the Discovery Museum on the Downtown Mall. Admission fee and reservations required.

NOVEMBER

Greek Bazaar
Charlottesville
Friday before Thanksgiving   (804) 295-5337

Greek culture including food, pastries, music and dance is celebrated at the Greek Orthodox Church on Perry Drive. Free admission, but fee for food.

Governor Jefferson's Thanksgiving Festival
Charlottesville
Mid-November   (804) 296-8548

Revolutionary War period recreated with reenactments, trade demonstrations, living history interpreters, games and food all around the Downtown Mall and Court Square area. Lots of children's activities and games. Free admission.

Blessing of the Hounds
Keswick
Thanksgiving Day   (804) 293-3549

Hounds are blessed by the Rector at Grace Episcopal Church in Keswick at the beginning of the Hunt Club fox hunt at 10 AM. Formally-clad horseback riders and lots of hounds, but typically no foxes! Free admission.

Thanksgiving at Wintergreen

Wintergreen

Thanksgiving   (804) 325-2200

Huge Thanksgiving feasts at Devil's Grill and The Copper Mine, kid's Olympics, a family theater performance, and a holiday decoration workshop at the Wintergreen Resort. Fee and reservations for dinner.

Christmas Parade

Charlottesville

Day after Thanksgiving   (804) 977-4583

Community and civic organizations, elves, clowns, live animals at the Barracks Road Shopping Center at 9 AM. Free.

Ash Lawn-Highland Cut-Your-Own Christmas Tree

Charlottesville

Late November–Christmas Eve   (804) 293-9539

Fields around Ash Lawn-Highland are open for Christmas tree cutting on weekends until Christmas. Donations suggested.

DECEMBER

Fantasy in Lights

Richmond

Thanksgiving–New Year's   (804) 228-3200

Drive through more than 1-1/4 miles of holiday scenes in lights including Winter Wonderland, Toy Land, Candy Land, Elves' Village, and much more at the state fairground at Strawberry Hill from 6 PM–10 PM nightly. On select nights, wagon rides through the light display on Strawberry Hill's draft horse wagon are available by reservation. Admission fee.

A Victorian Christmas Celebration

Richmond

First weekend in December (804) 358-7166

Carriage rides, holiday decorations, visits with Father Christmas and a Kids Only Holiday Store (so kids can buy small gifts for parents) at the Maymont House in Maymont Park. Free admission, but some activities have a fee.

Free Union Christmas Tree Lighting

Free Union

First Sunday in December (804) 978-1351

Stories, caroling and lighting of the Christmas tree at the doctors' office in Free Union at 4:30 PM. Free.

The Charlottesville Tradition

Charlottesville

Early December (804) 977-1783

City-wide extravaganza centered around the Downtown Mall featuring the Grand Illumination, arrival of Santa on an antique fire engine, professional and community theater holiday performances, holiday tours and events at area historic sites, and much more. Many children's activities and performances. Some events are free, some charge admission.

Scottish Christmas Walk

Alexandria

First weekend in December (703) 549-0111

Many Scottish clans dressed in their traditional tartans march through Old Town Alexandria. Bake sales, crafts show and other events as well. Free.

Yuletide Feast at Michie Tavern

Charlottesville

Mid-December (804) 977-1234

Holiday food, period decorations, strolling musicians in "The Ordinary" at Michie Tavern. Fee and reservations required.

Christmas at Wintergreen
Wintergreen
December 18–31   (804) 325-2200

Special family activities in celebration of the holidays including horse-drawn carriage rides, Santa on the Slopes and more.

First Night Virginia
Charlottesville
New Year's Eve   (804) 296-8269

Huge, safe, alcohol-free New Year's Eve celebration with events throughout the Downtown Mall area and beyond. Many children's events and activities. Admission fee.

CHARLOTTESVILLE

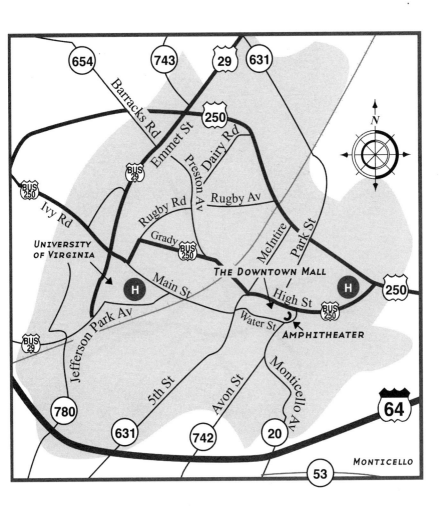

GREATER CHARLOTTESVILLE

This map shows
the main routes in, around and
through Charlottesville.

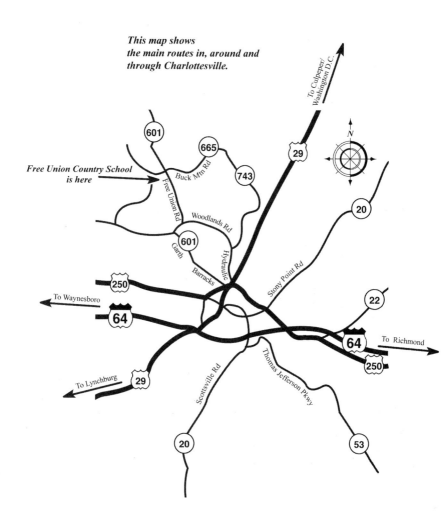

HARRISONBURG

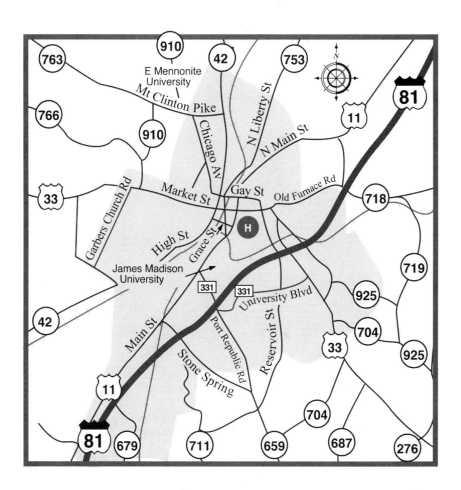

STAUNTON

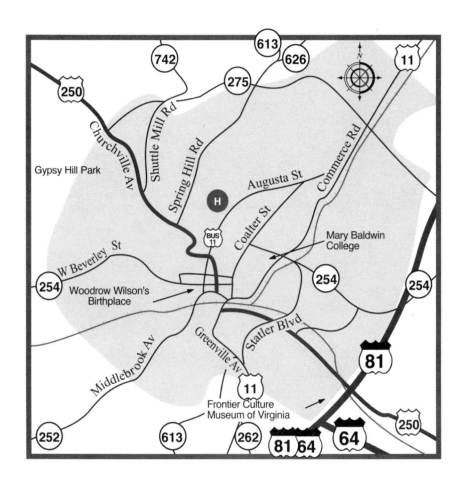

WAYNESBORO

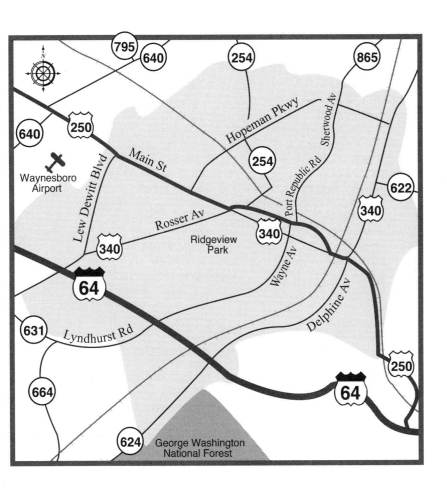

Greatest Hits

Every attraction in this book is a worthwhile stop for families, however the following attractions were mentioned again and again on our family surveys for the following age groups.

Under 6

All parks
Big Meadows Campground
Children's Community Theater productions (4 and up)
Children's Museum of Richmond
Claudius Crozet Park Pool
Dark Hollow Falls (upper section)
The Flying Circus
Fridays After Five concerts (3 and up)
Frontier Culture Museum of Virginia
Ivy Creek Natural Area
Little Calf Mountain
Luray Reptile Center
Morefield Gem Mine (4 and up)
Mountain Farm Trail
Northside Library
On the Wild Side Zoo
The Paintin' Place
Pick-Your-Own Fruit and Veggie farms
Planet Fun (3 and up)
Playland at Taco Bell, et. al
Putt-Putt Miniature Golf
Skyland Campground
Splashdown Water Park
Virginia Discovery Museum
Washington Park Pool
The Water Mine Family Swimmin' Hole
Whteoak Canyon (4 and up)

Ages 6-12

All hiking and camping
All water parks
Ashlawn-Highland during peak season
Both amusement parks
Both climbing walls
Both paint your own pottery studios
Charlottesville Ice Park

Children's Community Theater productions
The Flying Circus
Four County Players Productions
Fridays After Five concerts
Frontier Culture Museum of Virginia
Luray Caverns
Luray Reptile Center
Maymont Park
Michie Tavern
Monticello grounds and family tours
Montpelier
Natural Bridge
Pick your own fruit and veggie farms (especially kids under ten)
Planet Fun
Richmond Braves games
Richmond Kickers games
Ridgeview Park
Science Museum of Richmond
Skiing at Wintergreen
Star Base Alpha
Theater IV Productions
Tonsler Park
Tubing at Massenutten
U.Va. soccer games
U.Va. Women's basketball games
Virginia Discovery Museum (8 and under)

Ages 12 and up

All high ropes courses
All Richmond sporting events
All U.Va. sporting events
Ashlawn-Highland
Ash Lawn-Highland mainstage productions
Bayly Art Museum
Both amusement parks
Charlottesville Ice Park
Crabtree Falls
Four County Players productions
Fridays After Five concerts
Frontier Culture Museum of Virginia
Glaze 'N Blaze
Grass Skiing at Bryce
Graves Mountain Lodge overnight trips
Humpback Rock

Indoor and outdoor rock climbing
Lime Kiln productions
Loft Mountain Campground
Massanutten Skate Park
McCormick Observatory
Monticello
Montpelier
Newseum
Old Rag Mountain
Prism Coffee house
Sherando Lake
Skiing and tubing at Massenutten
Spelunking with Highland Adventures
Virginia Museum of Fine Arts
Washington Mystics' games
Water Country USA
Whiteoak Canyon

The Paintin' Place
Paramount's King's Dominion
PJ's Arcade and Pizzeria
Planet Fun
Playland at Pizza Hut, et. al
Putt-Putt
Richmond Braves
Richmond Kickers
Richmond Renegades
Science Museum of Virginia
Skatetown USA (both locations)
Virginia Discovery Museum

Birthday Parties

The following attractions either offer
birthday parties or are very familiar with
birthday parties on the premises. But
don't stop here. Be creative. For older
kids, how about a day on a local ropes
course? How about a pick-your-own fruit
party, an evening at the Fork Union Drive-
In, a hike at Ivy Creek, or a camp-out at
Camp Albemarle? For kids under five,
any local park is a great choice for a
birthday party, and many offer picnic
shelter rentals, too.

Auntie Ann's (for pretzel making)
The Bull Pen
Carver Recreation Center (roller skating)
Charlottesville Ice Park
Children's Museum of Richmond
Chuck E. Cheese
Classics Gymnastics
Discovery Zone
Fridays After Five concerts
Glaze 'N Blaze
Greenwood Community Center (roller
skating)
Keglers
Morefield Gem Mine
On the Wild Side Zoo

A

B

C

R

S

Y

Z